D0072039

SOME AMERICAN PIONEERS IN SOCIAL WELFARE

SELECT DOCUMENTS WITH EDITORIAL NOTES

BY EDITH ABBOTT

NEW YORK / RUSSELL & RUSSELL

COPYRIGHT 1937 BY THE UNIVERSITY OF CHICAGO
COPYRIGHT 1965 BY THE ESTATE OF EDITH ABBOTT
PUBLISHED 1963 BY RUSSELL & RUSSELL
A DIVISION OF ATHENEUM HOUSE, INC.
BY ARRANGEMENT WITH THE UNIVERSITY OF CHICAGO PRESS
L. C. CATALOG CARD NO.: 62-16198
PRINTED IN THE UNITED STATES OF AMERICA

PREFACE

THE material in this volume may be called a "preprint" from a documentary history of social welfare in England and America which will be published during the year 1938. In another sense this may be considered a "reprint" from the early numbers of the *Social Service Review*, in which these chapters have all appeared.

The group of men and women presented in this volume as representative of the vigorous attempts made to provide some pioneer social services at a time when there was dire need of such services, have been selected on the basis of the availability of certain material for classroom use. When the publication of the larger volume from which this material has been selected is possible, an attempt will be made to deal with the work of other pioneers in the same field who have made even more noteworthy contributions to the general welfare than some of those who appear in this volume.

Some of these early leaders, like Dorothea Dix, who advocated federal aid for public welfare purposes more than three-quarters of a century before federal aid became a reality in this field were pioneers with social vision which outran the years. Others were social reformers only for a brief period, when their ideas ceased to be constructive or useful. Both Miss Dix and her friend, Dr. Samuel Gridley Howe, had the large vision which led them at once to attempt to frame constructive legislation, while others, like Charles Loring Brace, worked exclusively in the field of private philanthropy. But they are all of interest to students, and the collection of material is therefore preprinted here for student use, pending the final issue of the larger volume.

The University of Chicago Press and the Board of the *Social Service Review* have made possible the publication of this volume.

EDITH ABBOTT

April 15, 1937

TABLE OF CONTENTS

BENJAMIN RUSH
1745–1813

A PHYSICIAN PHILANTHROPIST IN THE
EIGHTEENTH CENTURY
BENJAMIN RUSH, 1745–1813

EDITORIAL NOTE[1]

BENJAMIN RUSH was perhaps the leading American philanthropist of the eighteenth century. He was a great physician and was called "The American Sydenham" and the "Father of Experimental Medicine"; but, like many of the distinguished members of his profession, he was also a great citizen. He served from 1761 to 1766 as a medical student and apprentice in one of the early Philadelphia doctor's "shops" and then went to Edinburgh for two years of further study, and later to the hospital of St. Thomas in London for additional experience. Immediately upon his return home in 1769, he became identified with the movement for medical education through appointment to the faculty of the College of

---

[1] An adequate bibliography of the writings and life of Benjamin Rush would occupy several pages, and the following list contains only selected references which are of special interest to the social worker. The most conveniently available biography is Harry G. Good, *Benjamin Rush and His Services to American Education* (1918); but Rush's autobiography, *A Memorial Containing Travels through Life or Sundry Incidents in the Life of Dr. Benjamin Rush; Written by Himself,* edited by Louis Alexander Biddle (1905), is extremely interesting. See, also, David Ramsay, *An Eulogium upon Benjamin Rush, M.D.* (1813); John Graver Johnson, *A Criticism of Mr. William B. Reed's Aspersions on the Character of Dr. Benjamin Rush* (1867); Thomas D. Mitchell, *The Character of Rush* (1848); William Pepper, *Benjamin Rush* (1890); Benjamin Rush, *Report of an Action for Libel, Brought by Dr. Benjamin Rush against William Cobbett in the Supreme Court of Pennsylvania* (1800). Among his own writings, in addition to those listed in footnotes to the Documents on pp. 282 and 295, are *An Address to the Inhabitants of the British Settlements in America, upon Slave-Keeping* (1773); *Considerations on the Injustice and Impolicy of Punishing Murder by Death* (1792); *An Inquiry into the Effects of Public Punishments upon Criminals, and upon Society* (1787); *An Account of the Manners of the German Inhabitants of Pennsylvania* (written in 1789) (Pennsylvania-German Society, 1910). See also the recent volume which appeared after this material had been published, Nathan G. Goodman, *Benjamin Rush, Physician and Citizen* (1934).

One of his biographers (Good, *op. cit.*, pp. 95–96) says that "his numerous publications were for the most part intended and regarded as the means of advancing the various 'causes' in which he was interested." The titles "will show what these causes were.

Philadelphia, where the earliest medical school in the country was being established.

From the beginning he gave his services generously to the destitute. He recalled later in life that he had been much struck when a boy by reading that a celebrated physician had said that "the poor were his *best* patients because God was their paymaster." His natural disposition made this practice among the poor attractive to him, for he confessed to "a natural sympathy with distress of every kind." He wrote in his later years of this early period as follows:

From the time of my settlement in Philadelphia in 1769 until 1775 I led a life of constant labor and self denial. My shop was crowded with the poor in the morning and at meal times, and nearly every street and alley in the city was visited by me every day. There are few old huts now standing in the ancient parts of the city in which I have not attended sick people. Often have I ascended the upper story of these huts by a ladder, and many hundred times have I been obliged to rest my weary limbs upon the bedside of the sick, from the want of chairs, where I was sure I risked, not only taking their disease, but being infected by vermin. More than once did I suffer from the latter. Nor did I hasten from these abodes of poverty and misery. Where no other help was attainable, I have often remained in them long enough to administer my prescriptions, particularly bleeding with my own hands. I review these scenes with heartfelt pleasure. I believed at the time that they would not lose their reward. "Take care of him, and I will repay thee," were words which I have repeated a thousand times to myself in leaving the rooms of this class of sick people.[1]

They will show that he was throughout life a lover of his kind; a friend of the poor, the distressed, the unfortunate and the criminal. He was one of the first champions of the slave; one of the founders and for many years an officer in the first abolition society in America. He was one of the earliest advocates of temperance. He had the vision, the wisdom and the courage to urge the reformation of the bibulous habits of his time. He rests from his labors in the shadow of a tree which is thus described in a tablet over his grave: 'On the 3rd of November, 1885, the officers and delegates of the National Women's Christian Temperance Union from forty states and numbering 300 by their representatives planted this oak tree in token of their reverence for the memory of Dr. Benjamin Rush, instaurator of the American temperance reform, one hundred years ago.' He labored early for penal reform, for the abolition of the death penalty, for humane treatment and enlightened care of the insane, for humanity in the handling of animals. And it is to be mentioned as bearing on the last subject that he urged the establishment of a school of veterinary medicine."

[1] From *A Memorial, etc.*, pp. 58–59.

In this early period he also showed his interest in public affairs in his *Address to the Inhabitants of the British Settlements upon Slave-Keeping,* in which he said he "endeavored to show the iniquity of the slave trade." He thought, however, that this pamphlet had injured his growing practice "by giving rise to an opinion that I had meddled in a controversy that was foreign to my business." He found, in his own words, "that a physician's studies and duties were to be limited by the public and that he was destined to walk in a path as contracted as the most humble mechanic."

Of the critical year 1775, he wrote: "I now resolved to bear my share of the distress and burdens of the approaching revolution." Later in the same year he was appointed surgeon for the fleet of gunboats constructed for the protection of Philadelphia. It was also in the same eventful year that he suggested to Thomas Paine the preparation of the pamphlet *Common Sense.*

In the summer of 1776 he was elected a member of the delegation from Pennsylvania to the Continental Congress, and his name appears next to that of Franklin on the Declaration of Independence. In the following year he became surgeon general of the armies of the middle states and later physician general of the military hospitals. His career in these offices was a stormy one because of his hatred of the incompetency that he believed to be responsible for needless loss of life among the young soldiers of the Revolution. He wrote as follows of the conditions which confronted him:

The American army had suffered greatly in the campaign of 1776, from the want of system and perhaps of knowledge in the management of the medical department. I wished to introduce order and economy in our hospitals, and for this purpose recommended the system which time and experience had proved to be a good one in the British army. Its principal merit and advantage consisted in the directing and purveying business being independent of each other. In vain did I plead publicly and privately for the adoption of this system. Such was the temper of Congress at that time that its British origin helped to produce its rejection. The system established by Congress placed the directing or supreme medical power, and the purveyorship in the same hands. I reluctantly accepted the commission of physician general of the military hospitals under it, and entered upon my duty with a heart devoted to the interests of my country. The evils of the system soon developed themselves. A fatal hospital fever was generated in the month of May in 1777 in the house of employment by our sick being too much crowded. Several of the attending surgeons and mates died of it and most of them were infected by it. I called upon the Director and asked for more rooms for the sick. This was denied. Here was the beginning of sufferings and mortality in the American army which had nearly destroyed it. A physician who practises in a hospital or elsewhere should have no check upon his prescriptions. Air, water, fire and everything necessary to the relief and cure of the sick should be made to obey him. The reverse of this was the case in the military hospitals of the United States. No order was given or executed for food, medicines, liquors, or even apartments for the sick without the consent of the Director General.[1]

His further account of the situation and his indictment of Dr. Shippen, who, as director general, was his superior officer, must be quoted in full:

In April or May, 1777, I accepted of the appointment of physician-general of the military hospitals of the United States under the direction of Dr. Shippen. Here I saw scenes of distress touching to humanity, and disgraceful to a civilized country. I can never forget them. I still see the sons of our yeomanry brought up in the lap of plenty and domestic comforts, shivering with cold upon the bare floors without a blanket to cover them, calling for fire, for water, for suitable food, for medicines and calling in vain. I hear the complaints they utter against their country,—I hear their sighs for their fathers' firesides,—I hear their groans,—I see them expire. While hundreds of the flower of our youth were dying under such accumulated sufferings, Dr. Shippen was feasting with the general officers at the camp, or bargaining with tavern keepers in Jersey and Pennsylvania for the sale of Madeira wine from our hospital stores, bought for the use of the sick. Nor was this all. No officer was ever sent to command or preserve discipline in our hospital (a practice universal in European armies) in consequence of which our soldiers sold their blankets, muskets, and even clothing for the necessaries of life or for ardent spirits. In this situation of our hospital I addressed two letters to General Washington, the one complaining of the above abuses and pointing out their remedies,—the other complaining of Dr. Shippen for mal-practices. I expected that a court would be ordered to inquire into Dr. Shippen's conduct in consequence of my second letter. In this I was disappointed. Both my letters were sent to Congress, and a committee appointed to hear my complaints against the Director-General. On my way to Yorktown where the Congress then sat, I passed through the Army at Valley Forge where I saw similar marks of filth, waste of public property and want of discipline which I had recently witnessed in the hospitals. General Sullivan (at whose quarters I breakfasted) said to me, "Sir, this is not an army, it is a mob." Here a new source of distress was awakened in my mind. I now felt for the safety and independence of my country as well as for the sufferings of the sick under my care. . . . . .

[1] *A Memorial, etc.*, pp. 99–100.

In the year 1779 Dr. Morgan dragged Dr. Shippen before a court-martial at Morristown where I was summoned as a witness. During the trial several members of the court-martial were changed,—a thing I believed never done in such courts, nor in juries except in cases of sickness or death. The Doctor was acquitted, but without honor, and by a majority of a single vote. Soon after this cold and bare acquittal he resigned. Gen. Washington gave him a certificate approving of his conduct while Director-General of the hospitals, and saying that the distresses of the sick arose from a state of things inseparable from the new and peculiar situation of our country.

The change which took place in the army by the appointment of Baron Steuben, Inspector General, Mr. Morris, Financier, and Colonel Hamilton, a member of General Washington's family, restored him to the universal confidence of his country. You may easily conceive the nature of this change when I add that Baron Steuben said the clothes destroyed by our army would clothe the largest army in Europe (previously to his appointment) and of course that an immense saving of money and health and lives was the consequence of the economy he introduced into the army in that article alone; also, that Mr. Morris informed me that the expenses of the hospital department alone after he took charge of the finances were reduced from five million to one million of dollars in one year, estimating the value of paper money in gold and silver coin in both years.[1]

Dr. Rush was generous in his treatment of the enemies of the Revolution in spite of his ardent devotion to the cause of independence. He made repeated efforts to secure the release of a British officer who was ill and a prisoner of war, but without success. He then tried "to render his confinement as easy to him as possible until he was exchanged." As a result he was the object of attack in certain quarters for lack of patriotism and was charged with "always taking the part of Tory rascals."

After the evacuation of Philadelphia by the British he returned to that city with his family. In his *Memorial* he writes, "From the filth left by the British army in all the streets the city became sickly, and I was suddenly engaged in extensive and profitable business."

His activity during the Revolution involved heavy financial sacrifices. He thought that the depreciation of paper money and the loss of business to which he exposed himself by taking part in the Revolution had cost him not less than £10,000. He was proud of

[1] This account is to be found in the Rush MSS of the Ridgway Library of Philadelphia, XXIX, 136. It is quoted in full in several publications including Good, *op. cit.*, pp. 56–60.

the fact that during the whole of the war he never charged an officer or soldier of the American army anything for medicines or attendance. Toward the close of his life, in writing of this subject, he said that he thought he had not been paid for more than one-fifth of the labor of his life.

Only the briefest account of the numerous philanthropic interests of Dr. Rush is possible here, but it must be mentioned that he was an early contributor to, and member of, the staff of the Pennsylvania Hospital; and, as the author of *Inquiries and Observations upon the Diseases of the Mind*, he was called the "Father of American Psychiatry." He was the founder in 1786 of the Philadelphia Dispensary, apparently the earliest of our free dispensaries. He was active in the attempt to secure a hospital for the insane which should be separate from the Pennsylvania Hospital, which had cared both for the mentally and the physically ill. In his notebook[1] on March 1, 1792, he made the following entry:

> Yesterday a vote passed the Lower House of Assembly to allot $15,000 to build a mad-house. The idea of this building, etc. originated last winter in a conversation with Bartholomew Wister in the Hospital and the public mind was first awakened to it by a short publication I threw out in Dunlap's paper. I mention this to encourage my boys to expect great things from slender beginnings and weak instruments.

Before the Revolution he was already known as a young physician with an interest in reform movements. As early as 1774 he had been one of the founders of the Pennsylvania Society for Promoting the Abolition of Slavery and the Relief of Free Negroes Unlawfully Held in Bondage (the first American antislavery society). After the war his interests broadened. He was opposed to capital punishment and wrote one of the earliest articles published in America which set out the reasons for its abolition.[2] He was a member of the Society for Alleviating the Miseries of Public Prisons, and his notebook records a visit to the new jail (1794) with Caleb Lownes, the Quaker prison-reformer; and in 1796 he complained that the jail is

---

[1] From *A Memorial, etc.*, p. 133.

[2] See this *Review*, I (December, 1927), 645, for quotation from this article, which was entitled "An Enquiry into the Effects of Public Punishments upon Criminals and upon Society" and was first published in the *American Museum*.

"crowded with persons sent there for debt." He thought the "republican ferment" caused by the "revolution of republican principles" was responsible for new views of various social questions. He observed "a precipitation of the feculencies of error, upon the subject of education, penal laws and capital punishments." He published various essays upon each of these subjects, and in his autobiography we find this statement:

My opinions upon the latter subjects subjected me to some abuse and ridicule in the public newspapers. I met with but three persons in Philadelphia who agreed with me in denying the right of human laws over human life, when my publication against capital punishments first made its appearance, but in less than two years I had the satisfaction of observing that opinion to be adopted by many hundred people; more especially among the Society of Friends.

But I did not content myself by merely attacking old errors and prejudices from the press. I assisted in the institution of societies to carry them into effect. I was likewise for a while an active member of several societies whose objects were altogether of a humane nature.

The extract which we are publishing from his account of the yellow-fever epidemic gives a vivid picture of the services of Dr. Rush during that terrible period, and outlines the various controversies that separated him from some of the leading physicians of Philadelphia. When he became convinced that the fever was a disease of domestic origin, he insisted on stating publicly the reasons for his belief; but the College of Physicians went on record with a contrary report which said, "No instance has ever occurred of the disease called yellow fever having been generated in this city, or in any other parts of the United States, as far as we know: but there have been frequent instances of its having been imported."

Attacks upon his character in 1793 and the year following he attributed to the dislike of his opinions and the desire on the part of those who disagreed with him to lessen "the influence of a man who had aimed to destroy the credit of their city by ascribing to it a power of generating yellow fever." Of this hostility he wrote as follows:

Their design proved successful. They lessened my business, and they abstracted so much of the confidence of my patients as to render my practice extremely difficult and disagreeable among them. To put a stop to their injurious effects upon my business, and the lives of my patients, I commenced civil action. . . . .

From the year 1793 till 1797 my business was stationary in Philadelphia, after 1797 it sensibly declined. I had no new families except foreigners, added to the list of my patients and many of my old patients deserted me. Even the cures that I performed added to the detraction that had taken place against my character, when they were effected by remedies that were new and contrary to the feelings of citizens. No ties of ancient school fellowship, no obligations of gratitude, no sympathy in religious or philosophical opinions, were able to resist the tide of public clamor that was excited against my practice. My name was mentioned with horror in some companies, and to some of the weakest and insignificant of my brethren false tales of me became a recommendation to popular favor.[1]

Rush was an early advocate of free education; and, what was even more remarkable, he believed that women as well as men should have educational opportunities. He published in 1786 *A Plan for the Establishment of Public Schools and the Diffusion of Knowledge in Pennsylvania* and *Thoughts upon the Mode of Education Proper in a Republic*. In the following year he published *Thoughts upon Female Education*. In the same year he issued an *Address to the People of the United States* on the subject of education.

On March 20, 1792, he wrote in his "commonplace book" that he had witnessed a "day of triumph," in which "great good" had been accomplished. "This day," he wrote, "was spent in debating about the establishment of free schools in our legislature. I had great pleasure in living to see this event, for I had ten years ago and ever since inculcated the necessity and advantage of them from the press."

He was liberal in his attitude toward immigration; and at a time when even Benjamin Franklin had misgivings as to the effect of German immigration on Pennsylvania, Rush prepared a fine appreciation of his German fellow-citizens.[2]

The historian George Bancroft published, many years after the death of Rush, a discriminating estimate of his character and work. Bancroft knew that Rush made mistakes and that he had been overhasty in a quarrel with Washington, which the latter generously forgave. But Bancroft, weighing all the evidence with the caution of a historian, wrote of him as follows:

[1] From *A Memorial, etc.*, pp. 72–73.

[2] See E. Abbott, *Historical Aspects of the Immigration Problem*, pp. 415–16, 544–45, and 422–24, for the views of Franklin and Rush on this subject.

On the second of August, 1776, Rush signed the Declaration of Independence, and kept with truth and firmness the pledge which he then gave of life, fortune, and sacred honor. . . . . I once had in my custody fragments of diaries and auto-biographical sketches of Rush, written at various periods of his life, as well as two bound volumes of his most private correspondence, so that I was able to study his character thoroughly. He did not deny his faults, but claimed to "aim well." The key to his character is, that he was of an impatient and impulsive nature, fond of quick decision and quick action, and in consequence capable, under sudden excitement, of writing in terms of extravagance, or judging character, for the moment, unfairly. As a physician he inclined to powerful remedies and the free use of the lancet, and in public life he was eager for drastic measures, so that he sometimes fell into controversy with men of a calmer temperament than his own. But the tone of his own opinions is always the same. From his early life to his old age, his patriotism could not be doubted, and whenever a question regarding freedom arose he was sure to take the side of freedom. As he was one of the first to speak for independence, he was one of the first, publicly as well as privately, to speak for the abolition of slavery, and to treat the colored people as fellow-men and fellow-citizens; and to his last breath he was devoted to those principles of Jefferson which were humane and liberal. The profession of medicine, no less than that of war, has its bead-roll of heroes who have defied death in the discharge of duty. When an infectious pestilence, raging in Philadelphia, rapidly swept nearly four thousand to the grave, Rush despised every consideration of personal safety, and was so true day and night to his patients that it was said of him in Europe: "Not Philadelphia alone but mankind should raise to him a statue."[1]

E. A.

A Physician in the Epidemic of 1793[2]

The first reports of the existence of this fever were treated with neglect or contempt. A strange apathy pervaded all classes of people. While I bore my share of reproach for "terrifying our citizens with imaginary danger," I answered it by lamenting "that they were not terrified enough." The publication from the college of physicians soon dissipated this indifference and incredulity. Fear or terror now sat upon every countenance. The disease appeared in many parts of the town, remote from the spot

[1] George Bancroft, *Joseph Reed: A Historical Essay* (New York, 1867), pp. 31–32.

[2] Extract from Benjamin Rush, "An Account of the Bilious Remitting Yellow Fever, as It Appeared in Philadelphia in the Year 1793," *Medical Inquiries and Observations* (4th ed.; Philadelphia, 1815), III, 93–101, 181–93.

Good (*op. cit.*, p. 86) notes that Dr. Trotter said his "account" was the best history of an epidemic that had ever been written. It was translated into three languages. "As a mark of respect for his medical character and writings, especially his record of the yellow fever, both the King of Prussia and the Queen of Etruria presented him with

where it originated; although, for a while, in every instance, it was easily traced to it. This set the city in motion. The streets and roads leading from the city were crowded with families flying in every direction for safety to the country. Business began to languish. Water-street, between Market and Race-streets, became a desert.

The poor were the first victims of the fever. From the sudden interruption of business they suffered for a while from poverty as well as from disease. A large and airy house at Bush-hill, about a mile from the city was opened for their reception. This house, after it became the charge of a committee appointed by the citizens on the 14th of September, was regulated and governed with the order and cleanliness of an old and established hospital. An American and French physician had the exclusive medical care of it after the 22d of September.

The disease, after the second week in September, spared no rank of citizens. Whole families were confined by it. There was a deficiency of nurses for the sick, and many of those who were employed were unqualified for their business. There was likewise a great deficiency of physicians, from the desertion of some, and the sickness and death of others. At one time there were but three physicians who were able to do business out of their houses, and at this time there were probably not less than 6,000 persons ill with the fever.

During the first three or four weeks of the prevalence of the disease I seldom went into a house the first time without meeting the parents or children of the sick in tears. Many wept aloud in my entry or parlour, who came to ask for advice for their relations. Grief after a while descended below weeping, and I was much struck in observing that many persons submitted to the loss of relations and friends without shedding a tear, or manifesting any other of the common signs of grief.

A cheerful countenance was scarcely to be seen in the city for six weeks. I recollected once, in entering the house of a poor man, to have met a child of two years old that smiled in my face. I was strangely affected with this sight (so discordant to my feelings and the state of the city) before I recollected the age and ignorance of the child. I was con-

medals, the latter of gold; and the Czar of Russia sent him a costly diamond. Two medals, dated 1808, were also struck in his honor at the U.S. Mint in Philadelphia." His other writings on the yellow fever include *An Inquiry into the Origin of the Late Epidemic Fever in Philadelphia* (Philadelphia, 1793; pp. 15); *Observations upon the Origin of Malignant Bilious, or Yellow Fever in Philadelphia, and upon the Means of Preventing It; Addressed to the Citizens of Philadelphia* (Philadelphia, 1799; pp. 28); *A Second Address to the Citizens of Philadelphia Containing Additional Proofs of the Domestic Origin of the Malignant Bilious, or Yellow Fever* (Philadelphia, 1799; pp. 40).

fined the next day by an attack of the fever, and was sorry to hear, upon my recovery, that the father and mother of this little creature died a few days after my last visit to them.

The streets everywhere discovered marks of the distress that pervaded the city. More than one half the houses were shut up, although not more than one third of the inhabitants had fled into the country. In walking for many hundred yeards, few persons were met, except such as were in quest of a physician, a nurse, a bleeder, or the men who buried the dead. The hearse alone kept up the remembrance of the noise of carriages or carts in the streets. Funeral processions were laid aside. A black man, leading or driving a horse, with a corpse on a pair of chair wheels, with now and then half a dozen relations or friends following at a distance from it, met the eye in most of the streets of the city, at every hour of the day, while the noise of the same wheels passing slowly over the pavements, kept alive anguish and fear in the sick and well, every hour of the night.

But a more serious source of the distress of the city arose from the dissentions of the physicians, about the nature and treatment of the fever. It was considered by some as a modification of the influenza, and by others as the jail fever. Its various grades and symptoms were considered as so many different diseases, all originating from different causes. There was the same contrariety in the practice of the physicians that there was in their principles. The newspapers conveyed accounts of both to the public, every day. The minds of the citizens were distracted by them, and hundreds suffered and died from the delays which were produced by an erroneous opinion of a plurality of diseases in the city, or by indecision in the choice, or a want of confidence in the remedies of their physician.

The science of medicine is related to everything, and the philosopher as well as the Christian will be gratified by knowing the effects of a great and mortal epidemic upon the morals of a people. It was some alleviation of the distress produced by it, to observe its influence upon the obligations of morality and religion. It was remarked during this time, by many people, that the name of the Supreme Being was seldom profaned, either in the streets, or in the intercourse of the citizens with each other. But two robberies, and those of a trifling nature, occurred in nearly two months, although many hundred houses were exposed to plunder, every hour of the day and night. Many of the religious societies met two or three times a week, and some of them every evening, to implore the interposition of Heaven to save the city from desolation. Humanity and charity kept pace with devotion. The public have already seen accounts of their benevolent exercises in other publications. It was my lot to witness the uncommon activity of those virtues upon a smaller scale. I saw little to blame, but much to admire and praise in persons of different professions, both sexes, and of all colours. It would be foreign to the design of this work to draw from the obscurity which they sought, the many acts of humanity and charity, of fortitude, patience, and perseverance, which came under my notice. They will be made public and applauded elsewhere.

But the virtues which were excited by our calamity were not confined to the city of Philadelphia. The United States wept for the distresses of their capital. In several of the states, and in many cities and villages, days of humiliation and prayer were set apart to supplicate the Father of Mercies in behalf of our afflicted city. Nor was this all. From nearly every state in the union the most liberal contributions of money, provisions, and fuel were poured in for the relief and support of such as had been reduced to want by the suspension of business, as well as by sickness and the death of friends.

The number of deaths between the 1st of August and the 9th of November amounted to four thousand and forty-four. . . . . Several of the deaths in August were from other acute diseases, and a few in the succeeding months were from such as were of a chronic nature. . . . . The principal mortality was in the second week of October. A general expectation had obtained, that cold weather was as fatal to this fever as heavy rains. The usual time for its arrival had come, but the weather was still not only moderate, but warm. In this awful situation, the stoutest hearts began to fail. Hope sickened, and despair succeeded distress in almost every countenance. On the fifteenth of October, it pleased God to alter the state of the air. The clouds at last dropped health in showers of rain, which continued during the whole day, and which were succeeded for nights afterwards by cold and frost. The effects of this change in the weather appeared first in the sudden diminution of the sick, for the deaths continued for a week afterwards to be numerous, but they were of persons who had been confined before, or on the day in which the change had taken place in the weather.

The appearance of this rain was like a dove with an olive branch in its mouth to the whole city. Public notice was given of its beneficial effects, in a letter subscribed by the mayor of Philadelphia, who acted as president of the committee, to the mayor of New York. I shall insert the whole of this letter. It contains, besides the above information, a record of the liberality of the city to the distressed inhabitants of Philadelphia.

Sir,

I am favoured with your letter of the 12th instant, which I have communicated to the committee for the relief of the poor and afflicted of this city.

It is with peculiar satisfaction that I execute their request, by making in their name, on behalf of our suffering fellow-citizens, the most grateful acknowledgments for the seasonable benevolence of the common council of the city of New York. Their sympathy is balm to our wounds.

We acknowledge the Divine interposition, whereby the hearts of so many around us have been touched with our distress, and have united in our relief.

May the Almighty Disposer of all events be graciously pleased to protect your citizens from the dreadful calamity with which we are now visited; whilst we humbly kiss the rod, and improve by the dispensation.

The part, sir, which you personally take in our afflictions, and which you have so pathetically expressed in your letter, excites in the breasts of the committee the warmest sensations of fraternal affection.

The refreshing rain which fell the day before yesterday, though light, and the cool weather which hath succeeded, appear to have given a check to the prevalence of the disorder: of this we have satisfactory proofs, as well in the decrease of the funerals, as in the applications for removal to the hospital.

I have, at your request, this day drawn upon you, at sight, in favour of the president and directors of the Bank of North America, for the sum of five thousand dollars, the benevolent donations of the common council of the city of New York.

With sentiments of the greatest esteem and regard,

I am, sir,

Your most obedient humble servant,

Matth. Clarkson

. . . . From the 15th of October the disease not only declined, but assumed more obvious inflammatory symptoms. It was, as in the beginning, more necessarily fatal where left to itself, but it yielded more certainly to art than it did a few weeks before. The duration of it was now more tedious than in the warm weather.

There were a few cases of yellow fever in November and December, after the citizens who had retired to the country returned to the city.

I heard of but three persons who returned to the city being infected with the disease: so completely was its cause destroyed in the course of a few weeks.

In consequence of a proclamation by the governor, and a recommendation by the clergy of Philadelphia, the 12th of December was observed as a day of thanksgiving throughout the state, for the extinction of the disease in the city.

It was easy to distinguish, in walking the streets, the persons who had returned from the country to the city, from those who had remained in it during the prevalence of the fever. The former appeared ruddy and healthy, while the latter appeared of a pale sallow colour.

It afforded a subject of equal surprise and joy to behold the suddenness with which the city recovered its former habits of business. In the course of six weeks after the disease had ceased, nothing but fresh graves, and the black dresses of many of the citizens, afforded a public trace of the distress which had so lately prevailed in the city. . . . .

A NARRATIVE OF THE STATE OF THE BODY AND MIND OF THE AUTHOR, DURING THE PREVALENCE OF THE FEVER

Narratives of escapes from great dangers of shipwreck, war, captivity, and famine have always formed an interesting part of the history of the body and mind of man. But there are deliverances from equal dangers which have hitherto passed unnoticed; I mean from pestilential fevers. I shall briefly describe the state of my body and mind during my intercourse with the sick in the epidemic of 1793. The account will throw additional light upon the disease, and probably illustrate some of the laws of the animal economy: It will, moreover, serve to furnish a lesson to all who may be placed in similar circumstances to commit their lives, without fear, to the protection of that Being, who is able to save to the uttermost, not only from future, but from present evil.

Some time before the fever made its appearance, my wife and children went into the state of New Jersey, where they had long been in the habit of spending the summer months. My family, about the 25th of August, consisted of my mother, sister, who was on a visit to me, a black servant man, and a mulatto boy. I had five pupils, viz. Warner Washington and Edward Fisher, of Virginia; John Alston, of South Carolina, and John Redman Coxe (grandson to Dr. Redman) and John Stall, both of this city. They all crowded around me upon the sudden increase of business, and with one heart devoted themselves to my service, and to the cause of humanity.

The credit which the new mode of treating the disease acquired, in all parts of the city, produced an immense influx of patients to me from all quarters. My pupils were constantly employed; at first in putting up purging powders, but, after a while, only in bleeding and visiting the sick.

Between the 8th and the 15th of September I visited and prescribed for between a hundred and a hundred and twenty patients a day. Several of my pupils visited a fourth or fifth part of that number. For a while we refused no calls. In the short intervals of business, which I spent at my meals, my house was filled with patients, chiefly the poor, waiting for advice. For many weeks I seldom ate without prescribing for numbers as I sat at my table. To assist me at these hours, as well as in the night, Mr. Stall, Mr. Fisher, and Mr. Coxe accepted of rooms in my house, and became members of my family. Their labours now had no remission.

Immediately after I adopted the antiphlogistic mode of treating the disease, I altered my manner of living. I left off drinking wine and malt liquors. The good effects of the disuse of these liquors helped to confirm me in the theory I had adopted of the disease. A troublesome head-ache, which I had occasionally felt, and which excited a constant apprehension that I was taking the fever, now suddenly left me. I likewise, at this time, left off eating solid animal food, and lived wholly, but sparingly, upon weak broth, potatoes, raisins, coffee, and bread and butter.

From my constant exposure to the sources of the disease, my body became highly impregnated with miasmata. My eyes were yellow, and sometimes a yellowness was perceptible in my face. My pulse was preternaturally quick, and I had profuse sweats every night. . . . . But my nights were rendered disagreeable, not only by these sweats, but by the want of my usual sleep, produced in part by the frequent knocking at my door, and in part by anxiety of mind, and the stimulus of the miasmata upon my system. I went to bed in conformity to habit only, for it ceased to afford me rest or refreshment. When it was evening I wished for morning; and when it was morning, the prospect of the labours of the day, at which I often shuddered, caused me to wish for the return of evening. The degrees of my anxiety may be easily conceived when I add, that I had at one time upwards of thirty heads of families under my care; among these were Mr. Josiah Coates, the father of eight, and Mr. Benjamin Scull and Mr. John Morell, both fathers of ten children. They were all in imminent danger; but it pleased God to make me the instrument of saving each of their lives. I rose at six o'clock, and generally found a number of persons waiting for advice in my shop or parlour. Hitherto the success of my practice gave a tone to my mind, which imparted preternatural vigour to my body. It was meat and drink to me to fulfil the duties I owed to my fellow-citizens, in this time of great and universal distress. From a hope that I might escape the disease, by avoiding every thing that could excite it into action, I carefully avoided the heat of the sun, and the coldness of the evening air. I likewise avoided yielding to everything that should raise or depress my passions. But at such a time, the events which influence the state of the body and mind are no more under our command than the winds or weather. On the evening of the 14th of September, after eight o'clock, I visited the son of Mrs. Berriman, near the Swedes' church, who had sent for me early in the morning. I found him very ill. He had been bled in the forenoon, by my advice, but his pulse indicated a second bleeding. It would have been difficult to procure a bleeder at that late hour. I therefore bled him myself. Heated by this act, and debilitated by the labours of the day, I rode home in the evening air. During the ensuing night I was much indisposed. I rose, notwithstanding, at my usual hour. At eight o'clock I lost ten ounces of blood, and immediately afterwards got into my chair, and visited between forty and fifty patients before dinner. At the house of one of them I was forced to lie down a few minutes. In the course of this morning's labours my mind was suddenly thrown off its pivots, by the last look, and the pathetic cries, of a friend for help, who was dying under the care of a French physician. I came home about two o'clock, and was seized, immediately afterwards, with a chilly fit and a high fever. I took a dose of the mercurial medicine, and went to bed. In the evening I took a second purging powder, and lost ten ounces more of blood. The next morning I bathed my face, hands, and feet in cold water for some time. I drank plentifully, during the day and night, of weak hyson tea, and of water, in which currant jelly had been dissolved. At eight o'clock I was so well as to admit persons who came for advice into my room, and to receive reports from my pupils of the state of as many of my patients as they were able to visit; for, unfortunately, they were not able to visit them all (with their own) in due time; in consequence of which several died. The next day I came downstairs, and prescribed in my parlour for not less than a hundred people. On the 19th of the same month, I resumed my labours, but in great weakness. It was with difficulty that I ascended a pair of stairs, by the help of a banister. A slow fever, attended with irregular chills, and a troublesome cough, hung constantly upon me. The fever discovered itself in the heat of my hands, which my patients often told me were warmer than their own. The breath and exhalations from the sick now began to affect me, in small and infected rooms, in the most sensible manner. On the morning of the 4th of October I suddenly sank down, in a sick room, upon a bed, with a giddiness in my head. It continued for a few minutes, and was succeeded by a fever, which confined me to my house the remaining part of the day.

Every moment in the intervals of my visits to the sick was employed in prescribing, in my own house, for the poor, or in sending answers to messages from my patients; time was now too precious to be spent in counting the number of persons who called upon me for advice. From circumstances I believe it was frequently 150, and seldom less than 50 in a day, for five or six weeks. The evening did not bring with it the least relaxation from my labours. I received letters every day from the country, and from distant parts of the union, containing inquiries into the mode of treating the disease, and after the health and lives of persons who had remained in the city. The business of every evening was to answer these letters, also to write to my family. These employments, by affording a fresh current to my thoughts, kept me from dwelling on the gloomy scenes of the day. After these duties were performed, I copied into my note book all the observations I had collected during the day, and which I had marked with a pencil in my pocket-book in sick rooms, or in my carriage.

To these constant labours of body and mind were added distresses from a variety of causes. Having found myself unable to comply with the numerous applications that were made to me, I was obliged to refuse many every day. My sister counted forty-seven in one forenoon before eleven o'clock. Many of them left my door with tears, but they did not feel more distress than I did from refusing to follow them. Sympathy, when it vents itself in acts of humanity, affords pleasure, and contributes to health; but the reflux of pity, like anger, gives pain, and disorders the body. In riding through the streets, I was often forced to resist the entreaties of parents imploring a visit to their children, or of children to their parents. I recollect, and even *yet* with pain, that I tore myself at one time from five persons in Moravian alley, who attempted to stop me, by suddenly whipping my horse, and driving my chair as speedily as possible beyond the reach of their cries.

The solicitude of the friends of the sick for help may further be conceived of, when I add, that the most extravagant compensations were sometimes offered for medical services, and, in one instance, for only a single visit. I had no merit in refusing these offers, and I have introduced an account of them only to inform such physicians as may hereafter be thrown into a similar situation, that I was favoured with an exemption from the fear of death, in proportion as I subdued every selfish feeling, and laboured exclusively for the benefit of others. In every instance in which I was forced to refuse these pathetic and earnest applications, my distress was heightened by the fear that the persons, whom I was unable to visit, would fall into improper hands, and perish by the use of bark, wine, and laudanum.

But I had other afflictions besides the distress which arose from the abortive sympathy which I have described. On the 11th of September, my ingenious pupil, Mr. Washington, fell a victim to his humanity. He had taken lodgings in the country, where he sickened with the disease. Having been almost uniformly successful in curing others, he made light of his fever, and concealed the knowledge of his danger from me, until the day before he died. On the 18th of September Mr. Stall sickened in my house. A delirium attended his fever from the first hour it affected him. He refused, and even resisted force when used to compel him to take medicine. He died on the 23d of September.[1] Scarce had I recovered from the shock of the death of this amiable youth, when I was called to weep for a third pupil, Mr. Alston, who died in my neighbourhood the next day. He had worn himself down, before his sickness, by uncommon exertions in visiting, bleeding, and even sitting up with sick people. At this time Mr. Fisher was ill in my house. On the 26th of the month, at 12 o'clock, Mr. Coxe, my only assistant was seized with the fever, and went to his grand-father's. I followed him with a look, which I feared would be the last in my house. At two o'clock my sister, who had complained for several days, yielded to the disease, and retired to her bed. My mother followed her, much indisposed, early in the evening. My black servant man had been confined with the fever for several days, and had on that day, for the first time quitted his bed. My little mulatto boy, of eleven years old, was the only person in my family who was able to afford me the least assistance. At eight o'clock in the evening I finished the business of the day. A solemn stillness at that time pervaded the streets. In vain did I strive to forget my melancholy situation by answering letters and by putting up medicines, to be distributed next day among my patients. My faithful black man crept to my door, and at my request sat down by the fire, but he added, by his silence and dulness, to the gloom, which suddenly overpowered every faculty of my mind.

[1] This accomplished youth had made great attainments in his profession. He possessed, with an uncommon genius for science, talents for music, painting, and poetry. The following copy of an unfinished letter to his father (who had left the city) was found among his papers after his death. It shows that the qualities of his heart were equal to those of his head.

"Philadelphia, September 15, 1793.

"My Dear Father, I take every moment I have to spare to write you, which is not many; but you must excuse me, as I am doing good to my fellow-creatures. At this time, every moment I spend in idleness might probably cost a life. The sickness increases every day, but most of those who die, die for want of good attendance. We cure all we are called to on the first day, who are well attended, but so many doctors are sick, the poor creatures are glad to get a doctor's servant."

On the first day of October, at two o'clock in the afternoon, my sister died. I got into my carriage within an hour after she expired, and spent the afternoon in visiting patients. According as a sense of duty, or as grief has predominated in my mind, I have approved, and disapproved, of this act, ever since. She had borne a share in my labours. She had been my nurse in sickness, and my casuist in my choice of duties. My whole heart reposed itself in her friendship. Upon being invited to a friend's house in the country, when the disease made its appearance in the city, she declined accepting the invitation, and gave as a reason for so doing, that I might probably require her services in case of my taking the disease, and that if she were sure of dying, she would remain with me, provided that, by her death, she could save my life. From this time I declined in health and strength. All motion became painful to me. My appetite began to fail. My night sweats continued. My short and imperfect sleep was disturbed by distressing or frightful dreams. The scenes of them were derived altogether from sick rooms and grave-yards. I concealed my sorrows as much as possible from my patients; but when alone, the retrospect of what was past, and the prospect of what was before me, the termination of which was invisible, often filled my soul with the most poignant anguish. I wept frequently when retired from the public eye, but I did not weep over the lost members of my family alone. I beheld or heard every day of the deaths of citizens, useful in public, or amiable in private life. It was my misfortune to lose as patients the Rev. Mr. Fleming and Mr. Graesel, both exhausted by their labours of piety and love among the poor, before they sickened with the disease. I saw the last struggles of departing life in Mr. Powell, and deplored, in his death, an upright and faithful servant of the public, as well as a sincere and affectionate friend. Often did I mourn over persons who had, by the most unparalleled exertions, saved their friends and families from the grave, at the expense of their own lives. Many of these martyrs to humanity were in humble stations. Among the members of my profession, with whom I have been most intimately connected, I had daily cause of grief and distress. . . . .

For the first two weeks after I visited patients in the yellow fever, I carried a rag wetted with vinegar, and smelled it occasionally in sick rooms: but after I saw and felt the signs of the universal presence of miasmata in my system, I laid aside this and all other precautions. I rested myself on the bed-side of my patients, and I drank milk or ate fruit in their sick rooms. Besides being saturated with miasmata, I had another security against being infected in sick rooms, and that was, I went into scarcely a house which was more infected than my own. Many of the poor people, who called upon me for advice, were bled by my pupils in my shop, and in the yard which was between it and the street. From the want of a sufficient number of bowls to receive their blood, it was sometimes suffered to flow and putrefy upon the ground. From this source streams of miasmata were constantly poured into my house, and conveyed into my body by the air, during every hour of the day and night.

The deaths of my pupils and sister have often been urged as objections to my mode of treating the fever. Had the same degrees of labour and fatigue, which preceded the attack of the yellow fever in each of them, preceded an attack of a common pleurisy, I think it probable that some, or perhaps all of them, would have died with it. But when the influence of the concentrated miasmata which filled my house was added to that of constant fatigue upon their bodies, what remedies could be expected to save their lives? Under the above circumstances, I consider the recovery of the other branches of my family from the fever (and none of them escaped it) with emotions, such as I should feel had we all been revived from apparent death by the exertions of a humane society. . . . .

I had read and taught, in my lectures, that fasting increases acuteness in the sense of touch. My low living had that effect, in a certain degree, upon my fingers. I had a quickness in my perception, of the state of the pulse in the yellow fever, that I had never experienced before in any other disease. My abstemious diet, assisted perhaps by the state of my feelings, had likewise an influence upon my mind. Its operations were performed with an ease and a celerity, which rendered my numerous and complicated duties much less burdensome than they would probably have been under other circumstances of diet, or a less agitated state of my passions.

My perception of the lapse of time was new to me. It was uncommonly slow. The ordinary business and pursuits of men appeared to me in a light that was equally new. The hearse and the grave mingled themselves with every view I took of human affairs. Under these impressions I recollect being as much struck with observing a number of men, employed in digging the cellar of a large house, as I should have been, at any other time, in seeing preparations for building a palace upon a cake of ice. I recollect, further, being struck with surprise, about the 1st of October, in seeing a man busily employed in laying in wood for the approaching winter. I should as soon have thought of making a provision for a dinner on the first day of the year 1800.

In the account of my distresses, I have passed over the slanders which were propagated against me by some of my brethren. I have mentioned them only for the sake of declaring, in this public manner, that I most heartily forgive them; and that if I discovered, at any time, an undue sense of the unkindness and cruelty of those slanders, it was not because I felt myself injured by them, but because I was sure they would irreparably injure my fellow-citizens, by lessening their confidence in the only remedies that I believed to be effectual in the reigning epidemic. One thing in my conduct towards these gentlemen may require justification; and that is, my refusing to consult with them. A Mahometan and a Jew might as well attempt to worship the Supreme Being in the same temple, and through the medium of the same ceremonies, as two physicians of opposite principles and practice attempt to confer about the life of the same patient. . . . .

After the loss of my health I received letters from my friends in the country, pressing me, in the strongest terms, to leave the city. Such a step had become impracticable. My aged mother was too infirm to be removed, and I could not leave her. I was, moreover, part of a little circle of physicians, who had associated themselves in support of the new remedies. This circle would have been broken by my quitting the city. The weather varied the disease, and, in the weakest state of my body, I expected to be able, from the reports of my pupils, to assist my associates in detecting its changes, and in accommodating our remedies to them. Under these circumstances it pleased God to enable me to reply to one of the letters that urged my retreat from the city, that "I had resolved to stick to my principles, my practice, and my patients, to the last extremity."

On the 9th of October, I visited a considerable number of patients, and, as the day was warm, I lessened the quantity of my clothing. Towards evening I was seized with a pain in the back, which obliged me to go to bed at eight o'clock. About twelve I awoke with a chilly fit. A violent fever, with acute pains in different parts of my body, followed it. At one o'clock I called for Mr. Fisher, who slept in the next room. He came instantly, with my affectionate black man, to my relief. I saw my danger painted in Mr. Fisher's countenance. He bled me plentifully, and gave me a dose of the mercurial medicine. . . . . The remaining part of the night was passed under an apprehension that my labours were near an end. I could hardly expect to survive so violent an attack of the fever, broken down, as I was, by labour, sickness, and grief. . . . . The next day the fever left me, but in so weak a state, that I awoke two successive nights with a faintness which threatened the extinction of my life. It was removed each time by taking a little aliment. My convalescence was extremely slow. I returned, in a very gradual manner, to my former habits of diet. . . . . During the month of November, and all the winter months, I was harassed with a cough and a fever somewhat of the hectic kind. The early warmth of the spring removed those complaints, and restored me, through Divine Goodness to my usual state of health.

I should be deficient in gratitude, were I to conclude this narrative without acknowledging my obligations to my surviving pupils, Mr. Fisher and Mr. Coxe, for the great support and sympathy I derived from them in my labours and distresses.

I take great pleasure likewise in acknowledging my obligations to my former pupil, Dr. Woodhouse, who assisted me in the care of my patients, after I became so weak as not to be able to attend them with the punctuality their cases required. The disinterested exploits of these young gentlemen in the cause of humanity, and their success in the treatment of the disease, have endeared their names to hundreds, and, at the same time, afforded a prelude of their future eminence and usefulness in their profession.

But wherewith shall I come before the great FATHER and REDEEMER of men, and what shall I render unto him for the issue of my life from the grave?

Here all language fails:
Come then expressive silence, muse his praise.

Life and Character of Christopher Ludwick[1]

There was a time, when the lives of men who occupied the first ranks in society were the only subjects of biographical history. Happily for the world, this species of writing has descended into the humble walks of life, and embracing the characters of men of different professions and occupations, has multiplied its usefulness, by holding up practicable examples of successful talents and virtue, to those classes of people who constitute the majority of mankind.

[1] From *An Account of the Life and Character of Christopher Ludwick, Late Citizen of Philadelphia, and Baker-General of the Army of the United States during the Revolutionary War*, by Benjamin Rush, M.D. First published in the year 1801. Reviewed and republished by direction of the Philadelphia Society for the Establishment and Support of Charity Schools. To which is added, "An Account of the Origin, Progress, and Present Condition of That Institution" (Philadelphia, 1831). The following introductory note appears in this edition:

"The Philadelphia Society for the Establishment and Support of Charity Schools, cherishing with feelings of respect and gratitude, the memory of its most distinguished

The history of the life and character of Christopher Ludwick, is calculated to show the influence of a religious education upon moral conduct; of habits of industry and economy, upon success in all enterprises; and to inspire hope and exertion in young men of humble employment, and scanty capital, to aspire to wealth and independence, by the only means in which they are capable of commanding respect and affording happiness.

Most of the incidents which are to compose the following memoir were obtained from Mr. Ludwick, by a person who often visited him in the evening of his life. Such of them as were not obtained from that source, were communicated by his family, or by persons who were the witnesses of them.

Christopher Ludwick was born on the 17th of October, 1720, at Giessen in Hesse Darmstadt, in the circle of the Upper Rhine, in Germany. His father was a Baker, in which business the son was instructed as soon as he was able to work. At fourteen years of age he was sent to a free school, where he was taught to read and write, and the common rules of arithmetic. He was carefully instructed at the same time, in the principles of the Christian religion as held by the Lutherans. Of this school he always retained a grateful remembrance, as will appear in the sequel of his life. At seventeen years of age, he enlisted as a private soldier in the army of the Emperor of Germany, and bore his part in the war carried on by the Austrians against the Turks, between the years 1737 and 1740. At the close of the war in Turkey, he set off with one hundred men for Vienna. Their march was through a dreary country, and in extremely cold weather. Seventy-five of his companions perished on the way. He spent some months in Vienna. The incident that made the deepest impression on his mind while he remained in that city, was the public execu-

---

benefactor, some time since appointed a committee to prepare for publication, a sketch of the life and character of Christopher Ludwick, to whose early and liberal endowment the Institution is deeply indebted. The committee reported at a subsequent meeting, that they had succeeded in obtaining a brief account of that singular, but worthy man, which appeared in Poulson's *American Daily Advertiser*, about thirty years ago, and which was written by the late Dr. Benjamin Rush, who was intimately acquainted with Mr. Ludwick. This memoir, having been revised by the committee, was ordered to be printed, and a copy to be furnished to each member of the Society.

"A brief sketch of the origin, progress, and present condition of the Society, has been added. It was a pioneer in the important cause of public free schools in Pennsylvania, and its history, like Mr. Ludwick's life, affords another evidence of what may be effected by industry and perseverance.

"Philadelphia, June 1831."

tion of the Commissary General of the Austrian army, for fraud and peculation.

From Vienna he went to Prague, where he endured all the distresses of a seventeen weeks' siege. After its surrender to the French arms in 1741, he enlisted as a soldier in the army of the King of Prussia. Upon the return of peace, he went to London, ... and passed the years between 1745 and 1752 in successive voyages from London to Holland, Ireland, and the West Indies, as a common sailor. In these voyages he saved twenty-five pounds sterling, with which he bought a quantity of ready made clothes, and embarked with them for Philadelphia, where he arrived in 1753. He sold these clothes for a profit of 300 per cent, and with the proceeds returned to London. Here he spent nine months in learning the confectionary business, and the making of gingerbread. In the year 1754, he returned to Philadelphia with a number of gingerbread prints, and immediately set up his business of family and gingerbread baker in Laetitia Court. . . . . He was much esteemed by all who did business with him, for his integrity and punctuality, and for his disposition to do kind offices. His neighbours treated him with so much respect, that he acquired among them the title of "The Governor of Laetitia Court."

In the year 1774, he felt, with a great majority of the people of America, the impulse of that spirit of liberty, which led them to oppose, first by petitions and afterwards by arms, the attempts of Great Britain to subjugate the American Colonies. He possessed at that time, nine houses in Philadelphia, a farm near Germantown, and three thousand five hundred pounds, Pennsylvania currency, at interest; all of which he staked with his life, in the scale of his country. He was elected successively, a member of all the Committees and Conventions, which conducted the affairs of the Revolution, in Pennsylvania, in 1774, 1775 and 1776. His principles and conduct were alike firm, under the most difficult and alarming events of those memorable years. In one of the Conventions of which he was a member, it was proposed by General Mifflin, to open a private subscription for purchasing fire-arms. To this motion some persons objected the difficulty of obtaining, by such a measure, the sum that was required. Upon this, Mr. Ludwick rose and addressed the chair, in the following laconic speech, which he delivered in broken English, but in a loud and animated voice: "Mr. President, I am but a poor gingerbread baker, but put my name down for two hundred pounds." The debate was closed by this speech, and the motion was carried unanimously in the affirmative.

In the summer of 1776, he acted as a volunteer in the flying camp, but drew neither pay nor rations for his services. He animated the soldiers with the love of liberty, by his example and conversation, and often pointed out to them the degrading nature of slavery, by describing the poverty and misery of his native country under the rapacious hands of arbitrary kings and princes. Upon one occasion he heard that a number of militia soldiers, who were dissatisfied with their rations, were about to leave the camp. He went hastily to them, and in the sight of them all, fell suddenly upon his knees. This solemn and humble attitude commanded general silence and attention. "Brother soldiers," said he, "listen for one minute to Christopher Ludwick"—for in this manner he often spoke of himself.—"When we hear the cry of fire in Philadelphia, on the hill at a distance from us, we fly there with our buckets to keep it from our houses. So let us keep the great fire of the British army from our town. In a few days you shall have good bread and enough of it." This speech had its desired effect. The mutinous spirit of a detachment of the militia was instantly checked. In the autumn of the campaign, eight Hessian prisoners were brought into the camp. A disagreement of opinion took place at head quarters, about the most proper place to confine them. "Let us," said Mr. Ludwick, who happened to be at head quarters, "take them to Philadelphia, and there show them our fine German churches. Let them see how our tradesmen eat good beef, drink out of silver cups every day, and ride out in chairs every afternoon; and then let us send them back to their countrymen, and they will all soon run away, and come and settle in our city and be as good whigs as any of us."

From a desire to extend the blessings of liberty and independence to his German countrymen, he once exposed his neck to the most imminent danger. He went, with the consent of the commanding officer of the flying camp, among that part of the British army which was composed of Hessian troops while they were encamped on Staten Island, in the character of a deserter. He opened to them the difference between the privileges and manner of life of an American freeman and those of a Hessian slave. He gave them the most captivating descriptions of the affluence and independence of their former countrymen in the German counties of Pennsylvania. His exertions were not in vain. They were followed by the gradual desertion of many hundred soldiers, who, now in comfortable freeholds or on valuable farms, with numerous descendants, bless the name of Christopher Ludwick. He escaped from the Hessian camp, without detection or suspicion.

In the spring of 1777, he received the following commission:

In Congress, May 3, 1777.

Resolved, That Christopher Ludwick be, and he is hereby appointed Superintendent of Bakers, and Director of Baking in the army of the United States; and that he shall have power to engage, and by permission of the Commander in Chief, or officer commanding at any principal post, all persons to be employed in this business, and to regulate their pay, making proper reports of his proceedings, and using his best endeavours to rectify all abuse in the articles of bread; that no person be permitted to exercise the trade of a baker in the said army without such license, and that he receive for his services herein, an allowance of seventy-five dollars a month, and two rations a day.

Extract from the minutes,

                                                     Charles Thomson, Secretary.

By order of Congress,

                                                     JOHN HANCOCK, President.

When this commission was delivered to him by a committee of Congress, they proposed, that for every pound of flour, he should furnish the army with a pound of bread. "No gentlemen," said he, "I will not accept of your commission upon any such terms; Christopher Ludwick does not want to get rich by the war; he has money enough. I will furnish one hundred and thirty-five pounds of bread for every cwt. of flour you put into my hands." The committee were strangers to the increase of weight which flour acquires by the addition of water and leaven.

From this time there were no complaints of the bad quality of bread in the army, nor was there a moment in which the movements of the army, or of any part of it, were delayed from the want of that necessary article of food. After the capitulation of Lord Cornwallis, he baked six thousand pounds of bread for his army by order of General Washington. "Let it be good," said he, "old gentleman," (the epithet which the general most commonly gave him) "and let there be enough of it, if I should want myself."

He often dined with the Commander in Chief in large companies, and was always treated by him upon such occasions, with particular marks of attention. He frequently spent two hours at a time with him in private, in conferring upon the business of the baking department. The General appreciated his worth, and occasionally addressed him in company, as "his honest friend." . . . . .

At the close of the war, he returned and settled on his farm near Germantown. His house had been plundered of every article of furniture, plate and wearing apparel, he had left in it, by the British army on their march to Philadelphia. As he had no more cash than was sufficient to satisfy the demands of the market, he suffered a good deal from the want of many of the conveniences of life. . . . .

The principal part of his bonds having been paid to him in depreciated paper money, he was obliged to sell part of his real property in order to replace his clothing and furniture.[1]

In the year 1795 . . . . he converted his farm and all his houses except one into private bonds and public stock, and removed to Philadelphia . . . . During the prevalence of yellow fever in 1797 the old gentleman volunteered his services to assist in making bread for distribution among the poor, in that period of awful distress. . . . .

In the last two years of his life he was frequently indisposed; he spent the intervals of his sickness in reading his bible and religious books and in visiting his friends. . . . . He had held his life for a year or two, by the tenure of a small and single thread; it broke on Wednesday, the 17th of the month. There appeared to be a revival of the languid powers of reason in his last illness; he ceased to speak, with a prayer upon his lips.

The event of Mr. Ludwick's death was thus noticed in the public papers:

Died, on the evening of the 17th inst. in the 80th year of his age, Christopher Ludwick, Baker General of the army of the United States during the Revolutionary war. His life was marked by a variety of incidents, which, if known, would prove interesting to every class of readers. In all the stations in which he acted, he was distinguished for his strong natural sense, strict probity, great benevolence, and uncommon intrepidity in asserting the cause of public and private justice. . . . .

Thus closed the long and chequered life of a most singular but worthy and useful man. Of the domestic virtues of Mr. Ludwick, the surviving branches of his family are the affectionate and grateful witnesses. Of his patriotism and integrity, the testimony of General Washington will be a lasting record. Of his liberality, there is scarcely a public institution in Philadelphia, established before his decease, that does not possess some

[1] The following certificate, which he had neatly framed and hung up in his parlour, not only reconciled him to these losses, but threw a large balance of pleasure in their favour.

"I have known Christopher Ludwick from an early period in the war, and have every reason to believe as well from observation as information, that he has been a true and faithful servant to the public; that he has detected and exposed many impositions, which were attempted to be practised by others in his department; that he has been the cause of much saving in many respects; and that his deportment in public life, has afforded unquestionable proofs of his integrity and worth.

"With respect to his losses, I have no personal knowledge, but have often heard that he has suffered from his zeal in the cause of his country.

"Geo. Washington

"April 25, 1785."

monument. Three Africans whom he had emancipated, proclaimed in tears over his grave, his regard to justice and the equal rights of man; while more than fifty persons who had been taught reading, writing and arithmetic at his expense, in different schools in the city and its neighbourhood, summed up the evidence of his uncommon public beneficence. His private charities were like the fires that blazed perpetually upon the Jewish altar. The principal part of his business for many years before he died was to find out and relieve objects of distress. This was done with a delicacy and secrecy that conferred a double pleasure and obligation. He discriminated, it is true, in the distribution of his charities. To the tippler, and drunkard, his hand was always closed; when applied to by such persons for relief, he used to say, "he had not carried packs of flour upon his back for twenty years, to help people to destroy themselves by strong drink."

The same just and charitable disposition which governed his actions in life, manifested itself in an eminent degree in his will; in which after bequeathing various family legacies, he gives five hundred pounds, in equal shares, to the German Reformed Church in Philadelphia, to the German Society, to the University of Pennsylvania, and the Lutheran Church at Beggarstown, to be employed in educating poor children. To the Pennsylvania Hospital, he gives one hundred pounds for the relief of poor patients, and to the Guardians of the Poor, two hundred pounds, to be laid out in fire wood for the use of the poor in Philadelphia. The residue of his estate is then disposed of by the following bequest, viz:

ITEM. As I have, ever since I arrived to the years of discretion, seen the benefit and advantage that arise to the community by the education and instruction of poor children, and have earnestly desired that an institution could be established in this city or liberties, for the education of poor children of all denominations gratis, without any exception to country, extraction or religious principles of their friends or parents; and as the residue and remainder of my estate will, in my opinion, amount to upwards of three thousand pounds specie, I am willing that the same shall be my mite or contribution towards such institution, and flatter myself that many others will add and contribute to the fund for so laudable a purpose. And therefore I do will, devise, and direct that all the residue and remainder of my estate, real and personal, whatsoever and wheresoever, not hereinbefore otherwise disposed of, shall be appropriated as and towards a fund, for the schooling and educating gratis, of poor children of all denominations, in the city and liberties of Philadelphia, without any exception to the country, extraction, or religious principles of their parents or friends; and for that purpose shall be vested by my executors, or the survivers or surviver of them, or the executor of such surviver, in the public funds, or placed out at interest on good and sufficient land security, or in the purchase of well-secured ground rents, and the annual interest and income thereof, from time to time, used and applied by them my said executors and the survivers or surviver of them, and in case of all their deaths, then by the Guardians or Overseers of the Poor in the said city or liberties for the time being, and their successors, for the sole use and purpose of defraying the expense of schooling and educating of such poor children of the said city or liberties, whose parents or friends cannot afford to pay for the same, without any exception as above mentioned, until an institution and free school on the liberal principles as herein above mentioned, shall be established and incorporated in the said city or liberties, when all the said residue and remainder of my estate, whether in stock, mortgages or ground rents, and otherwise, shall vest in and be added to the fund of such charitable institution and free school, for the use and purpose of educating poor children as above mentioned forever.

If before the lapse of five years, such a school should not be established, he orders the said residue of his estate, to be divided in unequal shares among the German Lutheran, the German Reformed, the English Episcopal, the First and Second Presbyterian, the Roman Catholic, and the African Churches, and the University of Pennsylvania, to be employed by them, exclusively in educating poor children.—His reason for including the Roman Catholic Church, in this division of his property, he said, was to express his gratitude for the kindness he received from some Catholic peasants, above sixty years ago, when returning half starved and naked from Turkey to Vienna. . . . .

The incidents which have been related of the life and character of Mr. Ludwick, are replete with instruction to the statesman, the citizen, the moralist and the divine. They suggest many reflections: the following are a few of the most obvious.

1. The benefit of free schools: without the advantages Mr. Ludwick derived from one of them, he might have passed through life in obscurity, or ended his days prematurely, from the operation of vices which are the results of a defect of education. It was from a grateful sense of the usefulness of the knowledge he acquired in a free school, that he took so much pains during his life, and in his will, to render that degree of knowledge more general, by educating the children of the poor people. The greatest favour that can be conferred upon a poor child is to give him the knowledge of letters and figures. It is equal to imparting to him a sixth sense.

2. The wealth and independence which were acquired by Mr. Ludwick, forcibly exemplify the benefits of regular industry and economy in a mechanical employment. Could the aggregate product of labour in

agriculture and the mechanical arts, be compared with the product of commerce and speculation under equal circumstances in Pennsylvania, the balance would be greatly in favour of the former. This balance would be derived chiefly from economy which is connected with labour.

3. In every stage and situation of life, Mr. Ludwick appeared to be, more or less, under the influence of the doctrines and precepts of Christianity. Part of this influence, it has been said, was derived from his education. But it was much increased by the following circumstance. His father inherited from his grandfather, a piece of silver of the size of a French crown, on one side of which was marked in bas relief, a representation of John baptizing our Saviour, with the following words in its exergue, in the German language. "The blood of Christ cleanseth from all sin." 1 John I. vii. On the other side, was the representation of a new born infant, lying in an open field, with the following words in its exergue. "I said unto thee when thou wast in thy blood, live." Ezekiel xvi. vi. This piece of silver Mr. Ludwick carried in his pocket, in all his voyages and travels in Europe, Asia and America. It was closely associated in his mind, with the respect and affection he bore for his ancestors, and with a belief of his interest in the blessings of the Gospel. In looking at it in all his difficulties and dangers, he found animation and courage. In order to insure its safety and perpetuity, he had it fixed a few years ago in the lid of a silver tankard, in the front of which he had engraved the following device, a bible, a plough and a sword; and under it the following motto: "May the religion, industry and courage of a German parent, be the inheritance of his issue."

4. "If men were to record all their escapes from death," says a sensible writer, "they would find as many proofs of divine interposition in favour of their lives, as are recorded in the history of the life of Joseph." It is impossible to review the numerous causes of death to which Mr. Ludwick was exposed, from battles, famine, and casualties of a sailor's life, vicissitudes and heat of climates, an enemy's camp, and yellow fevers, and his wonderful preservation from death for eighty years, and not acknowledge that a particular providence presides over the lives and affairs of men.

The following epitaph is inscribed on the tomb stone of Mr. Ludwick, in the grave yard of the Lutheran church at Germantown.

In Memory of Christopher Ludwick, and of his wife Catharine, She died at Germantown the 21st September, 1796, Aged eighty years and five months; He died at Philadelphia the 17th June, 1801, Aged eighty years and nine months.

He was born at Giessen in Hesse D'Armstadt in Germany, and learned the

Baker's trade and business; in his early life he was a soldier and a sailor, and visited the East and West Indies; in the year 1775, he came to and settled at Philadelphia, and by his industry at his trade and business, acquired a handsome competency, part of which he devoted to the service of his adopted country in the contest for the Independence of America; was appointed Baker General to the Army, and for his faithful services received a written testimony from the Commander in Chief General Washington. On every occasion his zeal for the relief of the oppressed was manifest; and by his last will, he bequeathed the greater part of his estate for the Education of the children of the poor of all denominations, gratis. He lived and died respected for his integrity and public spirit, by all who knew him. Reader, such was Ludwick. Art thou poor, Venerate his character. Art thou rich, Imitate his example.

BENJAMIN FRANKLIN'S ACCOUNT OF AN EIGHTEENTH-CENTURY HOSPITAL

EDITORIAL NOTE

BENJAMIN FRANKLIN'S account of the founding of the Pennsylvania Hospital by act of the provincial legislature in 1751 is important for many reasons. For one thing this document supplements the material in the preceding chapter dealing with Benjamin Rush; for another, because of Franklin's own interest in the project. Rush was of course younger than Franklin and was only six years old when the hospital was founded. But he became an early contributor to the hospital as well as a member of the staff. Franklin was one of the members of the first board of managers, the first "clerk" of the Board, and the annual reports of the Hospital were published in his *Gazette*. The history of this eighteenth-century hospital is interesting also as an early example of the co-operative method of financing charitable institutions. The plan here—whether Franklin's or someone else's is not clear—was to ask the legislature to provide funds for the erection of the building, to write to the proprietors (descendants of William Penn) in London with the request that they give land for a site, and to raise by subscriptions the funds needed for upkeep and maintenance.

The foundation stone of the original building, which was laid in May, 1755, bears the following inscription:

In the year of Christ
MDCCLV
George the Second happily Reigning
(For he sought the Happiness of his People)
Philadelphia Flourishing
(For its Inhabitants were public spirited)
This Building
By the Bounty of the Government,
And of many private persons,
Was piously founded
For the Relief of the Sick and Miserable.
May the God of Mercies
Bless the Undertaking.

THE PENNSYLVANIA HOSPITAL
Founded in 1751

From an early print

The plan of the hospital was interesting also because it was planned for the care of the insane as well as of those physically ill, and it represents the first attempt to provide institutional facilities for the insane in America.[1] The hospital board provided, from the beginning, not only for the poor, but for paying patients. Thus an early report says, "After the accommodation of as many poor patients as the state of their funds will justify, the managers have authority to receive pay patients; any profit derived from this source being devoted to increasing the fund for the maintenance of the poor."[2] An effort was made, however, to prevent the hospital from becoming a refuge for chronic cases, or a superior poorhouse. "As this institution," says one of the reports, "is intended to be a hospital for the cure of disease, not a permanent asylum for poverty and decrepitude, the managers can admit none on the charity list whose diseases are chronic and incurable except those afflicted with insanity." And as regards the latter class, the report of 1828 noted that "It has been found necessary to limit the proportion of insane poor on account of the length of time they frequently remained in the house."

In a small pamphlet published in 1828 the need of a separate hospital for the insane is strongly urged: "The Managers of the institution have long had in view, the necessity of providing funds for the erection of a separate asylum for the insane. A very desirable measure, on many accounts, for both classes: the repose of the sick being liable to much disturbance from the noise of the insane; while the narrow limits in which so many of the latter are confined, prevent the adoption of various means, probably adequate to the recovery of many individuals."[3] An appeal is therefore made again in 1828 urging "the wealthy and charitable" not to forget the Pennsylvania

---

[1] The Virginia Hospital for the Insane was founded in 1769, the first institution exclusively devoted to the care of this group. The Virginia statute establishing the hospital, "An Act to Make Provision for the Support and Maintenance of Idiots, Lunatics, etc.," may be found conveniently reprinted in Breckinridge, *Public Welfare Administration* (Chicago: University of Chicago Press, 1927), pp. 73–76.

[2] *Some Account of the Origin, Objects, and Present State of the Pennsylvania Hospital*, prepared by William G. Malin, clerk, Roberts Vaux, secretary (Philadelphia, 1828) p. 10.

[3] *Ibid.*, pp. 22–23.

Hospital in the disposition of their estates. "The want of an asylum for the insane, founded upon a liberal scale, with the advantage of the increased light which modern science has shed on the history of the human intellect," said the report of 1828, "is more urgent than anyone who has not deeply investigated the subject can imagine." The insane were partly accommodated in basement rooms, in a "long garret in which about twelve of the most quiet male patients usually sleep," as well as in the building west of the center, where "the whole range" from basement to attic was occupied by the insane and their attendants.

Another interesting feature of the Pennsylvania Hospital is that it was, from the beginning, a "teaching hospital." In 1828 the report notes that "the students of medicine who attend the practice of the hospital physicians pay a fee of $10 each for the privilege." The report adds that the fees, which in European hospitals would have been a perquisite of the medical staff, were generously given by the attending physicians to the foundation and endowment of a medical library. Franklin's early account of the hospital needs no introductory comment.

Some Account of the Pennsylvania Hospital[1]

About the end of the year 1750, some persons, who had frequent opportunities of observing the distress of such distempered poor as from time to time came to Philadelphia, for the advice and assistance of the

[1] Extract from Benjamin Franklin, *Some Account of the Pennsylvania Hospital; from Its First Rise to the Beginning of the Fifth Month, Called May, 1754* (Philadelphia: Printed at the Office of the *U.S. Gazette*, 1817; pp. 145); the first edition was published in Philadelphia by B. Franklin and D. Hall, in 1754 (pp. 77). Both editions contain "Continuation of the Account of the Pennsylvania Hospital from the First of May, 1754, to the Fifth of May, 1761, with an alphabetical list of the contributors and the legacies which have been bequeathed for promotion and support thereof from its first rise to that time." The "Continuation" was not written by Franklin, but was issued by the managers of the hospital and prepared by the Committee on Publication, of which Samuel Rhodes was chairman.

The printed reports and accounts of the hospital are of course the most important source of information about it, but various descriptions of it are available, of which a partial list follows: *Some Account of the Origin, Objects, and Present State of the Pennsylvania Hospital*, prepared by William G. Malin, clerk, Roberts Vaux, secretary (Philadelphia, 1828; pp. 24); Philadelphia Citizens' Committee on an Asylum for the Insane Poor of Pennsylvania, *An Appeal to the People of Pennsylvania on the Subject of an Asylum for the Insane Poor of the Commonwealth* (Philadelphia, 1838; pp. 24); *ibid., A*

physicians and surgeons of that city; how difficult it was for them to procure suitable lodgings, and other conveniences proper for their respective
cases, and how expensive the providing good and careful nurses, and other
attendants, for want whereof, many must suffer greatly, and some probably perish, that might otherwise have been restored to health and comfort, and become useful to themselves, their families, and the publick, for
many years after; and considering moreover, that even the poor inhabitants of this city, though they had homes, yet were therein but badly
accommodated in sickness, and could not be so well and so easily taken
care of in their separate habitations, as they might be in one convenient
house, under one inspection, and in the hands of skilful practitioners; and
several of the inhabitants of the province, who unhappily became dis-
ordered in their senses, wandered about, to the terrour of their neighbours,
there being no place (except the house of correction) in which they might
be confined, and subjected to proper management for their recovery, and
that house was by no means fitted for such purposes; did charitably consult together, and confer with their friends and acquaintances, on the best
means of relieving the distressed, under those circumstances; and an
Infirmary, or Hospital, in the manner of several lately established in
Great Britain, being proposed, was so generally approved, that there was
reason to expect a considerable subscription from the inhabitants of this
city, towards the support of such a Hospital; but the expense of erecting
a building sufficiently large and commodious for the purpose, it was
thought would be too heavy, unless the subscription could be made general through the province, and some assistance could be obtained from the
assembly; the following petition was therefore drawn, and presented to
the house on the 23d of January, 1750–51.

To the honourable House of Representatives of the Province of Pennsylvania,
The petition of sundry inhabitants of the said Province,
    Humbly Showeth,

Second Appeal (1840; pp. 35); George Bacon Wood, *An Address on the Occasion of the
Centennial Celebration of the Founding of the Pennsylvania Hospital, Delivered June 10,
1851* (Philadelphia, 1851; pp. 141); Philadelphia, Pennsylvania, Hospital for Insane,
*Proceedings on the Occasion of Laying the Cornerstone of the New Pennsylvania Hospital
for the Insane* (Philadelphia, 1856; pp. 30); *ibid., Reports of the Pennsylvania Hospital for
the Insane, with a Sketch of Its History, Buildings, and Organizations,* by Thomas S.
Kirkbride (Philadelphia, 1851; pp. 437); *ibid., Code of Rules and Regulations for the
Government of those Employed in the Care of the Patients of the Pennsylvania Hospital
for the Insane near Philadelphia,* prepared and printed by authority of the Board of
Managers (Philadelphia, 1850; 2d ed., pp. 51); John Forsyth Meigs, *A History of the First
Quarter of the Second Century of the Pennsylvania Hospital* (Philadelphia, 1877; pp. 145).

That with the number of people the number of lunaticks, or persons dis-tempered in mind, and deprived of their rational faculties, hath greatly increased in this province.

That some of them going at large, are a terrour to their neighbours, who are daily apprehensive of the violences they may commit; and others are contin-ually wasting their substance, to the great injury of themselves and families, ill disposed persons wickedly taking advantage of their unhappy condition, and drawing them into unreasonable bargains, &c.

That few or none of them are so sensible of their condition as to submit voluntarily to the treatment their respective cases require, and therefore con-tinue in the same deplorable state during their lives; whereas it has been found, by the experience of many years, that above two thirds of the mad people re-ceived into Bethlehem Hospital, and there treated properly, have been perfectly cured.

Your petitioners beg leave further to represent, that though the good laws of this province have made many compassionate and charitable provisions for the relief of the poor, yet something farther seems wanting in favour of such whose poverty is made more miserable by the additional weight of a grievous disease, from which they might easily be relieved, if they were not situated at too great a distance from regular advice and assistance, whereby many languish out their lives, tortured perhaps with the stone, devoured by the cancer, de-prived of sight by cataracts, or gradually decaying by loathsome distempers; who, if the expense in the present manner of nursing and attending them sepa-rately when they come to town, were not so discouraging, might again, by the judicious assistance of physick and surgery, be enabled to taste the blessings of health, and be made in a few weeks useful members of the community, able to provide for themselves and families.

The kind care our assemblies have heretofore taken for the relief of sick and distempered strangers, by providing a place for their reception and accom-modation, leaves us no room to doubt their showing an equal tender concern for the inhabitants. And we hope they will be of opinion with us, that a small provincial Hospital, erected and put under proper regulations, in the care of persons to be appointed by this house, or otherwise, as they shall think meet, with power to receive and apply the charitable benefactions of good people towards enlarging and supporting the same, and some other provisions in a law for the purposes abovementioned, will be a good work, acceptable to God, and to all the good people they represent.

We therefore humbly recommend the premises to their serious considera-tion.

On the second reading of the petition, January 29, the house gave leave to the petitioners to bring in a bill, which was read the first time on the first of February. For some time it was doubtful whether the bill would not miscarry, many of the members not readily conceiving the necessity or usefulness of the design; and apprehending moreover, that the expense of paying physicians and surgeons, would eat up the whole of any fund that could be reasonably expected to be raised; but three of the profession, viz. Doctors Lloyd Zachary, Thomas Bond, and Phineas Bond, generously offering to attend the Hospital gratis for three years, and the other objections being by degrees got over, the bill, on the seventh of the same month, passed the house, *Nemine Contradicente*, and in May following it received the governour's assent, and was enacted into a law.[1]

As soon as the law was published, the promoters of the design set on foot a subscription, which in a short time amounted to considerable more than the sum required by the act. And on the first of the month called July, 1751, a majority of the contributors met at the state house in Philadelphia, and, pursuant to the act, chose by ballot twelve managers, and a treasurer. . . . .

The managers met soon after the choice, and viewed several spots of ground in and near the city, which were thought suitable to erect buildings on for this purpose; and agreeing in judgment, that one particular lot,

---

[1] [The law was called "An act to encourage the establishing of a Hospital for the relief of the sick poor of this province, and for the reception and cure of lunaticks," the preamble being as follows: "WHEREAS the saving and restoring useful and laborious members to a community, is a work of publick service, and the relief of the sick poor is not only an act of humanity, but a religious duty; and whereas there are frequently, in many parts of this province, poor distempered persons, who languish long in pain and misery under various disorders of body and mind, and being scattered abroad in different and very distant habitations, cannot have the benefit of regular advice, attendance, lodging, diet and medicines, but at a great expense and therefore often suffer for want thereof; which inconveniency might be happily removed by collecting the patients into one common provincial Hospital, properly disposed and appointed, where they may be comfortably subsisted, and their health taken care of at a small charge, and by the blessing of God on the endeavours of skilful physicians and surgeons, their diseases may be cured and removed: And whereas it is represented to this assembly, that there is a charitable disposition in divers inhabitants of this province to contribute largely towards so good a work, if such contributors might be incorporated with proper powers and privileges for carrying on and completing the same, and some part of the publick money given and appropriated to the providing a suitable building for the purposes aforesaid: Therefore, for the encouragement of so useful, pious, and charitable a design, ... be it enacted etc. . . . ."

[The law provided that when the sum of 2,000 pounds had been raised, the treasurer of the Province was to pay 2,000 pounds "in two yearly payments to the Treasurer of the said Hospital to be applied to the founding, building, and furnishing of the same." The law also required an annual publication of expenditures and donations "in the *Gazette* or other newspapers" and provided that the managers must submit "the books, accounts, affairs, and economy thereof, to the inspection and free examination of visitors who might be appointed by the Assembly "to visit and inspect the same."]

belonging to the proprietaries, would suit as well or better than any other, they drew up the following respectful address, and sent it (with the following letter) to Thomas Hyam, and Sylvanus Bevan, to be presented by them to the proprietaries. . . . .

LETTERS TO THE PROPRIETORS AND THE REPRESENTATIVES

To the honorable Thomas Penn, and Richard Penn, esquires, proprietaries of the province of Pennsylvania, &c.:

The address of the managers of the Pennsylvania Hospital.

May it please the proprietaries,

It hath been long observed, that this your province, remarkable for the goodness of its constitution, laws, and government, and many other advantages, is yet deficient of a common Hospital or Infirmary, for the relief of such poor as are afflicted with curable diseases.

Your good people here, to supply this defect, and out of a tender charitable regard for their fellow creatures, have voluntarily subscribed, and are still subscribing, large sums towards a stock for the support of such a Hospital: And the general assembly being petitioned by a number of the inhabitants of all ranks and denominations, have passed an act to encourage the same, and granted two thousand pounds for the founding, building, and furnishing thereof.

In pursuance of that act, we the subscribers were, on the first of this instant, chosen by the contributors to be managers of the said Hospital, and think it our duty to take this first opportunity of laying the affair before our proprietaries, in the humble confidence that so good and pious an undertaking will not fail of their approbation; hoping withal, from the accustomed bounty of the proprietary family, in encouraging former designs of publick utility to the people of their province, the present will also receive their kind assistance; and as private persons raise a stock to support the Hospital, and the assembly build the house, so (that all concerned in the province may share in the honour, merit, and pleasure of promoting so good a work) the proprietaries will be pleased to favour us with the grant of a piece of ground for the buildings and their necessary accommodations.

If anything should occur to the proprietaries, that they may think of service with respect to the management or rules of the Hospital, we should be obliged to them for their sentiments, being desirous that what falls within our duty, may be done to the greatest advantage for the publick. . . . .

We are with great respect, your very affectionate friends, Joshua Crosby, Benjamin Franklin, Thomas Bond, Samuel Hazard, Israel Pemberton, Jr., Hugh Roberts, Samuel Rhodes, Joseph Morris, John Smith, Evan Morgan, Charles Norris.

Philadelphia, July 6, 1751.

PHILADELPHIA, JULY 6, 1751

Esteemed Friends, Thomas Hyam, and Sylvanus Bevan:

The opinion we have of your beneficent principles, induces us to make this application to you, and we hope the opportunity of exerting your tenderness to the afflicted and distressed, will be so acceptable, as to render any apology unnecessary for our freedom in requesting your friendship in delivering and soliciting the address we herewith send to our proprietaries, Thomas and Richard Penn.

The circumstances of this province have, in a few years past, been much altered, by the addition of a great number of persons who arrive here from several parts of Europe, many of whom are poor, and settle in remote parts of the country, where suitable provision cannot be made for their relief from the various disorders of body and mind some of them labour under; the consideration of which hath lately raised in many of the inhabitants of this city a benevolent concern, and engaged them to apply for the assistance of the legislature, by whom a law is passed, and some provision made out of the provincial treasury for the erecting a publick Hospital, or Infirmary, under the direction of a corporation, by whom we have lately been elected the managers; but as the publick funds are not sufficient to answer the expense of endowing it, a charitable subscription for that purpose hath been proposed and begun with good success. The necessity and advantages of this institution are so apparent, that persons of all ranks unite very heartily in promoting it; and as several of our most eminent physicians and surgeons have freely offered their service for some years, we have good grounds to expect that this undertaking may be of general service much sooner than was at first expected, and that our legislature will soon make a further provision for the building, which we apprehend it will be prudent to contrive and erect in such manner, as to admit of such additions as the future state of the province may require. The principal difficulty we now labour under, is the want of a commodious lot of ground, in a healthy situation; for (though we have so great encouragement as we have mentioned) we cannot flatter ourselves with speedily raising a sum sufficient to enable us to provide for all other necessary charges, and to purchase a suitable piece of ground so near the built part of the city, as the constant attendance of the physicians, and other considerations, will necessarily require: We are therefore under the necessity of laying the state of our case before our proprietaries, and we hope the same motives which have induced others, will have due weight with them to promote this good work, and that they will generously direct a piece of ground to be allotted for this service.

There are several lots in different parts of this city very suitable, but from their situation, &c. are of great value for other purposes; we have therefore thought of one, which is in a part of the town quite unimproved, and where, in all probability, there will be the conveniency of an open air for many years; it is the vacant part of the square between the Ninth and Tenth streets from

Delaware, on the south side of Mulberry street, and is 396 feet east and west, and 360 feet north and south. The lots in this part of the city have not advanced in value for several years past, and are not likely to be soon settled; so that we are in hopes, if you will favour us with your application for this piece of ground, you will meet with no difficulty in obtaining it.

The interest of the proprietaries and people, are so nearly connected, that it seems to us self-evident that they mutually share in whatever contributes to the prosperity and advantage of the province; which consideration, added to the satisfaction arising from acts of charity and benevolence, will, we hope, have so much weight with them, as to render any other argument superfluous; but as your own prudence will suggest to you the most effectual method of soliciting this address successfully, we rely thereon so much as to think it unnecessary to add any thing more on this occasion, than that your friendship therein will be exceedingly grateful to us and our fellow citizens in general; and next to obtaining the lot we ask for, the most agreeable service you can do us, is to obtain a speedy answer; for the promoting this undertaking appears to us so necessary, that all concerned therein are unanimous in determining to prepare for the building early in the spring next year.

We are, with much respect, your obliged and real friends,

[Signed as before.]

LONDON, JANUARY 17, 1752

To Messieurs Sylvanus Bevan and Thomas Hyam

GENTLEMEN: You may inform the directors of the Hospital at Philadelphia, that we sent orders to the Governour, the nineteenth of December, by way of New England, to grant them a piece of ground to build the Hospital upon, though not the piece they asked, yet one of the same size, and where, if it should be necessary, we can grant them an addition.

I am, Gentlemen, your affectionate friend,

THOMAS PENN

REMARKS

The design of the Hospital being in itself so beneficent and our honourable proprietaries having fully expressed their approbation of it in strong terms, as well as declared their kind intentions of aiding and assisting it, by granting a valuable tract of land, in a proper place, for a Hospital; all therefore that seems necessary for us to do, is to convince our honourable proprietaries, that the methods by which they have proposed to aid and assist the Hospital, will by no means answer these good intentions, but are really inconsistent therewith.

We must then beg leave to remark in the first place, with regard to the charter, that, as the act of assembly is undoubtedly the best grant of incorporation that we can possibly have, and as the representatives of the freemen of this province have generously contributed towards the design, we should fail of the respect that is justly due to them, were we to accept of any other, without obtaining some very great and manifest advantage by it; but that there are no such advantages in the charter proposed, is evident at first view: On the contrary, we should by it be confined to stricter limits than we now are, particularly with respect to the power of making by-laws, and being subjected to visitors of the proprietaries' appointment. But that clause which makes the lot (and of consequence the buildings on it) revert to the proprietaries on failure of a succession of contributors, is so weighty an objection, that were there no other, we could not entertain the least thoughts of accepting the charter; for as the sum allowed for support of the Hospital is limited, we may reasonably conclude, that in time there will cease to be a succession of contributors, and no person can imagine that when that happens to be the case, the lot and buildings ought to become the private property of any man. And though the act of assembly hath made provision in a manner which may be liable to some inconveniences, yet it can scarce fail of answering to purposes first intended. The proprietaries, to be sure, have not attended to these consequences, or they never would have proposed any thing so inconsistent with the design they intended to promote.

As to the lot that the proprietaries designed for the Hospital, it is so situated, and so circumstanced, that it will by no means be suitable for the purpose. It is a moist piece of ground, adjoining to the brick yards, where there are ponds of standing water, and therefore must be unhealthy, and more fit for a burying place (to which use part of it is already applied) than for any other service; besides, as it is part of a square allotted by the late honourable proprietary for publick uses, as the old maps of the city will show, our fellow citizens would tax us with injustice to them, if we should accept of this lot by a grant from our present proprietaries, in such terms as would seem to imply our assenting to their having a right to the remainder of the square. . . . .

LETTER FROM THE REPRESENTATIVES OF THE PROPRIETORS

To the Managers of the Pennsylvania Hospital

RESPECTED FRIENDS: We attended your proprietary, Thomas Penn, esquire, and presented to him your remarks on the grant of land made by him and his brother Richard to your society (dated the eight of October, 1751) and requested instead thereof that spot which your memorial mentioned, and desired might be granted for the intended Hospital. He perused the remarks, and made objections to them, alleging that the ground which you desired was contiguous to that which they have offered, consequently no difference in the healthiness thereof. And as to the remark against its reverting to the proprietaries he very readily declared nothing more was intended by the clause in the grant, than that provided the scheme for the establishment and continuance of the Hospital should not succeed, either for the want of the sum proposed to be raised as a fund, or through any other cause, that then the ground should revert, &c. but as to the erections thereon, they should be at the managers disposal. We desired his answer in writing, but he refused the giving it in that manner, and added the governour should have the necessary instructions on the affair, unto whom you might apply concerning it. On the whole, he came to this resolution, not to make any alteration in what was before granted, nor to let or sell the spot of ground you pitch upon; and therefore we are of opinion, you should either accept the proprietaries' offer, with the clause relating to the reverting to them being explained, or else to fix on some other piece of ground. And if there is no other objection than the small distance of a mile to the place which one of the contributors hath offered to give you, may not that be more fit for a Hospital or Infirmary, than to have it in the city, where infectious diseases may be much more liable to spread. We observe, with pleasure, the success that hath attended the beginning of the good work you are engaged in, and hope it will go forward, and be happily completed, and are, with hearty salutes,

Your real friends,
Thomas Hyam
Sylvanus Bevan

Pennsylvania Hospital, 30th 6th Mo., 1763

Esteemed friends, Thomas Hyam, and Sylvanus Bevan:

We have lately received your favour of thirty-first first month last, with duplicate of your former letters to our president, and being sensible that you have solicited our address to the proprietaries with all the diligence and care we could desire or expect, we gratefully acknowledge your friendship, and think ourselves under the same obligations we should have been if your kind endeavours had obtained the desired effect.

The accounts of the affairs of the Hospital, and of its present state, will be laid before the assembly at their next meeting, and soon after published, of which we shall direct duplicates to be sent you; and as you have interested yourselves in the promotion of it, and we are convinced of your good wishes for its success, when we can give you a pleasing account of its advancement, shall take the liberty of communicating the same, being, with real respects,

Your obliged friends,

(Signed on behalf of the board of managers) Joshua Crosby

. . . . On the sixteenth of August, it being made appear, to the satisfaction of the assembly, that the contributions amounted to upwards of two thousand pounds, an order was obtained for the two thousand pounds that had been conditionally granted by the act, one thousand pounds to be paid immediately, the other in twelve months: The money, when received, was let out at interest on good security, that it might be improving till it should be wanted for the building, which the managers were obliged to postpone, till a piece of ground could be obtained, that would afford sufficient room in an airy, healthy situation; and yet so nigh the built streets of the city, as that the managers, physicians and surgeons might readily and conveniently visit the house on every occasion. But that some good might be doing in the meantime, the managers concluded to hire a house, and take in some patients for a beginning; but some doubts arising concerning the power and duty of the managers, a general meeting of the contributors was called to settle the same. . . . .

The managers hired the most convenient house that could be procured, with gardens, etc., agreed with a matron to govern the family, and nurse the sick, and provided beds and other necessary furniture; and prepared the following rules respecting the admission and discharge of patients, a number of which were printed and dispersed among the contributors, viz.:

RULES AGREED TO BY THE MANAGERS OF THE PENNSYLVANIA HOSPITAL, FOR THE ADMISSION AND DISCHARGE OF PATIENTS

First, That no patients shall be admitted whose cases are judged incurable, lunaticks excepted; nor any whose cases do not require the particular conveniences of a Hospital.

Secondly, That no person, having the small-pox, itch, or other infectious distempers, shall be admitted, until there are proper apartments prepared for the reception of such as are afflicted with those diseases; and if any such persons should be inadvertently admitted they shall forthwith be discharged.

Thirdly, That women having young children shall not be received, unless their children are taken care of elsewhere, that the Hospital may not be burthened with the maintenance of such children, nor the patients disturbed with their noise.

Fourthly, That all persons desirous of being admitted into the Hospital (not inhabitants of Philadelphia) must, before they leave their abode, have their cases drawn up in a plain manner, and sent to the managers, together with a certificate from a justice of peace, and the overseer or overseers of the poor of the township in which they reside, that they have gained a residence in such township, and are unable to pay for medicines and attendance; to which an answer shall speedily be returned, informing them whether and when they may be admitted. All persons employed in drawing up their cases, are desired to be particular in enumerating the symptoms, and to mention the patient's age, sex, and place of abode, with the distance from the city of Philadelphia.

Fifthly, That all persons who have thus obtained a letter of license to be received into the Hospital, must be there at the time mentioned for their reception, and bring with them that letter, and must likewise deposit in the hands of the treasurer so much money, or give such security as shall be mentioned in their respective letters of license, to indemnify the Hospital either from the expense of burial, in case they die, or to defray the expense of carrying them back to their place of abode, and that they may not become a charge to the city.

Sixthly, If several persons, not excluded by the preceding exceptions, are applying when they cannot be received, without exceeding the number allowed by the managers to be entertained at one time in the Hospital, the preference will be given, when the cases are equally urgent, first to such as are recommended by one or more of the contributors, members of this corporation, residing in the township to which the poor persons belong; secondly, to those who stand first in the list of applications; but if some cases are urgent, and others can admit of delay, those with the most urgent symptoms shall be preferred.

Seventhly, Notwithstanding such letters of license, if it shall appear by a personal examination of any of the patients, that their cases are misrepresented, and that they are improper subjects of the Hospital, the managers shall have the power of refusing them admission.

Eighthly, That at least one bed shall be provided for accidents that require immediate relief.

Ninthly, That if there shall be room in the Hospital to spare, after as many poor patients are accommodated as the interest of the capital stock can support, the managers shall have the liberty of taking in other patients, at such reasonable rates as they can agree for; and the profits arising from boarding and nursing such patients, shall be appropriated to the same uses as the interest money of the publick stock. Provided that no such persons, under pretence of coming to board in the Hospital, shall be admitted, unless, on the first application made on his behalf, a certificate be produced from the overseer or overseers of the poor of the township in which he lives, of his having gained a residence in the said township; and unless sufficient security be given to the managers to indemnify the city and Hospital from all charges and expenses whatsoever, occasioned by his removing hither.

Tenthly, That those who are taken into the Hospital at a private expense, may employ any physicians or surgeons they desire.

Eleventhly, That all persons who have been admitted into the Hospital, shall be discharged as soon as they are cured, or, after a reasonable time of trial, are judged incurable.

Twelfthly, that all patients when cured, sign certificates of their particular cases, and of the benefit they have received in this Hospital, to be either published or otherwise disposed of, as the managers may think proper.

Thirteenthly, That no patient go out of the Hospital without leave from one of the physicians or surgeons, first signified to the matron: That they do not swear, curse, get drunk, behave rudely or indecently, on pain of expulsion after the first admonition.

Fourteenth, That no patient presume to play at cards, dice, or any other game within the Hospital, or to beg any where in the city of Philadelphia, on pain of being discharged for irregularity.

Fifteenth, That such patients as are able, shall assist in nursing others, washing and ironing the linen, washing and cleaning the rooms, and such other services as the matron shall require.

The foregoing rules were agreed to by a board of managers of the Pennsylvania Hospital, the twenty-third day of the first month (January), 1752.

BENJAMIN FRANKLIN, *Clerk*

We do approve of the foregoing rules:

WILLIAM ALLEN, *Chief Justice*
ISAAC NORRIS, *Speaker of the Assembly*
TENCH FRANCIS, *Attorney-General*

Through the industry of the managers, everything was ready for the admission of patients by the tenth of February, 1752, and the first were accordingly taken in on that day. From which time the physicians and surgeons, with a committee of the managers, have constantly and cheerfully given attendance at the house twice a week, to visit the sick, examine cases, admit and discharge patients, etc., besides the daily attendance of the former. . . . . .

The practitioners charitably supplied the medicines gratis till December, 1752, when the managers, having procured an assortment of drugs from London, opened an apothecary's shop in the Hospital; and, it being found necessary, appointed an apothecary to attend and make up the medicines daily, according to the prescriptions, with an allowance of fifteen pounds per annum for his care and trouble, he giving bond, with two sufficient sureties, for the faithful performance of his trust. To pay for these medicines, which cost one hundred twelve pounds, fifteen shillings, and two pence half-penny, sterling, a subscription was set on foot among the charitable widows, and other good women of the city, and £104 18s. were contributed. . . . . .

From this bounty the managers have since been enabled to furnish medicines to many poor out-patients, who, at their request have been kindly visited by the physicians gratis, besides the service of them to those in the Hospital.

About the beginning of this year, twelve tin boxes were provided, on which were written these words in gold letters, *Charity for the Hospital*. One box for each manager, to be put up in his house, ready to receive casual benefactions, in imitation of a good custom practised in some foreign countries, where these kind of boxes are frequent in shops, stores, and other places of business, and into which the buyer and seller (when different prices are proposed) often agree to throw the difference, instead of splitting it: In which the successful in trade sometimes piously deposit a part of their extraordinary gains, and magistrates throw their petty fees; a custom worthy imitation. But these boxes among us have produced but little for the Hospital as yet, not through want of charity in our people, but from their being unacquainted with the nature and design of them. . . . .

In the beginning of 1754, spinning-wheels were provided by the managers, for the employment of such of the women patients as may be able to use them.

The accounts of the Hospital were laid before the house of assembly, and a committee appointed to examine them, and to visit the Hospital, who having accordingly done so, made their report in writing, which (having recited the foregoing general state of the said accounts) concludes thus:

We also report, that by the list of patients, we find that from the eleventh of second month, 1752, to the fourth of fifth month, 1753, there were sixty-four patients received into the Hospital, afflicted with lunacy and various other disorders, which required the conveniences of such a place; of which number thirty-two were cured and discharged, and some others received considerable relief. We likewise report, that we have visited the Hospital, and find a considerable number of distempered patients there, who are well taken care of, and the whole appears to us to be under very regular and good management, and likely to answer the original design. All which we submit to the House. . . . .

About this time a seal was procured by the managers; it was engraven on silver, the device, the good Samaritan taking the sick man, and delivering him to the inn keeper, with these words underneath: "Take care of him, and I will repay thee."

The twenty-seventh of fourth month, 1754, John Reynell, and John Smith, the committee appointed for that purpose, reported an account of patients remaining on the twenty-eighth of fourth month, 1753, and of such as have been admitted into the Pennsylvania Hospital from that time to the twenty-seventh of fourth month, 1754, from which it appears that there were sixty-one patients. Of which 28 were cured and discharged, 7 received considerable benefit, 2 discharged at the request of their friends, 1 discharged for disobedience to rules, 2 judged incurable, 5 died, and 16 remained. In all, 61. . . . .

From the foregoing accounts it appears: That from the tenth of February, 1752, to the twenty-seventh of April, 1754, which is but about two years and two months, sixty persons, afflicted with various distempers, have been cured, besides many others that have received considerable relief, both in and out patients; and if so much good has been done by so small a number of contributors, how much more then may reasonably be expected from the liberal aid and assistance of the well disposed who hitherto have not joined in the undertaking? Experience has more and more convinced all concerned, of the great usefulness of this charity. The careful attendance afforded to the sick poor; the neatness, cleanness, and regularity of diet with which they are kept in the Hospital, are found to contribute to their recovery much sooner than their own manner of living at home, and render the physick they take more effectual. Here they have the best advice, and the best medicines, which are helps to recovery, that many in better circumstances in different parts of the province do not enjoy. In short, there is scarce any one kind of doing good, which is not hereby in some manner promoted; for not only the sick are visited and relieved, but the stranger is taken in, the ignorant instructed, and the bad reclaimed; present wants are supplied, and the future prevented, and (by easing poor families of the burthen of supporting and curing their sick) it is also the means of feeding the hungry and clothing the naked.

It is therefore hoped, that by additional benefactions from pious and benevolent persons (an account of which will be published yearly according to law) this charity may be farther extended, so as to embrace with open arms all the sick poor that need the relief it affords, and that the managers will not in time to come, be under a necessity, from the narrowness of the funds, of refusing admittance to any proper object.

It is hoped that a deaf ear will not be turned to the cries of those, in whose favour both religion and humanity strongly plead; who are recommended by the great pattern of human conduct; who in sickness are lost to society; who contribute greatly to the instruction of those youth to whom the lives of high and low may hereafter be intrusted, whose prayers are to be sent up for their deliveries; but that all will assist to render the funds of this Hospital answerable to the necessities of the poor. Incapacity of contributing can by none be pleaded; the rich only indeed can bestow large sums, but most can spare something yearly, which collected from many, might make a handsome revenue, by which great numbers of distressed objects can be taken care of, and relieved, many of whom may possibly one day make a part of the blessed company above, when a cup of cold water given to them will not be unrewarded. Let people but reflect what unnecessary expenses they have been at in any year for vain superfluities or entertainments, for mere amusements or diversions or perhaps in vicious debauches; and then let them put the question to themselves, whether they do not

wish that money had been given in the way now proposed? If this reflection
has influence on their future conduct, the poor will be provided for. The least
mite may be here given without a blush; for what people would not choose to
give the treasurer, or any manager, the trouble to receive, may be put into their
charity boxes, or into the box which is fixed in the entry of the Hospital: where
money cannot so well be spared, provision or linen, blankets, and any kind of
furniture, herbs and roots for the kitchen, or the apothecary, or other necessaries of a family, may be delivered to the matron or governess; old linen, and
even rags, for lint, bandages, and other chyrurgical dressings, are acceptable,
being scarce to be purchased sometimes for money; and though they are of little
or no value to those who have them, they are absolutely necessary in such a
Hospital, and will be thankfully received.

It ought in justice to be here observed, that the practitioners have not
only given their advice and attendance gratis, but have made their visits
with even greater assiduity and constancy than is sometimes used to their
richer patients; and that the managers have attended their monthly
boards, and the committees the visitations of two days in every week,
with greater readiness and punctuality than has been usually known in
any other publick business, where interest was not immediately concerned; owing, no doubt, to that satisfaction which naturally arises in
humane minds from a consciousness of doing good, and from the frequent
pleasing sight of misery relieved, distress removed, grievous diseases
healed, health restored, and those who were admitted languishing, groan-
ing, and almost despairing of recovery, discharged sound and hearty, with
cheerful and thankful countenances, gratefully acknowledging the care
that has been taken of them, praising God, and blessing their benefactors,
who by their bountiful contributions founded so excellent an institution. . . . .

The contributions which have been generously made this year, have
enabled the managers to proceed in completing some necessary conveniences, which were immediately wanted, and to receive and entertain a
much larger number of patients in the house, than their stock would
permit before; and if the spirit of charity towards this institution continues, with equal warmth hereafter, it will soon become more extensively
useful. To give it its proper weight with the publick, let it be considered,
that in a city of large trade, many poor people must be employed in carrying on a commerce, which subjects them to frequent terrible accidents.
That in a country, where great numbers of indigent foreigners have been
but lately imported, and where the common distresses of poverty have
been much increased, by a most savage and bloody war, there must be

many poor, sick, and maimed. That poor people are maintained by their labour, and, if they cannot labour, they cannot live, without the help of the more fortunate. We all know many mouths are fed, many bodies clothed, by one poor man's industry and diligence; should any distemper seize and afflict this person; should any sudden hurt happen to him, which should render him incapable to follow the business of his calling, unfit him to work, disable him to labour but for a little time; or should his duty to his aged and diseased parents, or his fatherly tenderness for an afflicted child, engross his attention and care, how great must be the calamity of such a family! How pressing their wants! How moving their distresses! And how much does it behove the community to take them immediately under their guardianship, and have the causes of their misfortunes as speedily remedied as possible! Experience shows, this will be more effectually and frugally done in a publick Hospital, than by any other method whatever.

Can any thing in this checkered world, afford more real and lasting satisfaction to humane minds, than the reflection of having made such a social use of the favours of Providence, as renders them, in some measure, instruments which open the door of ease and comfort to such as are bowed down with poverty and sickness; and which may be a means of increasing the number of people, and preserving many useful members to the publick from ruin and distress.

That this is a satisfaction which the contributors to the Pennsylvania Hospital have a just claim to, all may be assured, by visiting the house, examining the patients, and considering the extraordinary cases which are there received, and happily treated; among which, it is hoped, they will find sufficient instances to convince them, that every individual, in this and the adjacent provinces, are interested in the prosperity of this charitable institution; and induce them to consider, that "riches make themselves wings, and flee away; but blessed is he that considereth the weak, sick, and needy, the Lord will deliver him in time of trouble." And that it is better to give alms, than to lay up gold. . . . .

THOMAS EDDY'S PROPOSALS REGARDING THE CARE
OF THE INSANE, 1815

EDITORIAL NOTE

A GOOD biography of Thomas Eddy (1758–1827) was published less than ten years after his death by Samuel Lorenzo Knapp, *The Life of Thomas Eddy; Comprising an Extensive Correspondence with Many of the Most Distinguished Philosophers and Philanthropists of This and Other Countries* (New York, 1834; pp. 394).

Eddy was born in Philadelphia in 1758. His parents were originally "Scotch Presbyterians" living in Ireland. His father was born in Belfast and his mother in Dublin. His parents later became "Friends" and emigrated to this country. His mother had sixteen children, but only two survived to adult life.

The Eddys were Tories during the Revolution. He says that his mother carried on the hardware business in Philadelphia from his father's death in 1758. "She was induced to quit the city on account of the bitter spirit of persecution of the Whigs (the advocates of American independence, against the Tories, so called on account of their attachment to the mother country); and our family being of the latter description, we suffered considerable from the opposite party. Schools were then badly conducted, and many of them broken up, on account of the teachers being Tories so that I had but a poor chance of getting an education." Eddy discusses the political division and bitterness in the few years preceding the revolution.

Everyone seemed to take a decided and warm part and was attached and marked as belonging to one or the other of the parties. It now appears very clearly to my mind that it would have been more wise and consistent with the principles of Friends, if they had carefully avoided the intemperate political zeal, then manifested by all parties. The advice of George Fox was for Friends to keep out of all civil commotions, as they are mostly carried on in a temper very opposite to the meek and quiet spirit of the Gospel.

*Thy Assured Friend,
Thomas Eddy*

1758–1827

In 1777 the British troops took possession of Philadelphia. Eddy rode out to Germantown with a friend after the battle there "and had a view, a mournful view, of the killed and wounded on the ground." A month earlier, a number of Friends including Eddy's brother Charles "were arrested by a general warrant, by order of the Executive Council of Pennsylvania and without being admitted to a hearing were unjustly banished to Winchester in Virginia. . . . . The alleged charge against them was, that, they were unfriendly to the independence of America." They were allowed to return when the British occupied Philadelphia.

After the British evacuated Philadelphia in 1778 there were several trials for treason on the charge of having aided the British. "As is common in all civil wars, the minds of people were extremely irritated against each other, and those who were attached to the British government were often very bitterly persecuted by the opposite party." Two Friends, John Roberts and Abraham Carlisle, were executed. Their funerals were very large, says Eddy, who attended that of Carlisle, who was buried in the Friends' burial ground in Philadelphia.

When the British evacuated Philadelphia (June, 1778) Charles fled to New York, where in April, 1779, Thomas Eddy followed. "At this period it was very dangerous traveling without a passport. I was put over to Staten Island (possessed by the British troops) at night and next day reached New York." His brother had some time before left for England. Later the brother returned, bringing with him imports from Irish cities. A firm, of which Thomas Eddy was a member, to carry on business chiefly in consignments from England and Ireland and some shipping business, was formed under the name Eddy, Sykes, and Company. Thus the Eddys were busy making money while the Americans were chiefly occupied with the war. So also they were alert to capture profitable business connected with the war. Thus by his firm "an arrangement was made with the consent of General Washington, to supply the British and foreign troops with money, who were taken with Lord Cornwallis at York Town. . . . . By an agreement made with Sir Henry Clinton we were paid 6 per cent commission. The whole amount paid amounted to a very large sum and proved a profitable contract."

In 1780 he went to Sandy Hook to call on Hannah Hartshorne, his future wife, was arrested and taken prisoner as a spy by the New Jersey militia, and taken to Monmouth courthouse to Judge Symmes and committed to prison. He and Lawrence Hartshorne were put in a small room about 6 or 7 feet square in which were four or five other prisoners, some of whom had been there for some time. "We were much crowded and had nothing to lie on but extremely dirty straw which I believe had not been changed since the other prisoners occupied the room. On first entering this miserable dungeon, the stench occasioned by foul and noxious air exceedingly alarmed me, and it was strongly fixed on my mind that it would put an end to my life in less than half an hour. However, in time it did not feel so very offensive, and becoming habituated to it, I was able to eat my meals with good appetite; Elisha Boudinot([later] President of the American Bible Society) was then commissary of prisoners; I consulted with him, and he behaved very friendly to me." After eight or ten days "in this loathsome place," Eddy and his friend were taken to Springfield near Elizabethtown, where they had the liberty of a mile round the village. At first he was charged with being a spy, but in about a month he and Hartshorne were exchanged for two soldiers of the militia and returned to New York City. In November, 1783, the British evacuated New York. Eddy wrote, "This was a trying period to myself and others, who had taken refuge in New York, as all persons of our description had thereby incurred the ill-will of those of the opposite party, and we much feared that we should be exceedingly persecuted by them." Many went to Nova Scotia, but Eddy could not be reconciled to leaving his mother and near connections in Philadelphia and he decided to stay. Before the Americans entered New York he moved back to Philadelphia.

In 1778 "it became necessary for Thomas and George Eddy to make a settlement with their creditors." Eddy wrote, "We were discharged under a general Act of Bankruptcy for the State of Pennsylvania." Thomas Eddy had been trying to carry on a business in Fredericksburg, Virginia, and had failed (see *Life* [London, 1836], p. 39).

In 1785 he went to England but stayed only three months. In 1791 he went back to New York and went into the insurance business

as an insurance broker. "At this period and for some years afterwards," he wrote, "there were no insurance offices in New York."
He again made money indirectly out of the war in connection with
the funding of the national debt, which was largely, of course, a debt
incurred during the Revolutionary War. "About 1792," he says, "the
public debt of the United States was founded; this afforded an opportunity for people to speculate in the public funds. In this business I made a good deal of money" (*ibid.*, p. 39). In 1794 he was
elected a director of the Mutual Insurance Company and soon after
a director in the Western Inland Lock Navigation Company, of
which he became treasurer in 1797.

Some time before the close of the eighteenth century, Thomas
Eddy, being then quite wealthy and continuing his interest as a
Quaker in various public questions that the Society of Friends was
interested in, began a long connection with various charitable and
philanthropic activities. His biographer says, "Mr. Eddy at this
time being in easy circumstances had leisure to turn his attention to
some of those charities that are of permanent benefit to mankind"
(*ibid.*, p. 40). Eddy wrote as follows:

From early life, all improvement of a public nature, that tended to benefit the
country, or in any manner to promote the happiness and welfare of mankind
were considered by me as highly important and claimed my attention. I have
been connected with a number of public institutions and have providentially
been the means of their being established.

In 1796 Eddy was on a journey to Philadelphia with General
Philip Schuyler of New York, who was very influential and a member of the New York Senate. According to Knapp, Thomas Eddy
interested him in reforming the penal code and penitentiary of New
York along Pennsylvania lines (see *ibid.*, pp. 41–42).

As the title of the Knapp biography indicates, Eddy carried on an
active correspondence for the period with several Englishmen dis-
tinguished for their interest in philanthropic work. In writing to
Patrick Colquhoun (the author of *A Treatise on the Police of the
Metropolis* [London, 1796], *A Treatise on Indigence* [London, 1806],
A New and Appropriate System of Education for the Labouring People
[London, 1806]), on May 19, 1815, Eddy said:

I send by my friend Gallaudet, a packet containing a few pamphlets.
1. *A view of New York State Prison*, published the present year.

2. *Hints for introducing an improved Mode of treating the Insane,* by T. Eddy.

3. *Report of the Philadelphia Association of Friends for the Instruction of Poor Children.*

4. *Report of the Governors of the New York Hospital.*

5. *Report of the Free School Society of New York.*

6. *A solemn Review of the Custom of War, showing that War is the effect of popular Delusion,* etc.

I do not know who wrote the view of our State prison; it appears to me the information it contains is very correct. The institution is now conducted by persons who are very capable of managing its concerns. The great benefits derived to the public, by the alterations of our present system, is acknowledged by all our citizens, and similar establishments of prisons have taken place in almost every State [*Life,* p. 184].

Thomas Eddy was an early supporter of the New York Free School Society, which in 1824 had under care "about 4,000 children who received gratuitous education at the schools under their charge; yet notwithstanding their care and diligence in endeavoring to prevail on parents to send their children to school, it is believed that there are 8,000 children in the city who are brought up without the advantage of school learning."

In 1816 Colquhoun wrote to him as follows (*ibid.,* p. 191):

To Mr. Thomas Eddy, New York

LONDON, 14th June, 1816

. . . . It is a pleasing circumstance, to find your country is following our example, with respect to free schools. We at last discover here, that the general education of youth is not only the best prop to the State, but to the happiness and prosperity of the people. I trust your schools are established on a staple basis, which can undergo no unfavourable change by the death or removal of the first benevolent founders. For want of this, many excellent institutions have fallen into decay, when their original founders were no more. As yet, our Legislature has afforded no pecuniary aid to the numerous schools established in this country; they are entirely supported by the benevolence of the public. I trust ere long, their permanence will be secured by a national institution, embracing the whole population. . . . .

Yours, truly and affectionately,

P. COLQUHOUN

Thomas Eddy was also interested in the Society for the Reformation of Juvenile Offenders in the City of New York, which established the House of Refuge (see *ibid.,* p. 64).

Eddy also became one of the commissioners for erecting a State

Prison in New York and in 1801 published an account of the State Prison of New York.

The following letter from Thomas Eddy to Colquhoun, written May 4, 1816 (see *ibid.*, pp. 187–90), is also very interesting because of its account of some of the philanthropic interests of the period:

My Good Friend,

I scarce know how to begin this letter, as I feel ashamed and mortified that I have so long neglected replying to thy last very acceptable communication.

I rejoice to find such a number of your good people in England are engaged so devoutly in improving the condition of the lower classes in society; your Bible Society, and the immense sums raised for the poor, who have suffered by the calamity of war on the continent, is truly astonishing, and I sincerely trust and believe, will procure the blessings of Divine Providence on your nation. The communications of the British and Foreign Bible Society show that genuine religion is held in veneration, in many parts of the continent, to a much greater extent than many heretofore believed. I trust it will yet appear more fully in France, notwithstanding that deluded nation seemed to have been dead to any sense of it. As the spirit of our most holy religion spreads over the world, the condition of mankind will be meliorated—the minds of men will be softened; instead of being filled with bitterness, revenge, and hatred, they will learn of Christ to love each other, and thus, in God's own time, an end be put to war and bloodshed. Owing to the late war, the morals of the people of this country have been (as was reasonably to be expected) much injured. Notwithstanding this, there is a general religious improvement evidently increasing amongst all denominations of Christians, so that I entertain a hope, which, I trust, is well grounded, that, on the whole, we are growing better. Bible Societies are established in all directions of the United States, except Virginia, and other slave States, and great attention is paid to schools, and otherwise to improve the state of the common people.

Prisons, on the plan of our State prison, are established nearly in every State. The affairs of our prisons have been, of late years, sadly mismanaged, otherwise the avails of the labour of the convicts would be sufficient to defray the annual expenses.

I have been, for some time, much engaged in improving a plan of an establishment for the accommodation of insane persons; the mode of treatment that ought to be pursued (and which was recommended by me to the Governors of the New York Hospital, in April last year, of which communication I now send a copy) is the one adopted at the Retreat, by the Society of Friends, near New York.

The Governors have purchased thirty-eight acres of land, about six miles from the city; and propose to erect a building to accommodate two hundred lunatic patients; the thirty-eight acres to be divided, and laid out in walks, gardens, &c. for the amusement and exercise of the patients who are fit to partake of useful employment and recreation. Our Legislature has acted very liberally, and generously granted us 10,000 dollars a year, payable quarterly; one half of this sum will enable us to make a loan of 80,000 dollars, so that we shall have very ample funds for erecting suitable buildings, and making every necessary improvement. I send thee the last report of the governors, which contains a memorial to the Legislature on the subject, and fully explains the plan we propose to pursue. About a month ago, I attended the Legislature, at Albany, for the purpose of aiding our application, and obtained the law alluded to, granting us the above-mentioned annuity for and during the term of forty-one years.

It is a considerable time since, that I met with, in the *Quarterly Review*, an account of the very important publication on the wealth, power, resources, &c. of the British nation, and I have been extremely anxious to procure a copy; it is highly spoken of by those who have met with it in England, and it is wonderfully strange, that I cannot meet with a single copy in this city of Philadelphia.

Our Free School Society, under the patronage of the State, is in a flourishing situation; we have two schools under our care in this city, containing about one thousand scholars; we have ample funds, and propose to erect two other schoolhouses next year.

There is now a school in every town in each of the counties; throughout the State, all under the patronage of the State; the sum of 60,000 dollars is now divided among them, according to the number of scholars in each school, and this fund, in a few years, will reach 200,000 dollars; besides this, they are obliged, each town, to raise by tax, a sum equal to what they respectively receive from the State.

I shall esteem it as a very particular favour, if thou will be so good as to continue thy correspondence on the general state and improvements of the numerous benevolent establishments in England.

It is owing to thy very valuable correspondence with me, that our New York Free School is in so flourishing a situation as it is at present, and that the condition of the poor, in many respects, have been considerably improved.

I am, with the warmest sentiments of esteem and regard, thy affectionate friend,

THOMAS EDDY

Another letter written by Thomas Eddy to Patrick Colquhoun in the following year (*ibid.*, pp. 197–99) is also very interesting and explains his sending a package of pamphlets a few years earlier by "my friend Gallaudet":

NEW YORK, 4th mo. 9th, 1817

To Patrick Colquhoun, Esq.

. . . . I have the pleasure to state, that at Hartford, in Connecticut, they have formed a valuable and extensive establishment for instructing the deaf and dumb, which has been aided by their Legislature, and considerable subscriptions of private individuals of that State, and citizens of this and other adjoining States. The Institution is to be under the superintendence and management of my friend, Gallaudet, who will have, as an assistant, a Frenchman who is deaf and dumb and who was a professor several years in the institution at Paris. Nothing of the kind exists in any other part of the United States; and, in my opinion, the Hartford establishment will be sufficient to serve all the States north of Pennsylvania.

Among the many philanthropic institutions with which your country abounds, there is none that appears to me more likely to be useful than saving-banks. They are certainly most admirably calculated to be beneficial to the poor, by promoting amongst them a spirit of independence, economy, and industry. Immediately on receiving from thee an account of the provident institution in your metropolis, I proposed to a number of friends to establish a similar one in this city. A plan was formed, and a number of our most respectable citizens agreed to undertake the management of it; but we found that we could not go into operation without an act of incorporation, for which we made an application to the Legislature, and the result is not yet known.

An act is now before our Legislature, for completing a canal from Lake Erie to the Hudson. Our mutual friend, John Grieg, Esq., has with him a map and profile of the track of the canal, the inspection of which will be interesting to thee.

We have now, in this city, twenty-seven *Sunday* schools, at which 5,000 scholars are instructed. I lately visited two of them, kept for black people, adults; at one of them, I noticed two black women, one of them seventy, and the other ninety years old. They both seemed to please themselves very much with the prospect of being soon able to read the Bible.

Our Legislature passed a law about two weeks ago declaring that every person now held in slavery, shall be free after 4th July, 1827. In the eastern States, and in the State of Ohio, slavery is prohibited.

Free schools and Sunday schools are spread, and are increasing throughout our State, and our Government have made very liberal provision for their support and Bible Societies receive great patronage, and are established in almost every part of the United States.

I have lately lost thy excellent and very valuable work on *Indigence*, published in 1806, and shall esteem it as a particular favour, if thou wilt be pleased to send me another copy.

The asylum for lunatics, mentioned in my letter of 4th May, is intended to be commenced building this season. The plan being adopted through my recommendation, I feel myself under an obligation to pay attention to it, and this occupies, at present, a great portion of my time. We propose to have separate buildings for men and women patients, about 300 feet distant from each other, besides one other building, remote from these, for *violent noisy patients;* this will be a great improvement on the *old* system, of having them *all* under one roof.

There is no one evil prevalent in this country, we have so much reason to lament and deplore, as the intemperate use of ardent spirits. It is distilled mostly from grain, in every part of the United States, and sold at about seventy-five cents per gallon. The quantity of brandy, gin, and rum imported from Europe and the West Indies, and whiskey &c., made in this country, is equal to twenty-four millions of gallons; so that supposing the population of the United States to be eight millions, this gives to each man, woman, and child, three gallons a year! In the late war, it is supposed six thousand persons lost their lives, owing to that dreadful calamity, and that a greater number of persons were destroyed during that period by the use of spirituous liquors. This vice enervates the mind to such a degree, that of the individuals whose habits are fixed in the use of it, scarcely one in one thousand leave it off; attention to wives, children, friends; their own interest, health, character, rank in life, and reputation, are all sacrificed to gratifying their inclination for this most dreadful poison. There appears no remedy sufficient to cure this disease of the mind, but the operation of the power of religion.

I am with sentiments of great regard and esteem

Thy affectionate friend,

THOMAS EDDY

A list of pamphlets sent by Thomas Eddy to William Roscoe in August, 1818, shows Eddy's careful interest in social-welfare problems of his day.

A Memorial and Petition of the Society of Friends, by B. Bates.

A Discourse on the Death of Captain Paul Cuffee.

Report of the Society of Philadelphia on Charity Schools.

Information of the Progress of the Asylum near Philadelphia.

Governor Clinton's Discourse before the New York Historical Society.

Report of the New York Hospital Society (1817).

Report of the Female Association (1818).

Historical Sketch of Massachusetts State Prison.

Report of the Commissioners on Internal Navigation, State of New York (1811, 1812, 1817).

Account of the New York State Prison (1801), by Thomas Eddy.

View of New York State Prison (1815).

Account of Massachusetts State Prison.

Statistical View of the Operation of the Penal Code of Pennsylvania.

In concluding this brief sketch, it is interesting to quote from Eddy's biographer who begins his *Life* thus:

At no period in the history of nations has the mind of man been more active in the great business of ameliorating his condition, than that which has elapsed since the close of the American Revolution. Invention, industry, and enterprises have been abroad, and multiplied conveniences, comforts, and even elegancies, beyond enumeration. Nor has this been all; those charitable institutions, which are at the same time the medicine for natural and moral evils . . . . have every-where been built up, especially in this country; and it is not too much to say that, in many instances, our institutions have become patterns for other nations, even those of the old world, from which, in other things, we have taken so much in organizing societies among ourselves. . . . .

America has been so intimately connected with England in science and let-ters, that all that has been done in that country was soon known in this, and has generally been imitated, when found to be good; at first, by small beginning which were, from time to time, increased and improved as information and wealth advanced. The privations and sufferings of a new people taught them to be kind to one another and gave them the habits as well as the spirit of benevo-lence.

E. A.

Proposals for Improving the Care of the Insane, 1815[1]

Of the numerous topics of discussion, on subjects relating to the cause of humanity, there is none which has stronger claims to our attention, than that which relates to the treatment of the insane.

Though we may reasonably presume this subject was by no means overlooked by the ancients, we may fairly conclude, it is deservedly the boast of modern times, to have treated it with any degree of success.

It would have been an undertaking singularly interesting and instruc-tive, to trace the different methods of cure which have been pursued in different ages, in the treatment of those labouring under mental derange-ment; and to mark the various results with which they were attended. The radical defect, in all the different modes of cure that have been pur-sued, appears to be, that of considering mania a *physical* or *bodily* disease, and adopting for its removal merely physical remedies. Very lately, how-ever, a spirit of inquiry has been excited, which has given birth to a new system of treatment of the insane; and former modes of medical discipline, have now given place to that which is generally denominated *moral management.*

This interesting subject has closely engaged my attention for some years, and I conceive that the further investigation of it, may prove highly beneficial to the cause of humanity, as well as to science, and excite us to a minute inquiry, how far we may further contribute to the relief and comfort of the maniacs placed under our care. In pursuing this subject,

[1] A reprint of a paper read by Thomas Eddy before the governors of the New-York Hospital, April 4, 1815. The title of the paper, which was later republished in pamphlet form, was "Hints for Introducing an Improved Mode of Treating the Insane in the Asylum."

my views have been much extended, and my mind considerably enlightened, by perusing the writings of Doctors Creighton, Arnold, and Rush;
but, more particularly, the account of the Retreat near York, in England.
Under these impressions, I feel extremely desirous of submitting to the
consideration of the Governors, a plan, to be adopted by them, for introducing a system of moral treatment for the lunatics in the Asylum, to
a greater extent than has hitherto been in use in this country. The great
utility of confining ourselves almost exclusively to a course of moral treatment, is plain and simple, and incalculably interesting to the cause of
humanity; and perhaps no work contains so many excellent and appropriate observations on the subject, as that entitled, *The Account of the
Retreat.* The author, Samuel Tuke, was an active manager of that establishment, and appears to have detailed, with scrupulous care and minute-
ness, the effects of the system pursued towards the patients. I have, therefore, in the course of the following remarks, with a view of illustrating the
subject with more clearness, often adopted the language and opinions of
Tuke, but having frequently mixed my own observation with his, and his
manner of expression not being always adapted to our circumstances and
situation, I have attempted to vary the language, so as to apply it to our
own institution; this will account for many of the subsequent remarks not
being noticed as taken from Tuke's work.

It is, in the first place, to be observed, that in most cases of insanity,
from whatever cause it may have arisen, or to whatever extent it may
have proceeded, the patient possesses some small remains of ratiocination
and self-command; and although many cannot be made sensible of the
irrationality of their conduct or opinions, yet they are generally aware of
those particulars, for which the world considers them proper objects of
confinement. Thus it frequently happens, that a patient, on his first introduction into the asylum, will conceal all marks of mental aberration;
and, in some instances, those who before have been ungovernable, have
so far deceived their new friends, as to make them doubt their being insane.

It is generally received opinion, that the insane who are violent, may be
reduced to more calmness and quiet, by exciting the principle of *fear*, and
by the use of chains or corporal punishments. There cannot be a doubt
that the principle of fear in the human mind, when moderately and
judiciously excited, as it is by the operation of just and equal laws, has a
salutary effect on society. It is of great use in the education of children,
whose imperfect knowledge and judgment, occasion them to be less influenced by other motives. But where fear is *too much* excited, and espe-

cially, when it becomes the chief motive of action, it certainly tends to contract the understanding, weaken the benevolent affections, and to debase the mind. It is, therefore, highly desirable, and more wise, to call into action as much as possible, the operation of superior motives. Fear ought never to be induced, except when an object absolutely necessary cannot be otherwise obtained. Maniacs are often extremely irritable; every care, therefore, should be taken, to avoid that kind of treatment that may have any tendency towards exciting the passions. Persuasion and kind treatment, will most generally supersede the necessity of coercive means. There is considerable analogy between the judicious treatment of children and that of insane persons. Locke has observed, "the great secret of education, is in finding out the way to keep the child's spirit easy, active, and free; and yet, at the same time, to restrain him from many things he has a mind to, and to draw him to things which are uneasy to him." Even with the more violent and vociferous maniacs, it will be found best to approach them with mild and soft persuasion. Every pains should be taken to excite in the patient's mind, a desire of esteem. Though this principle may not be sufficiently powerful to enable them to resist the strong irregular tendency of their disease; yet, *when properly cultivated*, it may lead many to struggle to overcome and conceal their morbid propensities, or at least, to confine their deviations within such bounds, as do not make them obnoxious to those about them. This struggle is highly beneficial to the patient; by strengthening his mind, and conducing to a salutary habit of self-restraint, an object, no doubt, of the greatest importance to the cure of insanity by *moral means*.

It frequently occurs, that one mark of insanity, is a fixed false conception, and a total incapacity of conviction. In *such* cases, it is generally advisable, to avoid reasoning[1] with them, as it irritates and rivets their

---

[1] The following anecdotes illustrate the observation before made, that maniacs frequently retain the power of reasoning to a certain extent; and that the discerning physician, may oftentimes successfully avail himself of the remains of this faculty, in controlling the aberrations of his patient:—A patient, in the Pennsylvania Hospital, who called his physician his father, once lifted his hand to strike him. "What!" said his physician, (Dr. Rush,) with a plaintive tone of voice, "strike your father!" the madman dropped his arm, and instantly showed marks of contrition for his conduct. The following was related to me by Samuel Coates, president of the Pennsylvania Hospital:—A maniac had made several attempts to set fire to the Hospital; upon being remonstrated with, he said, "I am a salamander"; "but recollect," said my friend Coates, "all the patients in the house are not salamanders." "That is true," said the maniac, and never afterwards attempted to set fire to the Hospital.

Many similar instances of a degree of reason being retained by maniacs, and some of cures effected by pertinent and well directed conversations, are to be met with in the records of medical writers.

false perception more strongly on the mind. On this account, every means ought to be taken to seduce the mind from unhappy and favourite musings; and particularly with melancholic patients; they should freely partake of bodily exercises, walking, riding, conversations, innocent sports, and a variety of other amusements; they should be gratified with birds, deer, rabbits, &c. Of all the modes by which maniacs may be induced to restrain themselves, regular employment is perhaps the most efficacious; and those kinds of employment are to be preferred, both on a moral and physical account, which are accompanied by considerable bodily action, most agreeable to the patient, and most opposite to the illusions of his disease.

In short, the patient should be always treated as much like a *rational* being as the state of his mind will possibly allow. In order that he may display his knowledge to the best advantage, such topics should be introduced as will be most likely to interest him; if he is a mechanic or agriculturalist, he should be asked questions relating to his art, and consulted, upon any occasion in which his knowledge may be useful. These considerations are undoubtedly very material, as they regard the comforts of insane persons; but they are of far greater importance as they relate to the cure of the disorder. The patient, feeling himself of some consequence, is induced to support it by the exertion of his reason, and by restraining those dispositions, which if indulged, would lessen the respectful treatment he wishes to receive, or lower his character in the eyes of his companions and attendants.

Even when it is absolutely necessary to employ coercion, if on its removal the patient promises to control himself, great reliance may frequently be placed upon his word, and under this engagement, he will be apt to hold a successful struggle with the violent propensities of his disorder. Great advantages may also be derived, in the moral management of maniacs, from an acquaintance with the previous employment, habits, manners, and prejudices of the individual: this may truly be considered as indispensably necessary to be known, as far as can be obtained; and, as it may apply to each case, should be registered in a book, for the inspection of the Committee of the Asylum, and the physician; the requisite information should be procured immediately on the admission of each patient; the mode of procuring it will be spoken of hereafter.

Nor must we forget to call to our aid, in endeavouring to promote self-restraint, the mild but powerful influence of the precepts of our holy religion. Where these have been strongly imbued in early life, they become little less than principles of our nature; and their restraining power is frequently felt, even under the delirious excitement of insanity.   To encourage the influence of religious principles over the mind of the insane, may be considered of great consequence, as a means of cure, provided it be done *with great care and circumspection*. For this purpose, as well as for reasons still more important, it would certainly be right, to promote in the patient, *as far as circumstances would permit*, an attention to his accustomed modes of paying homage to his Maker.

In pursuing the desirable objects above enumerated, we ought not to expect too suddenly to reap the good effects of our endeavours; nor should we too readily be disheartened by occasional disappointments. It is necessary to call into action, as much as possible, every remaining power and principle of the mind, and to remember, that, "in the wreck of the intellect, the affections very frequently survive." Hence, the necessity of considering *the degree* in which the patient may be influenced by moral and rational inducements.

The contradictory features in their characters, frequently render it exceedingly difficult to insure the proper treatment of insane persons; to pursue this with any hopes of succeeding, so that we may in any degree ameliorate their distressed condition, renders it indispensably necessary that attendants only should be chosen who are possessed of good sense, and of amiable dispositions, clothed as much as possible with philosophical reflection, and above all, with that love and charity that mark the humble christian.

Agreeably to these principles, I beg leave to suggest the following regulations to be adopted, in accomplishing the objects in view:

1st. No patient shall hereafter be confined by chains.

2nd. In the most violent states of mania, the patient should be confined in a room with the windows, &c. closed, so as nearly to exclude the light, and kept confined, if necessary, in a strait-jacket, so as to walk about the room or lie down on the bed at pleasure; or by straps, &c. he may, particularly if there appears in the patient a strong determination to self-destruction, be confined on the bed, and the apparatus so fixed as to allow him to turn and otherwise change his position.

3d. The power of judicious kindness to be generally exercised, may often be blessed with good effects, and it is not till after other moral remedies are exercised, that recourse should be had to restraint, or the power of fear on the mind of the patient; yet it may be proper sometimes, by way of punishment, to use the shower bath.

4th. The common attendants shall not apply any extraordinary coercion by way of punishment, or change in any degree the mode of treatment prescribed by the physician; on the contrary, it is considered as their indispensable duty, to seek by acts of kindness the good opinion of the patients, so as to govern them by the influence of esteem rather than of severity.

5th. On the first day of the week, the superintendent, or the principal keeper of the Asylum, shall collect as many of the patients as may appear to them suitable and read some chapters in the Bible.

6th. When it is deemed necessary to apply the strait-jacket, or any other mode of coercion, by way of punishment or restraint, such an ample force should be employed as will preclude the idea of resistance from entering the mind of the patient.

7th. It shall be the duty of the deputy keeper, immediately on a patient being admitted, to obtain his name, age, where born, what has been his employment or occupation, his general disposition and habits, when first attacked with mania; if it has been violent or otherwise, the cause of his disease, if occasioned by religious melancholy, or a fondness for ardent spirits, if owing to an injury received on any part of the body, or supposed to arise from any other known cause, hereditary or adventitious, and the name of the physician who may have attended him, and his manner of treating the patient while under his direction.

8th. Such of the patients as may be selected by the physician, or the committee of the Asylum, shall be occasionally taken out to walk or ride under the care of the deputy keeper: and it shall be also his duty to employ the patients in such manner, and to provide them with such kinds of amusements and books as may be approved and directed by the Committee.

9th. The female keeper shall endeavour to have the female patients constantly employed at suitable work; to provide proper amusements, books, &c. to take them out to walk as may be directed by the Committee.

10th. It shall be the indispensable duty of the keepers, to have all the patients as clean as possible in their persons, and to preserve great order and decorum when they sit down to their respective meals.

11th. It shall be the duty of the physician to keep a book, in which shall be entered an historical account of each patient, stating his situation, and the medical and moral treatment used; which book shall be laid before the Committee, at their weekly meetings.

The sentiments and improvements proposed in the preceding remarks, for the consideration of the governors, are adapted to our present situation and circumstances; but a further and more extensive improvement has occurred to my mind, which I conceive, would very considerably conduce towards effecting the cure, and materially ameliorate the condition and add to the comfort of the insane; at the same time that it would afford an ample opportunity of ascertaining how far that disease may be removed by moral management alone, which it is believed, will, in many instances, be more effectual in controlling the maniac, than medical treatment, especially, in those cases where the disease has proceeded from causes operating directly on the mind.

I would propose, that a lot, not less than ten acres, should be purchased by the governors, conveniently situated, within a few miles of the city, and to erect a substantial building, on a plan calculated for the accommodation of fifty lunatic patients; the ground to be improved in such a manner as to serve for agreeable walks, gardens, &c. for the exercise and amusement of the patients: this establishment might be placed under the care and superintendence of the Asylum Committee, and be visited by them once every week: a particular description of patients to remain at this Rural Retreat; and such others, who might appear as suitable objects, might be occasionally removed there from the Asylum.

The cost, and annual expense of supporting this establishment, is a matter of small consideration, when we duly consider the important advantages it would afford to a portion of our fellow-creatures, who have such strong claims on our sympathy and commiseration.

But, it is a fact that can be satisfactorily demonstrated, that such an establishment would not increase our expenses; and, moreover, would repay us even the interest of the money that might be necessary to be advanced, for the purchase of the ground and erecting the buildings. The board of the patients (supposing fifty) would yield two hundred dollars per week, or ten thousand four hundred dollars per annum.

Supposing the ground, building, &c. to cost $50,000, the interest on this sum, at 6 per cent would be $3000, there would yet remain $7400, for the maintenance and support of the establishment; a sum larger than would be required for that purpose.

We had lately in the Asylum, more than ninety patients; and, at that time, had repeated applications to receive an additional number; the Committee, however, concluded, that as the building was not calculated to accommodate more than seventy-five, it would be an act of injustice to take in any more; they, therefore, concluded to reduce the number to seventy-five, and strictly to refuse receiving any beyond that number. This may serve clearly to show, that we might safely calculate, that we should readily have applications to accommodate one hundred and twenty-five patients.

This succinct view of the subject may suffice, at this time, as outlines of my plan; and which is respectfully submitted to the governors, for their consideration.

STEPHEN GIRARD, 1750–1831

EDITORIAL NOTE

T HE GIRARD College for Orphans, which was chartered by the legislature of the state of Pennsylvania nearly eighty years ago, was the greatest single charitable trust established by an American citizen in the first half of the nineteenth century. The founder, Stephen Girard,[1] who planned to make his riches "do his generous will forever," was a French immigrant who came to this country on the eve of the Revolutionary War. He had sailed for the French port of San Domingo as a master of a merchant ship. His cargo, however, was sold at a loss, and, fearing imprisonment for debt if he returned to his native country,[2] he secured a discharge from the ship, and went, not to France, but to New York, where he secured employment by which he hoped to pay off his French creditors. Two years later, in 1776, he became a resident of Philadelphia, where he took the oath of allegiance in 1778, and in 1779 took the subsequent oath prescribed for anyone who wished to become a "free citizen of the state."

The historian John Bach McMaster has prepared a substantial biography of Stephen Girard's life as mariner, merchant, and banker, based on a study of the rare collection of Girard manuscripts. In this biography, the historian shows Girard as a "bold and adventurous trader taking great risks, suffering heavy losses, reaping rich

---

[1] For accounts of Stephen Girard's life and work, the following may be consulted: Stephen Simpson, *Biography of Stephen Girard* (Philadelphia, 1832); Henry W. Arey, *The Girard College and Its Founder* (Philadelphia, 1853); Henry Atlee Ingram. *Illustrated Girard College, to Which Is Added a Short Biography of Stephen Girard* (Philadelphia, 1892); Cheesman A. Herrick, *Stephen Girard, Founder* (Philadelphia: Girard College, 1923); John Bach McMaster, *The Life and Times of Stephen Girard, Mariner and Merchant* (Philadelphia: Lippincott, 1918); J. Parton, "Girard College and Its Founder," *North American Review*, C (1865), pp. 70–101; Neva A. Deardorff, "The New Pied Pipers: Girard College, Sacrosanct Legacy of the Financier of the War of 1812," *Survey*, LII(1924), 31–33.

[2] See John Bach McMaster, *The Life and Times of Stephen Girard, Mariner and Merchant* (Philadelphia: Lippincott, 1918), I, 4.

STEPHEN GIRARD
1750–1831

profits." He also became, early in the nineteenth century, the most important private banker in the United States, and during the War of 1812 he "enabled the government to float a loan of $16,000,000, for which the people of the entire country had not subscribed 50 per cent. When the second Bank of the United States was chartered and the stock did not sell, it was his subscription of $3,000,000 that made it possible for the directors to complete the organization of the Bank and begin business."[1] But Girard's reputation as "mariner, merchant, and banker" and his public services as financier to his adopted country have long since been forgotten, and it is the dedication of his vast wealth to charitable uses that has made his name a household word for nearly three generations.

Girard, however, gave his personal services as well as his fortune to his fellow-citizens. The documents that follow contain a contemporary account of his work for the poor during the yellow fever epidemic of 1793. Again in the later epidemics of 1797 and 1798, 1802, and 1820 he was a conspicuous public servant. He served for several terms as a member of the city council of Philadelphia, and he served also as one of the wardens of the port. He was a supporter of most of the public charities of Philadelphia during his life, including the Pennsylvania Hospital, the Society for the Relief of Distressed Masters of Ships and their Widows, the public schools, the Pennsylvania Institution for the Deaf and Dumb, the Orphan Society, the Société de Bienfaisance Française, and the Fuel-Saving Society.

He apparently had had the "College for Orphans" or some similar bequest long under consideration. It is interesting that some French letters written as early as 1810 which were found among his papers contained suggestions looking toward some such foundation. With one of these letters was sent a copy of the Testament of Fortuné Ricard, whose benevolent bequests the writer earnestly called to the attention of Stephen Girard. An appeal was apparently made to Girard.

to induce him to transfer his great wealth to his native land. For this purpose they endeavor to appeal to the feeling, which is supposed never to be extinguished, of attachment to the fatherland, and give a glowing picture of France, her arts and arms. They refer to the distracted condition of this country, on the

---

[1] McMaster, I, vii–viii.

probable eve of a war with the most powerful nation of Europe, in which the United States "must" be subjugated, and assure him that in the anarchy following conquest, his fortune will be scattered and lost. They remind him that in Europe wealth gives rank and distinction, while here the man of silver is not respected, but only valued. Appealing to his well-known love for agricultural pursuits, they draw a striking picture of this "guide and patron of all French merchants" located in the fertile and beautiful fields of Languedoc, the owner of thousands of broad acres, of beautiful vineyards and splendid herds; and finally describe him as dying, after founding a magnificent institution of benevolence in Paris—his name descending to posterity, blessed by the poor and homeless. And they conclude with this striking expression, that he must remember that ' benevolence is the only treasure which the rich man can take with him to the grave."[1]

In spite of appeals to return to his native land, Girard remained a devoted citizen of the United States, and he apparently made up his mind at a relatively early date to dedicate his great fortune to some charitable use in his adopted country.

In his private library were found pamphlets on poor relief, the almshouse "rules," the "special rules for the Committee on the Children's Asylum"; and a copy of the act incorporating the "Society for the Relief of the Poor, Aged, and Infirm Masters of Ships, their Widows and Children." An early interest in the care of orphan children may have been one of the results of his work at the Bush-Hill pesthouse during the first yellow fever epidemic. The report of the citizen's committee, of which he was a member, showed that 192 orphan children had been under the care of the committee during this period.

A considerable portion of the Girard will is reprinted in the following pages as indicating the range of his generous bequests. At the time of his death he had been for many years a childless widower, and of his great estate, which was valued at $7,000,000, he left only $140,000 to his various relatives. The residuary estate, which went to his great foundation, the "college for poor white male orphans," was originally valued at $6,000,000, but the real estate has increased so enormously in value in the century since his death that the college endowment today is reported to be approximately $73,000,000. The Foundation was established at a time when, owing to the high

[1] Henry W. Arey (secretary of the Girard College), *The Girard College and Its Founder* (Philadelphia, 1853), pp. 22–23.

mortality rates and frequent epidemics, there were proportionately a large number of orphans, and when the state Pennsylvania made no provision for the education of its future citizens except *in forma pauperis*. The only free schools for the children of Pennsylvania were the charity schools, and free education was available only to those people who were willing to place a mark of pauperism on their children.[1] Whether if Girard were living today he would make the same disposition of his great fortune no one can say, but any study of Girard's beneficent bequest must give rise to discussions of the larger subject of endowments in their relation to the changing needs of those to whose service they are dedicated.

The attack made upon Girard after his death by those who sought to break the will and who charged him with being irreligious was answered by his long-time friend and attorney in his argument supporting Girard before the United States Supreme Court in the hearing of the case:

We have nothing to do with Mr. Girard's religious opinions. If any one thinks he can lead a better life, with equal humility and more zeal, let him try. Instead of there being anything against religion in the will, there is a manly and unaffected testimony in its favor. The boys are directed to "adopt such religious tenets as mature reason may prefer"; any tenet, without exception. The will then holds religion to be inseparable from human character, but thinks the best way of forming that portion of the character is by attending to it at mature age. It is a speculative question. Can it be said that Girard had no respect for religion? He showed a religious heart by bestowing upon the poor what God had given him, so that, like Franklin's legacy, "it might go round." His desire was that the children should be educated in the manner which he thought the best, to make them religious. Who is to decide whether it is the best way or not? The objection assumes that the Bible is not to be taught at all, or that laymen are incapable of teaching it. There is not the least evidence of an intention to prohibit it from being taught. On the contrary, there is an obligation to teach what the Bible alone can teach, viz., a pure system of morality.[2]

What his fellow-citizens thought of Stephen Girard is shown by the following extract from the resolutions adopted by the councils of Philadelphia at the time of his death:

Contemplating the humility of his origin, and contrasting therewith the variety and extent of his works and wealth, the mind is filled with admiration of

---

[1] See Cheesman A. Herrick, *Stephen Girard, Founder*, pp. 138–41.

[2] From the argument of Horace Binney, 2 Howard U.S., 170.

the man, and profoundly impressed with the value of his example. Numerous and solid as are the edifices which he constructed in the city and vicinity of Philadelphia, they will contribute but a transitory record of what he was when compared with the moral influence that must arise from a knowledge of the merits, and means, by which he acquired his immense estate. These merits and means were probity of the strictest kind, diligence unsurpassed, perseverance in all pursuits, and a frugality as remote from parsimony as from extravagance. The goodness of his heart was not manifested by ostentatious subscription or loud profession; but when pestilence stalked abroad, he risked his life to preserve from its ravages the most humble of his fellow-citizens, and wherever sorrow, unaccompanied by immorality, appeared at his door, it was thrown wide open. His person, his home, and his habits evinced the love of what was simple, and he was a devoted friend to those principles of civil and religious liberty which are the basis of the political fabric of his adopted country.[1]

Stephen Girard and the Yellow Fever Epidemic[2]

It was some time before the disorder attracted public notice. It had in the meanwhile swept off many persons. . . . . The removals from Philadelphia began about the 25th or 26th of August; and so great was the general terror, that, for some weeks, carts, wagons, coaches, gigs, and chairs were almost constantly transporting families and furniture to the country in every direction. Many people shut up their houses wholly; others left servants to take care of them. Business became extremely dull, ... and the streets wore the appearance of gloom and melancholy. . . . .

The 26th of the same month [August], the college of physicians had a meeting, at which they took into consideration the nature of the disorder, and the means of prevention and cure. They published an address to the citizens, signed by the president and secretary, recommending to avoid all unnecessary intercourse with the infected; to place marks on the doors or windows where they were; to pay great attention to cleanliness and airing the rooms of the sick; to provide a large and airy hospital in the neighborhood of the city for their reception; to put a stop to the tolling of the bells; to convey to the burying ground those who died of the disorder, in carriages and as privately as possible; to keep the streets and wharves clean; to avoid all fatigue of body and mind, and standing or sitting in the sun, or in the open air; to accommodate the dress to the weather, and to exceed rather in warm than in cool clothing; and to avoid intemperance; but to

---

[1] Quoted in Arey, p. 28.

[2] Extract from Mathew Carey, *A Short Account of the Malignant Fever Which Prevailed in Philadelphia, in the Year 1793.* 5th ed., improved. (Philadelphia, 1830), pp. 19–43. (This book was first published November 14, 1793.)

use fermented liquors, such as wine, beer and cider, with moderation. They likewise declared their opinion that fires in the streets were a very dangerous, if not ineffectual means of stopping the progress of the fever, and that they placed more dependence on the burning of gunpowder. The benefits of vinegar and camphor, they added, were confined chiefly to infected rooms; and they could not be too often used on handkerchiefs, or in smelling bottles, by persons who attended the sick.

In consequence of this address, the bells were immediately stopped from tolling. The expedience of this measure was obvious; as they had before been almost constantly ringing the whole day, so as to terrify those in health, and drive the sick, as far as the influence of imagination could produce that effect, to their graves. An idea had gone abroad that the burning of fires in the streets would have a tendency to purify the air, and arrest the progress of the disorder. The people had, therefore, almost every night, large fires lighted at the corners of the streets. The 29th, the Mayor, conformably with the opinion of the college of physicians, published a proclamation forbidding this practice. As a substitute, many had recourse to the firing of guns, which they imagined was a certain preventive of the disorder. This was carried so far, and attended with such danger, that it was forbidden by an ordinance of the Mayor.

The number of the infected daily increasing, and the existence of an order against the admission of persons labouring under infectious diseases into the Alms House precluding them from a refuge there,[1] some temporary place was requisite, and three of the guardians of the poor, about the 26th of August, took possession of the circus, in which Mr. Ricketts had lately exhibited his equestrian feats, being the only place that could be then procured for the purpose. Thither they sent seven persons afflicted with the malignant fever, where they lay in the open air for some time, and without any assistance.[2] Of these, one crawled out on the commons, where he died at a distance from the houses. Two died in the circus. . . . .

The inhabitants of the neighborhood of the circus took the alarm, and threatened to burn or destroy it, unless the sick were removed; and it is believed they would have actually carried their threats into execution, had compliance been delayed a day longer.

[1] At this period, the number of paupers in the Alms House was between three and four hundred; and the managers, apprehensive of spreading the disorder among them, enforced the above mentioned order, which had been entered into a long time before. They, however, supplied beds and bedding, and all the money in their treasury, for their relief, out of that house.

[2] High wages were offered for nurses for these poor people, but none could be procured.

On the 29th, seven of the guardians of the poor had a conference with some of the city magistrates on the subject of the fever, at which it was agreed to be indispensably necessary that a suitable house, as an hospital, should be provided near the city, for the reception of the infected poor.

In consequence, in the evening of the same day, the guardians of the poor agreed to sundry resolutions, viz., to use their utmost exertions to procure a house of the above description for a hospital (out of town, and as near thereto, as might be practicable, consistently with the safety of the inhabitants) for the poor who were or might be afflicted with contagious disorders, and be destitute of the means of providing necessary assistance otherwise; to engage physicians, nurses, attendants, and all necessaries for their relief in that house; to appoint proper persons in each district, to inquire after such poor as might be afflicted; to administer assistance to them in their own houses, and if necessary, to remove them to the hospital. They reserved to themselves at the same time the liberty of drawing on the Mayor for such sums as might be necessary to carry their resolves into effect.

Conformably with these resolves, a committee of the guardians was appointed to make inquiry for a suitable place; and after strict examination, they judged that a mansion house adjacent to Bushhill . . . .was the best calculated for the purpose. . . . . And the great urgency of the case admitting no delay, eight of the guardians, accompanied by one of the city aldermen, with the concurrence of the governor, ... took possession of the mansion house itself, to which, on the same evening, the 31st of August, they sent the four patients who remained at the circus.

Shortly after this, the guardians of the poor for the city, except three, ceased the performance of their duties, nearly the whole of them having removed out of the city. Before this virtual vacation of office, they passed a resolve against the admission of any paupers whatever into the Alms House during the prevalence of the disorder. The whole care of the poor of the city, the providing for Bushhill, sending the sick there, and burying the dead, devolved, therefore, on the above three guardians. . . . .

The consternation of the people of Philadelphia at this period was carried beyond all bounds. Dismay and affright were visible in almost every person's countenance. Most of those who could, by any means, make it convenient, fled from the city. Of those who remained, many shut themselves up in their houses, being afraid to walk the streets. The smoke of tobacco being regarded as a preventive, many persons, even women and small boys, had segars almost constantly in their mouths. Others, placing full confidence in garlic, chewed it almost the whole day; some kept it in their pockets and shoes. Many were afraid to allow the barbers or hair-dressers to come near them, as instances had occurred of some of them having shaved the dead, and many having engaged as bleeders. Some, who carried their caution pretty far, bought lancets for themselves, not daring to allow themselves to be bled with the lancets of the bleeders. Many houses were scarcely a moment in the day, free from the smell of gunpowder, burned tobacco, nitre, sprinkled vinegar, etc. Some of the churches were almost deserted, and others wholly closed. The coffee-house was shut up, as was the city library, and most of the public offices—three, out of the four, daily papers were discontinued, as were some of the others. Many devoted no small portion of their time to purifying, scour-ing, and whitewashing their rooms. Those who ventured abroad, had handkerchiefs or sponges, impregnated with vinegar or camphor, at their noses, or smelling-bottles full of thieves' vinegar. Others carried pieces of tarred rope in their hands or pockets, or camphor bags tied round their necks. The corpses of the most respectable citizens, even of those who had not died of the epidemic, were carried to the grave on the shafts of a chair, the horse driven by a negro, unattended by a friend or relation, and with-out any sort of ceremony. People uniformly and hastily shifted their course at the sight of a hearse coming towards them. Many never walked on the footpath, but went into the middle of the streets, to avoid being in-fected in passing houses wherein people had died. Acquaintances and friends avoided each other in the streets and only signified their regard by a cold nod. The old custom of shaking hands fell into such general disuse, that many shrunk back with affright at even the offer of the hand. A per-son with a crape, or any appearance of mourning, was shunned like a viper. And many valued themselves highly on the skill and address with which they got to windward of every person whom they met. Indeed it is not probable that London, at the last stage of the plague, exhibited stronger marks of terror than were to be seen in Philadelphia, from the 25th or 26th of August till late in September. When the citizens summoned resolution to walk abroad, and take the air, the sick cart conveying patients to the hospital, or the hearse carrying the dead to the grave, which were travel-ling almost the whole day, soon damped their spirits, and plunged them again into despondency. . . . . Men of affluent fortunes, who have given daily employment and sustenance to hundreds, have been abandoned to the care of a negro, after their wives, children, friends, clerks, and serv-ants, had fled away, and left them to their fate. In some cases, at the commencement of the disorder, no money could procure proper attend-ance. With the poor, the case was, as might be expected, infinitely worse than with the rich. Many of these have perished, without a human being to hand them a drink of water, to administer medicines, or to perform any charitable office for them. Various instances have occurred of dead bodies found lying in the streets, of persons who had no house or habitation, and could procure no shelter. . . . .[1]

A servant girl, belonging to a family in this city, in which the fever had prevailed, was apprehensive of danger, and resolved to remove to a relation's house, in the country. She was, however, taken sick on the road, and returned to town, where she could find no person to receive her. One of the guardians of the poor provided a cart, and took her to the Alms House, into which she was refused admittance. She was brought back, but the guardian could not procure her a single night's lodging. And, in fine, after every effort made to provide her shelter, she absolutely expired in the cart. This occurrence took place before Bushhill hospital was opened. . . . .

In the meantime, the situation of affairs became daily more and more serious. Those of the guardians of the poor, who continued to act, were quite oppressed with the labors of their office, which increased to such a degree, that they were utterly unable to execute them. I have already mentioned, that for the city there were but three who persevered in the performance of their duty. . . . . The mortality increased daily. Owing to the general terror, nurses, carters, and attendants could not be procured but with difficulty. Thus circumstanced, the Mayor of the city, on the 10th of September, published an address to the citizens, announcing that the guardians of the poor, who remained, were in distress for want of assistance, and inviting such benevolent people, as felt for the general distress, to lend their aid. In consequence of this advertisement, a meeting of the citizens was held at the City-Hall, on Thursday, the 12th of September, at which very few attended, from the universal consternation that prevailed. The state of the poor was fully considered; and ten citizens, Israel Israel, Samuel Wetherill, Thomas Wistar, Andrew Adgate, Caleb Lownes, Henry Deforest, Thomas Peters, Joseph Inskeep, Stephen Girard, and John Mason, offered themselves to assist the guardians of the poor. At this meeting, a committee was appointed to confer with the physicians who had the care of Bushhill, and make report of the state of that hospital. This committee reported next evening, that it was in very bad order, and in want of almost everything.

On Saturday, the 14th, another meeting was held, when the alarming

---

[1] The novel of *Arthur Mervyn*, by C. B. Brown, gives a vivid and terrifying picture, probably not too highly colored, of the horrors of that period.

state of affairs being fully considered, it was resolved to borrow fifteen hundred dollars of the Bank of North America, for the purpose of procuring suitable accommodations for the use of persons afflicted with the prevailing malignant fever. At this meeting, a committee was appointed to transact the whole of the business relative to the relief of the sick, and the procuring of physicians, nurses, attendants, etc. This is the committee, which, by virtue of that appointment, has, from that day to the present time, watched over the sick, the poor, the widow, and the orphan. . . . .

At the meeting on Sunday, September 15th, a circumstance occurred, to which the most glowing pencil could hardly do justice. Stephen Girard, a wealthy merchant, a native of France, and one of the members of the committee, sympathising with the wretched situation of the sufferers at Bushhill, voluntarily and unexpectedly offered himself as a manager to superintend that hospital. The surprise and satisfaction excited by this extraordinary effort of humanity can be better conceived than expressed. Peter Helm, a native of Pennsylvania, also a member, actuated by the like benevolent motives, offered his services in the same department. Their offers were accepted; and the same afternoon they entered on the execution of their dangerous and praiseworthy office.

To form a just estimate of the value of the offer of these citizens, it is necessary to take into consideration the general consternation which at that period pervaded every quarter of the city, and which caused attendance on the sick to be regarded as little less than a certain sacrifice. Uninfluenced by any reflections of this kind, without any possible inducement but the purest motives of humanity, they magnanimously offered themselves as the forlorn hope of the committee. I trust that the gratitude of their fellow citizens will be as enduring as the memory of their beneficent conduct, which I hope will not die with the present generation.

On the 16th, the managers of Bushhill, after personal inspection of the state of affairs there, made a report of its situation which was truly deplorable. It exhibited as wretched a picture of human misery as ever existed. A profligate, abandoned set of nurses and attendants (hardly any of good character could at that time be procured) rioted on the provisions and comforts prepared for the sick, who (unless at the hours when the doctors attended) were left almost entirely destitute of every assistance. The sick, the dying, the dead, were indiscriminately mingled together. The ordure, and other evacuations of the sick, were allowed to remain in the most offensive state imaginable. Not the smallest appearance of order or regularity existed. It was, in fact, a great human slaughter-house, where numerous victims were immolated at the altar of riot and intemperance. No wonder, then, that a general dread of the place prevailed through the city, and that a removal to it was considered as the seal of death. In consequence, there were various instances of sick persons locking their rooms, and resisting every attempt to carry them away. At length, the poor were so much afraid of being sent to Bushhill, that they would not acknowledge their illness, until it was no longer possible to conceal it. For it is to be observed, that the fear of the contagion was so prevalent, that as soon as any one was taken ill, of any disorder whatever, an alarm was spread among the neighbors, and every effort was used to have the sick person hurried off to Bushhill, to avoid spreading the disorder. The cases of poor people forced in this way to that hospital, though labouring under only common colds, and common fall fevers, were numerous and afflicting. There were not wanting instances of persons, only slightly ill, being sent to Bushhill by their panic-struck neighbors, and embracing the first opportunity of returning to Philadelphia. . . . .

The order and regularity introduced, and the care and tenderness with which the patients were treated soon removed the prejudices against the hospital; and in the course of a week or two, numbers of sick people, who had not at home proper persons to nurse them, applied to be sent to Bushhill. Indeed, in the end, so many people who were afflicted with other disorders procured admittance there, that it became necessary to pass a resolve, that before an order of admission should be granted, a certificate must be produced from a physician, that the patient laboured under the malignant fever; for, had all the applicants been received, this hospital, provided for an extraordinary occasion, would have been filled with patients whose cases fell within the cognizance of the managers of the Pennsylvania Hospital.

The number of persons received into Bushhill, from the 16th of September to this time, November 30, is about one thousand; of whom nearly five hundred are dead; there are now in the house, about twenty sick, and fifty convalescents. Of the latter class, there have been dismissed about four hundred and thirty.

The reason why so large a proportion died, of those received, is that, in a variety of cases, the early fears of that hospital had obtained such firm possession of the minds of some, and others were so much actuated by foolish pride, that they would not consent to be removed till they were past recovery. And in consequence of this, there were several instances of persons dying in the cart on the road to the hospital. Were it not for the operation of these two motives, the number of the dead in the city and in the hospital would have been much lessened; for many a man whose nice feelings made him spurn the idea of a removal to the hospital, perished in the city for want of that comfortable assistance he would have had at Bushhill. I speak within bounds when I say, that at least a third of the whole number of those received, did not survive their entrance into the hospital two days; and of those that died in the hospital, many would have been rescued had they been taken there in proper season.

Before I conclude this chapter, let me add, that the perseverance of the managers of that hospital has been equally meritorious with their original magnanimous beneficence. During the whole calamity to this time, they have attended uninterruptedly, for six, seven, or eight hours a day, renouncing almost every care of private affairs. They have had a laborious tour of duty to perform. Stephen Girard, whose office was in the interior part of the hospital, has had to encourage and comfort the sick—to hand them necessaries and medicines—to wipe the sweat off their brows—and to perform many disgusting offices of kindness for them, which nothing could render tolerable, but the exalted motives that impelled him to this heroic conduct.

The Will of Stephen Girard[1]

I, Stephen Girard, of the city of Philadelphia, in the Commonwealth of Pennsylvania, Mariner and Merchant, being of sound mind, memory, and understanding, do make and publish this my last Will and Testament, in manner following: that is to say—

I. I give and bequeath unto "The Contributors to the Pennsylvania Hospital," of which Corporation I am a member, the sum of *Thirty Thousand Dollars,* upon the following conditions, namely, that the said sum shall be added to their Capital, and shall remain a part thereof forever, to be placed at interest, and the interest thereof to be applied *in the first place,* to pay to my black woman Hannah (to whom I hereby give her freedom) the sum of two hundred dollars per year, in quarterly payments of fifty dollars each, in advance, during all the term of her life; and, *in the second place,* the said interest to be applied to the use and accommodation of the sick in the said Hospital, and for providing, and at all times having, competent matrons, and a sufficient number of nurses and assistant nurses, in order not only to promote the purpose of the said Hospital, but to increase this last class of useful persons, much wanted in our city.

II. I give and bequeath to "The Pennsylvania Institution for the Deaf and Dumb," the sum of *Twenty Thousand Dollars,* for the use of that Institution.

---

[1] Reprinted in Henry W. Arey, *The Girard College and Its Founder, Containing the Biography of Mr. Girard and the Will of Mr. Girard* (Philadelphia, 1853), p. 57.

III. I give and bequeath to "The Orphan Asylum of Philadelphia," the sum of *Ten Thousand Dollars* for the use of that Institution.

IV. I give and bequeath to "The Comptrollers of the Public Schools for the City and County of Philadelphia," the sum of *Ten Thousand Dollars*, for the use of the Schools upon the Lancaster system[1] in the first section of the first school district of Pennsylvania.

V. I give and bequeath to "The Mayor, Aldermen, and Citizens of Philadelphia," the sum of *Ten Thousand Dollars*, in trust safely to invest the same in some productive fund, and with the interest and dividends arising therefrom to purchase fuel, between the months of March and August in every year forever, and in the month of January in every year forever, distribute the same amongst poor white house-keepers and room-keepers, of good character, residing in the City of Philadelphia.

VI. I give and bequeath to the Society for the relief of poor and distressed Masters of Ships, their Widows and Children (of which Society I am a member), the sum of *Ten Thousand Dollars*, to be added to their Capital stock, for the uses and purposes of said Society.

VII. I give and bequeath to the Trustees of the Masonic Loan the sum of *Twenty Thousand Dollars* . . . . in trust for the use and benefit of "The Grand Lodge of Pennsylvania, and Masonic Jurisdiction thereto belonging," . . . . the interest whereof shall be applied from time to time to the relief of poor and respectable brethren; and in order that the real and benevolent purpose of masonic institutions may be attained, I recommend to the several lodges not to admit to membership, or to receive members from other lodges, unless the applicants shall absolutely be men of sound and good morals.

VIII. I give and bequeath unto Philip Peltz (and others), the sum of *Six Thousand Dollars*, in trust, that they or the survivors or survivor of them shall purchase a suitable piece of ground, as near as may be in the centre of said township, and thereon erect a substantial brick building, sufficiently large for a school house, and the residence of a school-master, one part thereof for poor male white children, and the other part for poor female white children, of said township; . . . . and I do hereby recommend to the citizens of said townships to make additions to the fund whereof I have laid the foundation. . . . .

IX–XVIII. [Various bequests to relatives, employees, and friends.]

---

[1] [For an account of the so-called "Lancaster system" of educating the poor, see John Bach McMaster, *A History of the People of the United States* (New York, 1900), V, chap. xlix, 355.]

XIX. [Bequeaths 280,000 acres of land in Louisiana to New Orleans "to such uses and purposes as shall most likely promote the health and general prosperity of the inhabitants of the City of New Orleans," and to Philadelphia, but this land was lost to the legatees by a decision of the Supreme Court.]

XX. And, whereas, I have been for a long time impressed with the importance of educating the poor, and of placing them, by the early cultivation of their minds, and the development of their moral principles, above the many temptations to which, through poverty and ignorance, they are exposed; and I am particularly desirous to provide for such a number of poor male white orphan children as can be trained in one institution, a better education as well as a more comfortable maintenance, than they usually receive from the application of the public funds. . . . . Now, I do give, devise and bequeath *all the residue and remainder of my real and personal estate* of every sort and kind wheresoever situate, unto the Mayor, Aldermen, and Citizens of Philadelphia, their successors and assigns, in trust, ... that is to say: so far as regards my real estate in Pennsylvania, in trust, that no part thereof shall ever be sold or alienated by the said Mayor, Aldermen, and Citizens of Philadelphia, or their successors, but the same shall forever thereafter be let from time to time, to good tenants, at yearly or other rents, and upon leases . . . . and that the rents, issues, and profits arising therefrom shall be applied . . . . to the same uses and purposes as are herein declared of and concerning the residue of my personal estate. . . . .

XXI. And so far as regards the residue of my personal estate, in trust, as to *two millions of dollars*, part thereof, to apply and expend so much of that sum as may be necessary, in erecting, as soon as practicably may be, in the centre of my square of ground[1] between High and Chestnut streets, and Eleventh and Twelfth streets, in the City of Philadelphia (which square of ground I hereby devote for the purposes hereinafter stated, and for no other, forever), a permanent college, with suitable out-buildings, sufficiently spacious for the residence and accommodation of at least three hundred scholars, and the requisite teachers and other persons necessary in such an institution as I direct to be established, and in supplying the said college and out-buildings with decent and suitable furniture, as well as books and all things needful to carry into effect my general design.

The said college shall be constructed with the most durable materials,

[1] [By a later addition to the will the site was changed to another which he had recently purchased.]

and in the most permanent manner, avoiding needless ornament, and attending chiefly to the strength, convenience, and neatness of the whole. . . . .[1]

When the College and appurtenances shall have been constructed and supplied with plain and suitable furniture and books, philosophical and experimental instruments and apparatus, and all other matters needful to carry my general design into execution; the income, issues, and profits of so much of the said sum of two millions of dollars as shall remain unexpended, shall be applied to maintain the said college according to my directions.

1. The Institution shall be organized as soon as practicable, and to accomplish the purpose more effectually, due public notice of the intended opening of the college shall be given—so that there may be an opportunity to make selections of competent instructors, and other agents, and those who may have the charge of orphans may be aware of the provision intended for them.

2. A competent number of instructors, teachers, assistants, and other necessary agents shall be selected, and when needful, their places, from time to time, supplied: they shall receive adequate compensation for their services; but no person shall be employed, who shall not be of tried skill in his or her proper department, of established moral character, and in all cases persons shall be chosen on account of their merit, and not through favor or intrigue.

3. As many poor white male orphans, between the age of six and ten years, as the said income shall be adequate to maintain, shall be introduced into the college as soon as possible; and from time to time, as there may be vacancies, or as increased ability from income may warrant, others shall be introduced.

4. On the application for admission, an accurate statement should be taken in a book, prepared for the purpose, of the name, birthplace, age, health, condition as to relatives, and other particulars useful to be known of each orphan.

[1] [The next six pages are devoted to very minute details relating to the construction of the college buildings and wall. The latter, for example, was to be "a solid wall, at least 14 inches thick, and 10 feet high, capped with marble and guarded with irons on the top, so as to prevent persons from getting over; there shall be two places of entrance into the square, one in the centre of the wall facing High street, and the other in the centre of the wall facing Chestnut street: at each place of entrance there shall be two gates, one opening inward, and the other outward, those opening inward to be of iron, and in the style of the gates north and south of my Banking House; and those opening outward to be of substantial wood work, well lined and secured on the faces thereof with sheet-iron."]

5. No orphan should be admitted until the guardians or directors of the poor, or a proper guardian or other competent authority, shall have given, by indenture, relinquishment, or otherwise, adequate power to the Mayor, Aldermen and Citizens of Philadelphia, or to directors, or others by them appointed, to enforce, in relation to each orphan, every proper restraint, and to prevent relatives or others from interfering with, or withdrawing such orphan from the institution.

6. Those orphans, for whose admission application shall first be made shall be first introduced, all other things concurring—and at all future times, priority of application shall entitle the applicant to preference in admission, all other things concurring; but if there shall be, at any time, more applicants than vacancies, and the applying orphans shall have been born in different places, a preference shall be given—*first*, to orphans born in the city of Philadelphia; *secondly*, to those born in any other part of Pennsylvania; *thirdly*, to those born in the city of New York (that being the first port on the continent of North America at which I arrived); and *lastly*, to those born in the City of New Orleans, being the first port on the said continent at which I first traded, in the first instance as first officer, and subsequently as master and part owner of a vessel and cargo.

7. The orphans admitted into the College, shall be there fed with plain but wholesome food, clothed with plain but decent apparel (no distinctive dress ever to be worn), and lodged in a plain but safe manner. Due regard shall be paid to their health, and to this end their persons and clothes shall be kept clean, and they shall have suitable and rational exercise and recreation: They shall be instructed in the various branches of a sound education, comprehending reading, writing, grammar, arithmetic, geography, navigation, surveying, practical mathematics, astronomy; natural, chemical, and experimental philosophy, the French and Spanish languages (I do not forbid, but I do not recommend the Greek and Latin languages)—and such other learning and science as the capacities of the several scholars may merit or warrant: I would have them taught facts and things, rather than words or signs; and especially, I desire, that by every proper means a pure attachment to our Republican Institutions, and to the sacred rights of conscience, as guaranteed by our happy constitutions, shall be formed and fostered in the minds of the scholars.

8. Should it unfortunately happen, that any of the orphans admitted into the College, shall, from malconduct, have become unfit companions for the rest, and mild means of reformation prove abortive, they shall no longer remain therein.

9. Those scholars, who shall merit it, shall remain in the College until

they shall respectively arrive at between fourteen and eighteen years of age; they shall then be bound out by the Mayor, Aldermen and Citizens of Philadelphia, or under their direction, to suitable occupations, as those of agriculture, navigation, arts, mechanical trades, and manufactures, according to the capacities and acquirements of the scholars respectively, consulting, as far as prudence shall justify it, the inclinations of the several scholars, as to the occupation, art or trade, to be learned.

In relation to the organization of the College and its appendages, I leave, necessarily, many details to the Mayor, Aldermen and Citizens of Philadelphia, and their successors; and I do so, with the more confidence, as, from the nature of my bequests, and the benefits to result from them, I trust that my fellow-citizens of Philadelphia will observe and evince especial care and anxiety in selecting members for their City Councils, and other agents.

There are, however, some restrictions, which I consider it my duty to prescribe, and to be, amongst others, conditions on which my bequest for said College is made, and to be enjoyed, namely; *first*, I enjoin and require, that if at the close of any year, the income of the fund devoted to the purposes of the said College shall be more than sufficient for the maintenance of the Institution during that year, then the balance of the said income, after defraying such maintenance, shall be forthwith invested in good securities, thereafter to be and remain a part of the capital; but in no event, shall any part of the said capital be sold, disposed of, or pledged, to meet the current expenses of the said Institution, to which I devote the interest, income and dividends thereof, exclusively: *Secondly*, I enjoin and require that *no ecclesiastic, missionary, or minister of any sect whatsoever, shall ever hold or exercise any station or duty whatever in the said College: nor shall any such person ever be admitted for any purpose, or as a visitor, within the premises appropriated to the purposes of the said college.* In making this restriction, I do not mean to cast any reflection upon any sect or person whatsoever; but as there is such a multitude of sects, and such a diversity of opinion amongst them, I desire to keep the tender minds of the orphans, who are to derive advantage from this bequest, free from the excitement which clashing doctrines and sectarian controversy are so apt to produce; my desire is, that all the instructors and teachers in the College, shall take pains to instil into the minds of the scholars *the purest principles of morality*, so that, on their entrance into active life, they may *from inclination and habit*, evince *benevolence toward their fellow creatures*, and *a love of truth, sobriety, and industry*, adopting at the same time such religious tenets as their *matured reason* may enable them to prefer. . . . .

In witness, I, the said Stephen Girard, have to this my last Will and Testament, contained in thirty-five pages, set my hand at the bottom of each page, and my hand and seal at the bottom of this page; the said Will executed, from motives of prudence, in duplicate, this sixteenth day of February, in the year one thousand eight hundred and thirty.

STEPHEN GIRARD (Seal)

February 16, 1830.

Opinion of the Court in the Girard Will Case[1]

Mr. Justice Story delivered the opinion of the court.

This cause has been argued with great learning and ability. Many topics have been discussed in the arguments, as illustrative of the principal grounds of controversy, with elaborate care, upon which, however, in the view which we have taken of the merits of the cause, it is not necessary for us to express any opinion, nor even allude to their bearing or application. . . . .

The late Stephen Girard, by his will dated the 25th day of December, A.D. 1830, after making sundry bequests to his relatives and friends, to the city of New Orleans, and to certain specified charities, proceeded in the 20th clause of that will to make the following bequest on which the present controversy mainly hinges. "XX, And whereas I have been for a long time impressed, etc."[2] . . . .

[The] objection is that the foundation of the college upon the principles and exclusions prescribed by the testator, is derogatory and hostile to the Christian religion, and so is void, as being against the common law and public policy of Pennsylvania; and this for two reasons: First, because of the exclusion of all ecclesiastics, missionaries, and ministers of any sect from holding or exercising any station or duty in the college, or even visiting the same; and Secondly, because it limits the instruction to be given to the scholars to pure morality, and general benevolence, and a love of truth, sobriety, and industry, thereby excluding, by implication, all instruction in the Christian religion.

In considering this objection, the court are not at liberty to travel out

---

[1] This document is part of the opinion of the U.S. Supreme Court in the famous case in which the relatives of Stephen Girard attempted to break the will and secure for their private use the funds bequeathed to Girard College. The extract is from *Vidal and Others, Citizens and Subjects of the Monarchy of France*, v. *The Mayor, Aldermen and Citizens of Phildelphia, the Executors of Stephen Girard* (1844), 2 Howard (U.S.), 182–201.

[2] [See the extract from the will, p. 483, above.]

of the record in order to ascertain what were the private religious opinions of the testator (of which indeed we can know nothing), nor to consider whether the scheme of education by him prescribed, is such as we ourselves should approve, or as is best adapted to accomplish the great aims and ends of education. Nor are we at liberty to look at general considerations of the supposed public interests and policy of Pennsylvania upon this subject, beyond what its constitution and laws and judicial decisions make known to us. The question, what is the public policy of a state, and what is contrary to it, if inquired into beyond these limits, will be found to be one of great vagueness and uncertainty, and to involve discussions which scarcely come within the range of judicial duty and functions, and upon which men may and will complexionally differ; above all, when that topic is connected with religious polity, in a country composed of such a variety of religious sects as our country, it is impossible not to feel that it would be attended with almost insuperable difficulties, and involve differences of opinion almost endless in their variety. We disclaim any right to enter upon such examinations, beyond what the state constitutions, and laws, and decisions necessarily bring before us.

It is also said, and truly, that the Christian religion is a part of the common law of Pennsylvania. But this proposition is to be received with its appropriate qualifications, and in connection with the bill of rights of that state, as found in its constitution of government. The constitution of 1790 (and the like provision will, in substance, be found in the constitution of 1776, and in the existing constitution of 1838) expressly declares: "That all men have a natural and indefeasible right to worship Almighty God according to the dictates of their own consciences; no man can of right be compelled to attend, erect, or support any place of worship, or to maintain any ministry against his consent; no human authority can, in any case whatever, control or interfere with the rights of conscience; and no preference shall ever be given by law to any religious establishment or modes of worship." Language more comprehensive for the complete protection of every variety of religious opinion could scarcely be used; and it must have been intended to extend equally to all sects, whether they believed in Christianity or not, and whether they were Jews or infidels. So that we are compelled to admit that although Christianity be a part of the common law of the state, yet it is so in this qualified sense, that its divine origin and truth are admitted, and therefore it is not to be maliciously and openly reviled and blasphemed against, to the annoyance of believers or the injury of the public. Such was the doctrine of the Supreme Court of Pennsylvania in *Updegraff* v. *The Commonwealth*, 11 Serg. & R. (Pa.), 394.

It is unnecessary for us, however, to consider what would be the legal effect of a device in Pennsylvania for the establishment of a school or college, for the propagation of Judaism, or Deism, or any other form of infidelity. Such a case is not to be presumed to exist in a Christian country; and therefore it must be made out by clear and indisputable proof. Remote inferences, or possible results, or speculative tendencies, are not to be drawn or adopted for such purposes. There must be plain, positive, and express provisions, demonstrating not only that Christianity is not to be taught; but that it is to be impugned or repudiated.

Now, in the present case, there is no pretense to say that any such positive or express provisions exist, or are even shadowed forth in the will. The testator does not say that Christianity shall not be taught in the college. But only that no ecclesiastic of any sect shall hold or exercise any station or duty in the college. Suppose, instead of this, he had said that no person but a layman shall be an instructor or officer or visitor in the college, what legal objection could have been made to such a restriction? And yet the actual prohibition is in effect the same in substance. But it is asked: why are ecclesiastics excluded if it is not because they are the stated and appropriate preachers of Christianity? The answer may be given in the very words of the testator: "In making this restriction," says he, "I do not mean to cast any reflection upon any.sect or person whatsoever, but as there is such a multitude of sects, and such a diversity of opinions, amongst them, I desire to keep the tender minds of the orphans, who are to derive advantage from this bequest, free from the excitement which clashing doctrines and sectarian controversy are so apt to produce." Here, then, we have the reason given; and the question is not, whether it is satisfactory to us or not; nor whether the history of religion does or does not justify such a sweeping statement; but the question is, whether the exclusion be not such as the testator had a right, consistently with the laws of Pennsylvania, to maintain upon his own notions of religious instruction. Suppose the testator had excluded all religious instructors but Catholics, or Quakers, or Swedenborgians; or, to put a stronger case, he had excluded all religious instructors but Jews, would the bequest have been void on that account? Suppose he had excluded all lawyers, or all physicians, or all merchants from being instructors or visitors, would the prohibition have been fatal to the bequest? The truth is, that in cases of this sort, it is extremely difficult to draw any just and satisfactory line of distinction in a free country as to the qualifications or disqualifications which may be insisted upon by the donor of a charity as to those who shall administer or partake of his bounty.

But the objection itself assumes the proposition that Christianity is not to be taught, because ecclesiastics are not to be instructors or officers. But this is by no means a necessary or legitimate inference from the premises. Why may not laymen instruct in the general principles of Christianity as well as ecclesiastics? There is no restriction as to the religious opinions of the instructors and officers. They may be, and doubtless, under the auspices of the city government, they will always be, men, not only distinguished for learning and talent, but for piety and elevated virtue, and holy lives and characters. And we cannot overlook the blessings, which such men by their conduct, as well as their instructions, may, nay, must impart to their youthful pupils. Why may not the Bible, and especially the New Testament, without note or comment, be read and taught as a divine revelation in the college—its general precepts expounded, its evidences explained, and its glorious principles of morality inculcated? What is there to prevent a work, not sectarian, upon the general evidences of Christianity, from being read and taught in the college by lay-teachers? Certainly there is nothing in the will, that proscribes such studies. Above all, the testator positively enjoins, "that all the instructors and teachers in the college shall take pains to instil into the minds of the scholars the purest principles of morality, so that on their entrance into active life, they may from inclination and habit evince benevolence towards their fellow-creatures, and a love of truth, sobriety, and industry, adopting at the same time such religious tenets as their mature reason may enable them to prefer." Now, it may well be asked, what is there in all this, which is positively enjoined, inconsistent with the spirit or truths of Christianity? Are not these truths all taught by Christianity, although it teaches much more? Where can the purest principles of morality be learned so clearly or so perfectly as from the New Testament? Where are benevolence, the love of truth, sobriety, and industry, so powerfully and irresistibly inculcated as in the sacred volume? The testator has not said how these great principles are to be taught, or by whom, except it be by laymen, nor what books are to be used to explain or enforce them. All that we can gather from his language is, that he desired to exclude sectarians and sectarianism from the college, leaving the instructors and officers free to teach the purest morality, the love of truth, sobriety, and industry, by all appropriate means; and of course including the best, the surest, and the most impressive. The objection, then, in this view, goes to this—either that the testator has totally omitted to provide for religious instruction in his scheme of education (which, from what has been already said, is an inadmissible interpretation) or that it includes but partial and imperfect instruction in those truths. In either view can it be truly said that it contravenes the known law of Pennsylvania upon the subject of charities, or is not allowable under the article of the bill of rights already cited? Is an omission to provide for instruction in Christianity in any scheme of school or college education a fatal defect, which avoids it according to the law of Pennsylvania? If the instruction provided for is incomplete and imperfect, is it equally fatal? These questions are propounded, because we are not aware that any thing exists in the constitution or laws of Pennsylvania, or the judicial decisions of its tribunals, which would justify us in pronouncing that such defects would be so fatal. Let us take the case of a charitable donation to teach poor orphans reading, writing, arithmetic, geography, and navigation, and excluding all other studies, and instruction; would the donation be void, as a charity in Pennsylvania, as being derogatory to Christianity? Hitherto it has been supposed, that a charity for the instruction of the poor might be good and valid in England even if it did not go beyond the establishment of a grammar-school. And in America, it has been thought, in the absence of any express legal prohibitions, that the donor might select the studies, as well as the classes of persons, who were to receive his bounty without being compellable to make religious instruction a necessary part of those studies. It has hitherto been thought sufficient, if he does not require anything to be taught inconsistent with Christianity.

Looking at the objection therefore in a mere juridical view, which is the only one in which we are at liberty to consider it, we are satisfied that there is nothing in the devise establishing the college, or in the regulations and restrictions contained therein, which are inconsistent with the Christian religion, or are opposed to any known policy of the state of Pennsylvania.

This view of the whole matter renders it unnecessary for us to examine the other and remaining question, to whom, if the devise were void, the property would belong, whether it would fall into the residue of the estate devised to the city, or become a resulting trust for the heirs at law.

Upon the whole, it is the unanimous opinion of the court that the decree of the Circuit Court of Pennsylvania dismissing the bill ought to be affirmed, and it is accordingly affirmed with costs.

SAMUEL GRIDLEY HOWE
1801–1876

EDITORIAL NOTE

D R. HOWE[1] has been described as "one of the most romantic characters" of the nineteenth century. Certainly few lives have been at once so adventurous, and at the same time so full of beneficent activity.

A graduate of Harvard Medical School at the age of twenty-three, he offered his services to the patriot army of Greece in its war for independence. He spent most of his time in Greece from 1824 to 1830, and became surgeon general of the Greek fleet and took charge of the organization of relief work.

He was thirty years old when he returned to the United States, and looked about for something worth doing. He did not like the idea of medical practice, for he objected to charging money for medical services. Suddenly he became interested in a project for teaching the blind. In a few days he had arranged to take charge of the enterprise, and left at once for Europe to study the new methods that had been developed there, and to secure teachers and equipment.

In the summer of 1832 he began this work for the Massachusetts School and Asylum for the Blind by taking six blind children into his father's spacious Boston house and teaching them there.

[1] For accounts of Dr. Howe's life and work the following books may be consulted: *Letters and Journals of Samuel Gridley Howe*, edited by his daughter Laura E. Richards . . . . with notes and a Preface by Franklin B. Sanborn (2 vols.; Boston, 1906-9); Julia Ward Howe, *Memoir of Dr. Samuel Gridley Howe*, published by the Howe Memorial Committee (Boston, 1876); Julia Ward Howe, *Reminiscences, 1819-1899* (Boston, 1899); Franklin B. Sanborn, *Dr. S. G. Howe, the Philanthropist* (New York, 1891); *Proceedings at the Celebration of the One Hundredth Anniversary of the Birth of Dr. Samuel Gridley Howe, November 11, 1901* (Boston, 1902); Maud Howe Elliott and Mrs. Florence Hall, *Laura Bridgman, Dr. Howe's Famous Pupil and What He Taught Her* (Boston, 1903); Laura E. Richards, *Samuel Gridley Howe* (1935); and Charles Dickens, *American Notes for General Circulation*, chap iii, "Boston."

The available published writings of Dr. Howe himself include the following: *Annual*

SAMUEL GRIDLEY HOWE
(During the early days at the Blind Asylum)

Few people had ever thought of teaching children except through the sense of sight, and his experiment aroused the greatest interest. Elizabeth Peabody, who visited the school in 1833, wrote of it with great enthusiasm as a place

where, in the simplest surroundings, we found Dr. Howe with the half-dozen first pupils he had picked up in the highways and byways. He had then been about six months at work and had invented and laboriously executed some books with raised letters to teach them to read, some geographical maps, and the geometrical diagrams necessary for instructions in mathematics. He had gummed twine, I think, upon cardboard, an enormous labor, to form the letters of the alphabet. I shall not, in all time, forget the impression made upon me by seeing the hero of the Greek Revolution, who had narrowly missed being that of the Polish Revolution also; to see this hero, I say, wholly absorbed, and applying all the energies of his genius to this apparently humble work, and doing it as Christ did, without money and without price.

The interest in the young doctor's work was widespread, for at that time the education of blind children was not thought possible. Dr. Howe found it necessary to take the blind children he had been teaching before the legislature to demonstrate that such children really could be taught. The result of his six months' work made such an impression that both houses voted, almost by acclamation, a grant of funds on condition that the institution should educate and support twenty poor blind children for the state. Other funds were promptly given, and a suitable home for the new institution was

Reports of the Massachusetts Board of State Charities (1865-74); Annual Report of the Perkins Institution and Massachusetts Asylum for the Blind (1833-75); Causes and Prevention of Idiocy (23 pp.; Boston, 1874; reprinted from the Massachusetts Quarterly Review, No. III [1848]); Cretan Refugees and Their American Helpers: A Statement Addressed to the Contributors for the Relief of Cretan Refugees (64 pp.; Boston, 1868); An Essay on Separate and Congregate Systems of Prison Discipline; Being a Report Made to the Boston Prison Discipline Society (90 pp.; Boston, 1846); An Historical Sketch of the Greek Revolution (2d ed.; 447 pp.; New York, 1828); A Letter on the Sanitary Condition of the Troops in the Neighborhood of Boston Addressed to His Excellency, the Governor of Massachusetts (16 pp.; Washington, D.C., 1861); A Letter to J. H. Wilkins, H. B. Rogers, and F. B. Fay, Commissioners of Massachusetts for the State Reform School for Girls (36 pp.; Boston, 1854); A Letter to Mrs.———and Other Loyal Women Touching the Matter of Contributions for the Army and Other Matters Connected with the War (27, 26 pp.; Boston, 1862); A Letter to the Governor of Massachusetts upon His Veto Bill Providing for an Increase of State Beneficiaries at the School for Idiotic Children (24 pp.; Boston, 1857); Letters on the Proposed Annexation of Santo Domingo (32 pp.; Boston, 1871); Refugees from Slavery in Canada West; Report to the Freedman's Inquiry Commission (110 pp.; Boston, 1864); Report Made to the Legislature of Massachusetts upon Idiocy (54 pp.; Boston, 1848).

soon established. This was one of the three pioneer schools for blind children in America. A school was being started at approximately the same time in New York, and Philadelphia established one in the following year. The portrait that is used in this volume was painted during the early years at the Blind Asylum.

Many years later, in speaking at a convention held on the subject of the instruction of the blind, he described his early experiment as follows:

> It seems but yesterday (though it is really more than twenty years) that I undertook to organize and put in operation an institution which had been incorporated four years before in Massachusetts, and I then looked around the country in vain for some one practically acquainted with the subject. There was not then upon this continent a school for the blind, a teacher of the blind, or even a blind person who had been taught by one. I had but an imperfect knowledge of the European schools, and supposed, therefore, that I should gain time, and start with greater chance of success in what was regarded by many as a visionary enterprise, by going to Europe for teachers and for actual knowledge of all that had been done there. I went, therefore, saw what little there was to be seen of schools for the blind, and soon returned, bringing a teacher of the intellectual branches from France, and of the mechanical branches from Scotland.

He also brought with him three books printed with raised characters, for the use of his prospective pupils. These were at that time the only three books printed for the blind, in the English language. He determined to print more books and to find a means of lessening the bulk and the cost. His appeal for funds was generously met, and he not only maintained a large printing-office, which was actively at work increasing the number of books for his blind students, but he himself compiled for their use an encyclopedia, an atlas, and some other works of reference.

Finally, he saw the need of a national printing-press for the blind; and in 1836–37 tried, unsuccessfully, for help from Congress. In 1845 he made a new appeal to Congress, enlisting the help of the principals of the New York and the Philadelphia schools. These three pioneers went to Washington, taking with them their most gifted pupils, and gave exhibitions before Congress, which made a deep and lasting impression. More than three decades passed, however, before Congress finally made an appropriation for publishing books for the blind.

Dr. Howe began his greatest experiment in education in the year 1837, when he undertook the teaching of Laura Bridgman, a little girl of seven who, in an attack of scarlet fever in infancy, had become blind, deaf, and dumb. His own account of Laura's educational development is given in pages which follow (pp. 300–306). More familiar today is the case of Helen Keller, but her education was made possible by Dr. Howe's earlier experiments. In 1901, at the time of the Howe centenary meeting in Boston, Helen Keller, then a student at Radcliffe College, sent the following message:

I hope you will express the heartfelt gratitude of those who owe their education, their opportunities, their happiness to him who opened the eyes of the blind and gave the dumb lip language.

Sitting here in my study, surrounded by my books, enjoying the sweet and intimate companionship of the great and the wise, I am trying to realize what my life might have been if Dr. Howe had failed in the great task God gave him to perform. If he had not taken upon himself the responsibility of Laura Bridgman's education, and led her out of the pit of Acheron back to her human inheritance.

I think only those who have escaped that death-like existence from which Laura Bridgman was rescued can realize how isolated, how shrouded in darkness, how cramped by its own importance is a soul without thought or faith or hope. Words are powerless to describe the desolation of that prison house, or the joy of the soul that is delivered out of its captivity. When we compare the needs and helplessness of the blind before Dr. Howe began his work with their present usefulness and independence, we realize that great things have been done in our midst. . . . . [1]

From the beginning, Dr. Howe was interested in education, in the largest sense of that word. He looked to restoring the blind child to a normal place in its family and the community. For example, in 1853, he wrote to a friend:

It is very desirable for the blind child that his claim upon his parents, friends, neighbors, or bondsmen should be kept alive. This is done in part by insisting that they provide him with clothing, and take him home at vacations. It is found, especially with the ignorant of our own and foreign population, that if a blind child is taken off their hands, fed and clad, and kept in an Institution, after a few years they come to look upon him as a stranger having no claim upon them; whereas if they had been obliged to provide him with shoes, and to receive him at home during vacations, the relationship would have grown and

[1] *Proceedings at the Celebration of the One Hundredth Anniversary of the Birth of Dr. Samuel Gridley Howe, November 11, 1901.*

strengthened. It is for the interest of the children, therefore, that we act, when we insist that the parents, or lacking parents, the relations, or lacking these, the neighborhood in which they are born shall be held responsible for them.

He was tireless also in helping the movement in other states. He appeared, sometimes alone, sometimes with some of his pupils, before the legislatures of seventeen different states, urging them to provide for the education of the blind.

Many years later, when the centenary of his birth was being celebrated in Boston, numerous messages came from these distant institutions which he had helped to found. One of these messages from Kentucky is typical of many others:

In behalf of the blind of Kentucky, the Board of Visitors of the Kentucky Institution for the Education of the Blind beg to assure you that the labours of Dr. Samuel G. Howe, in assisting in founding the Kentucky Institution for the Blind, are held in grateful remembrance to this day.

In the winter of 1841 he made the long and tiresome journey to Kentucky, and addressed the Legislature of our State upon the expediency of founding a school for the blind, with such success that in February, 1842, the Kentucky Institution for the Blind was established.

Even should the memory of his name, in the course of ages, pass from the minds of men, the beneficent influence of his deeds will abide to the last syllable of recorded time.

It was inevitable that Dr. Howe should also become interested in the education of mentally deficient children. In 1839 a blind child who was also "idiotic" was brought to the Asylum, and it was found possible to improve his condition very definitely. Later other blind and "idiotic" children were received and helped. Dr. Howe promptly became convinced "that if so much could be done for idiots who were blind, still more could be done for those who were not blind." He knew that schools for those who were then called "idiots" had been started in France and Germany, and he began planning an attempt to secure help from the legislature for such a project in Massachusetts. This appeal he made in the winter of 1845–46. In a letter to an influential member of the Massachusetts House he wrote:

There are about 600 idiotic children in Massachusetts, most of whom are born of poor and ignorant persons who can do nothing for them, and they soon become the children and the charge of the public. . . . . We thrust them out of sight into the almshouses; we feed them, indeed, and care for them, as we do for our cattle, but like cattle we let them go down to the grave without trying to kindle within them the light of reason which may guide them on their way to eternity.

The result of Dr. Howe's appeal was the appointment of a special commission, of which he was chairman, to report to the next legislature. In 1848, he submitted his report—the first official report on the condition of the feeble-minded in any American state. His daughter tells of the ridicule that followed his report. One man said the doctor's report was, in his opinion, a report for idiots as well as concerning them, and others laughed and said, "What do you think Howe is going to do next? He is going to teach idiots. Ha! Ha!"[1] As a result of this report the legislature appropriated the small sum of $2,500 a year for three years to allow Dr. Howe to experiment with the teaching of ten "idiotic" children, and the Massachusetts School for Idiotic and Feeble-minded Youth was incorporated in 1850. This was the beginning of the famous institution now known as the Walter E. Fernald School. Dr. Fernald himself said that he considered Dr. Howe's work with the imbecile as "truly the chief jewel in his crown. The other things he did other men might have done, but he alone among the philanthropists of that time was able to see the need of this work and to realize the possibilities."

Dr. Howe's own account of this school, written in 1852, is of special interest:

When the first steps were taken in this matter by the Legislature of Massachusetts, in 1846, it was the common belief—indeed, one might say that with very rare exceptions it was the universal belief—in this country, that idiots were beyond the reach of the most zealous educator's skill, and almost beyond the reach of human sympathy. . . . .

Our law considered them as paupers, but classed them with rogues and vagabonds; for it provided that they should be kept within the precincts of the House of Correction.

The most melancholy feature of the whole was that they were condemned as worthless and incapable of improvement; and the law required their removal from the only place where they were comfortable, the State Lunatic Asylum, whenever it was necessary to make room for the less unfortunate insane, and it sent them not to another asylum, but to the houses of correction. There was not, throughout this whole continent, any systematic attempt to lift them out of

[1] Quoted in *Letters and Journals of Samuel Gridley Howe* (edited by his daughter, Laura E. Richards), II, 213.

their brutishness. Even in Massachusetts, where the maniac is made to go clad and kept in mental quiet,—where the blind are taught to read, the mute to speak, yea, and even the blind mute to do both,—even here the poor idiot was left to that deterioration which certainly follows neglect. He had but little talent given him, and by neglect or abuse that little was lost. . . . .

Now, ... it has been shown here and elsewhere that even idiots are not beyond the educator's skill; and consequently, from every part of the country come eager inquiries from anxious parents, in whose breasts the hope has dawned that something may yet be done for children whom they had considered as beyond hope. . . . .

It is true that these children and youth speak and read but little, and that little very imperfectly compared with others of their age; but if one brings the case home, and supposes these to be his own children, it will not seem a small matter that a daughter who it was thought would never know a letter, can now read a simple story, and a son who could not say "father" can now distinctly repeat a prayer to his Father in heaven.[1]

With Horace Mann, who was an intimate personal friend, he became interested in attempting to teach deaf-mute children to speak, and thus to make them normal members of society. The Asylum for the Deaf at Hartford was using the old method of sign language; and as the deaf children of Massachusetts were being sent to this Asylum and paid for out of Massachusetts taxes, Mann found himself in opposition to the Hartford school and finally, with the support of Howe, engaged in a long controversy. Together these two men visited institutions in Switzerland, Holland, and Germany, where the deaf were being taught by the vocal method and where they saw deaf children progressing through every stage of attempted articulation "from the simultaneous utterance of unintelligible sounds to the very politeness and perfection of speech."

The introduction of this wonderful system of teaching deaf-mute children was resisted not only in Dr. Howe's day, but long afterward; and there are still, in the twentieth century, tax-supported schools for deaf children in the United States in which sign language is being taught.

But Dr. Howe was never acquiescent in a bad system where the welfare of children was at stake. If he could not persuade the Hart-

[1] Extract from the *Third and Final Report on the Experimental School for Teaching and Training Idiotic Children*, also the *First Report of the Trustees of the Massachusetts School for Idiotic and Feeble-minded Youth* (1852), quoted in *Letters and Journals*, II, 217-20.

ford Asylum to try the newer and better method, he would himself show that deaf-mute children could be taught to speak. He therefore took two deaf-mute children as an experiment, and not long afterward helped to establish a small school near Boston in which the articulate method of education was used for deaf mutes. He also taught mothers of such children how to educate them in large part at home.

It is not easy to give briefly an adequate account of Dr. Howe's varied interests. No social movement of his time was without his help. He was an active supporter of the movement to abolish imprisonment for debt, and of the Boston Prison Discipline Society, and the Prisoners' Aid Society. As physician he was a warm supporter of "temperance," and in his writings frequently set out the evil consequences of the use of liquor to the individual and to the race.

During the years between 1840 and 1846 he served as a member of the Massachusetts Legislature and as a member of the Boston School Committee. In the legislature he presented the first and most famous memorial of Dorothea Dix[1] and secured the appropriation for which she asked. As a member of the School Committee he instituted a very thorough overhauling of the Boston public schools. Horace Mann said of this episode, "It could only have been done by an angel—or by Sam Howe."

In 1846, as the conflict over slavery and its impending doom began to absorb the thoughts and fears of men, Dr. Howe became an ardent supporter of the abolition cause—a friend of Sumner, of Garrison, and of John Brown; a member of the Emigrant Aid Company that sent men and rifles to bleeding Kansas. He was chairman of the Faneuil Hall Committee that sent out clothes and money for the Kansas sufferers. Later he volunteered to go and carry the aid himself, and go he did in spite of his advancing years, his poor health, and the pressure of his other work. No one, he said, could die in a better cause.

During the war he was in Washington much of the time. He was one of the original members of the Sanitary Commission which pre-

[1] An account of the work of Miss Dix and a reprint of one of her "Memorials" will be found in the succeeding chapter, *supra*, p. 107.

ceded the Red Cross, and he served as chairman of the United States Freedman's Inquiry Committee, for which he wrote a report on the condition of the runaway slaves in Canada.

The latter part of Dr. Howe's life is better known. During the war Governor Andrew, of Massachusetts, had become interested in the state institutions and wrote asking for his views "in reference to general and systematic improvements in our methods of public charities." Dr. Howe replied in December, 1862, suggesting a "board or central commission . . . . to establish as far as may be a uniform and wise system of treatment of pauperism over the Commonwealth."

In 1863 such a board was actually organized, the first State Board of Charities in this country. In 1864 Dr. Howe became a member of the Board, although he was still occupied at that time with the momentous work of the war. In 1865 he became chairman of the Board, and in his *Annual Report* for that year he laid down his famous principles of public charity, which are reprinted in the pages which follow. Some of his large ideas of public charity had long been in his mind. As early as 1857 he had written regarding public institutions as follows:

The more I reflect upon the subject the more I see objections in principle and practice to asylums. What right have we to pack off the poor, the old, the blind into asylums? They are of us, our brothers, our sisters—they belong in families; they are deprived of the dearest relations of life in being put away in masses in asylums. Asylums generally are the offspring of a low order of feeling; their chief recommendation often is that they do cheaply what we ought to think only of doing well.

In the years from 1865 to 1874, he prepared a series of annual reports which set out in his vigorous and dramatic way the methods of making the state charitable administration efficient and humane. If we ever have a science of public welfare administration, Samuel Gridley Howe will surely be looked upon as one of its founders.

After his death, in 1876, the General Court of Massachusetts passed the following resolutions:

Resolved, That the commonwealth of Massachusetts, ever mindful of the welfare of the poor and the claims of the unfortunate among its people, recalls with gratitude the constant and efficacious service devoted by the late Dr. Samuel G. Howe to the education of the blind, the deaf, and the feeble-minded children of this Commonwealth, to the improvement of the discipline of prisons and reform schools, to the better care of the insane, the prevention of pauperism, and, in general, to the public charities of Massachusetts, with which he has been for a whole generation officially connected.

Resolved, That especial mention ought to be made of that grand achievement of science and patient beneficence, the education by Dr. Howe of deaf, dumb, and blind children in such a manner as to restore them to that communication with their friends and with the world which others enjoy, but from which they seemed wholly debarred until his genius and benevolence found for them the key of language, accustomed it to their hands, and thus gave them freedom instead of bondage and light for darkness. . . . .

A more vivid picture of his work was given by his friend Dr. Edward Everett Hale:

You ask for his epitaph. It is a very simple epitaph. He found idiots chattering, taunted, and ridiculed by each village fool, and he left them cheerful and happy. He found the insane shut up in their wretched cells, miserable, starving, cold, and dying, and he left them happy, hopeful, and brave. He found the blind sitting in darkness, and he left them glad in the sunshine of the love of God.

E. A.

The Historic Case of Laura Bridgman[1]

Laura Dewey Bridgman was born in Hanover, New Hampshire, on the twenty-first of December, 1829. She is described as having been a very sprightly and pretty infant, with bright blue eyes. She was, however, so puny and feeble until she was a year and a half old, that her parents hardly hoped to rear her. . . . .

It was not until four years of age that the poor child's bodily health seemed restored, and she was able to enter upon her apprenticeship of life and the world. Sight and hearing were gone forever. Her sense of smell was almost entirely destroyed, and consequently, her taste was much blunted. . . . .

As soon as she could walk she began to explore the room, and then the house. She followed her mother and felt of her hands and arms; and her disposition to imitate led her to repeat everything herself. She even learned to sew a little and to knit. But though she received all the aid that a kind mother could bestow, she soon began to give proof of the importance of language to the development of human character. Caressing and

[1] This account of the development of Laura Bridgman's education is taken from Dr. Howe's reports in the *Ninth Annual Report of the Trustees of the Perkins Institution and Massachusetts Asylum for the Blind* (1841), pp. 23–31, and the *Eighteenth Annual Report* (1850), pp. 47–48. Other extracts are reprinted in F. B. Sanborn, *Dr. S. G. Howe, the Philanthropist* (1891), pp. 148–58.

chiding will do for infants and dogs, but not for children, and by the time Laura was seven years old, the moral effects of her privation began to appear. There was nothing to control her will but the absolute power of another, and humanity revolts at this; she had already begun to disregard all but the sterner nature of her father; and it was evident that, as the propensities should increase with her physical growth, so would the difficulty of restraining them increase. At this time I was so fortunate as to hear of the child, and immediately hastened to Hanover to see her. I found her with a well-formed figure; a strongly marked, nervous-sanguine temperament; a large and beautifully shaped head, and the whole system in healthy action. Here seemed a rare opportunity of benefiting an individual, and of trying a plan for the education of a deaf and blind person. The parents were easily induced to consent to her coming to Boston; and on the fourth of October, 1837, they brought her to the institution.

LAURA'S FIRST LESSONS

The first experiments were made by taking articles in common use, such as knives, forks, spoons, keys, etc., and pasting upon them labels with their names printed in raised letters. These she felt of very carefully, and soon, of course, distinguished that the crooked lines *spoon* differed as much from the crooked lines *key*, as the spoon differed from the key in form. Then small, detached labels, with the same words printed upon them, were put into her hands; and she soon observed that they were similar to the ones pasted on the articles. She showed her perception of this similarity by laying the label *key* upon the key, and the label *spoon* upon the spoon. She was here encouraged by the natural sign of approbation, patting on the head.

The same process was then repeated with all the articles which she could handle; and she very easily learned to place the proper labels upon them. It was evident, however, that the only intellectual exercise was that of imitation and memory. She recollected that the label *book* was placed upon a book, and she repeated the process, first from imitation, next from memory, with no other motive than the love of approbation, and apparently without the intellectual perception of any relation between the things. After a while, instead of labels, the individual letters were given to her on detached pieces of paper; they were arranged side by side, so as to spell *book*, *key*, etc.; then they were mixed up in a heap, and a sign was made for her to arrange them herself, so as to express the words *book*, *key*, etc., and she did so.

Hitherto, the process had been mechanical, and the success about as great as teaching a very knowing dog a variety of tricks. The poor child had sat in mute amazement, and patiently imitated everything her teacher did; but now the truth began to flash upon her, her intellect began to work, she perceived that here was a way by which she could herself make up a sign of anything that was in her own mind, and show it to another mind, and at once her countenance lighted up with a human expression; it was no longer a dog or parrot—it was an immortal spirit, eagerly seizing upon a new link of union with other spirits! I could almost fix upon the moment when this truth dawned upon her mind, and spread its light to her countenance; I saw that the great obstacle was overcome, and that henceforward nothing but patient and persevering, plain and straightforward efforts were to be used.

The result, thus far, is quickly related, and easily conceived; but not so was the process; for many weeks of apparently unprofitable labor were passed before it was effected.

The next step was to procure a set of metal types, with the different letters of the alphabet cast upon their ends; also a board, in which were square holes, into which holes she could set the types, so that the letters on their ends could alone be felt above the surface. Then, on any article being handed her—for instance, a pencil or a watch—she would select the component letters, and arrange them on her board, and read them with apparent pleasure. She was exercised for several weeks in this way, until her vocabulary became extensive; and then the important step was taken of teaching her how to represent the different letters by the position of her fingers, instead of the cumbrous apparatus of the board and types. She accomplished this speedily and easily, for her intellect had begun to work in aid of her teacher, and her progress was rapid. . . . . .

The whole of the succeeding year was passed in gratifying her eager inquiries for the names of every object which she could possibly handle; in exercising her in the use of the manual alphabet; in extending in every possible way her knowledge of the physical relations of things; and in taking proper care of her health.

[At the end of the year the report of her case said:] Of beautiful sights, and sweet sounds, and pleasant odors, she has no conception; nevertheless she seems as happy and playful as a bird or a lamb; and the employment of her intellectual faculties, the acquirement of a new idea, gives her a vivid pleasure, which is plainly marked in her expressive features. She never seems to repine, but has all the buoyancy and gaiety of childhood. She is fond of fun and frolic, and, when playing with the rest of the children, her shrill laugh sounds loudest of the group. When left alone, she seems very happy if she has her knitting or sewing, and will busy herself for hours; if she has no occupation, she evidently amuses herself by imaginary dialogues, or by recalling past impressions; she counts with her fingers, or spells out names of things which she has recently learned, in the manual alphabet of the deaf-mutes. In this lonely self-communion she reasons, reflects, and argues; if she spells a word wrong with the fingers of her right hand, she instantly strikes it with her left, as her teacher does, in sign of disapprobation; if right, then she pats herself upon the head and looks pleased. She sometimes purposely spells a word wrong with the left hand, looks roguish for a moment, and laughs, and then with the right hand strikes the left, as if to correct it. . . . .

When Laura is walking through a passage-way, with her hands spread before her, she knows instantly every one she meets, and passes them with a sign of recognition; but if it be a girl of her own age, and especially if one of her favorites, there is instantly a bright smile of recognition, an intertwining of arms, a grasping of hands, and a swift telegraphing upon the tiny fingers, whose rapid evolutions convey the thoughts and feelings from the outposts of one mind to those of the other. There are questions and answers, exchanges of joy or sorrow; there are kissings and partings, just as between little children with all their senses. . . . .

LAURA AND HER MOTHER

During this year [1838], and six months after she had left home, her mother came to visit her, and their meeting was an interesting one. The mother stood some time, gazing with overflowing eyes upon her unfortunate child, who, all unconscious of her presence, was playing about the room. Presently Laura ran against her, and at once began feeling of her hands, examining her dress, and trying to find out if she knew her; but, not succeeding in this, she turned away as from a stranger, and the poor woman could not conceal the pang she felt, at finding that her beloved child did not know her. She then gave Laura a string of beads which she used to wear at home, which were recognized by the child at once, who, with much joy, put them around her neck, and sought me eagerly, to say she understood the string was from her home. The mother now tried to caress her, but poor Laura repelled her, preferring to be with her acquaintances. Another article from home was now given her, and she began to look much interested; she examined the stranger much closer, and gave me to understand that she knew she came from Hanover; she even endured her caresses, but would leave her with indifference at the slightest signal. The distress of the mother was now painful to behold; for, although she had feared she should not be recognized, yet the reality of being treated with cold indifference by a darling child was too much for woman's nature to bear.

After a while, on the mother taking hold of her again, a vague idea seemed to flit across Laura's mind, that this could not be a stranger; she therefore felt of her hands very eagerly, while her countenance assumed an expression of intense interest; she became very pale, and then suddenly red; hope seemed struggling with doubt and anxiety, and never were contending emotions more strongly painted upon the human face. At this moment of painful uncertainty, the mother drew her close to her side, and kissed her fondly; when at once the truth flashed upon the child, and all mistrust and anxiety disappeared from her face, as with an expression of exceeding joy she eagerly nestled to the bosom of her parent, and yielded herself to her fond embraces.

After this, the beads were all unheeded; the playthings which were offered to her were utterly disregarded; her playmates, for whom but a moment before she gladly left the stranger, now vainly strove to pull her from her mother; and, though she yielded her usual instantaneous obedience to my signal to follow me, it was evidently with painful reluctance. She clung close to me, as if bewildered and fearful; and when, after a moment, I took her to her mother, she sprang to her arms, and clung to her with eager joy. . . . .

LAURA COINS WORDS AND WRITES

In her eagerness to advance her knowledge of words and to communicate her ideas, she coins words, and is always guided by analogy. Sometimes her process of *word-making* is very interesting; for instance, after some time spent in giving her an idea of the abstract meaning of *alone*, she seemed to obtain it, and understanding that being *by one's self* was to be alone, or *al-one;* she was told to go to her chamber, or school, or elsewhere, and return *alone;* she did so, but soon after, wishing to go with one of the little girls, she strove to express her meaning thus, "Laura go *al-two*." The same eagerness is manifested in her attempts to define for the purpose of classification. . . . .

Having acquired the use of substantives, adjectives, verbs, prepositions and conjunctions, it was deemed time to make the experiment of trying to teach her to *write*, and to show her that she might communicate her ideas to persons not in contact with her. It was amusing to witness the mute amazement with which she submitted to the process, the docility with which she imitated every motion, and the perseverance with which she moved her pencil over and over again in the same track, until she could form the letter. But when at last the idea dawned upon her, that by this mysterious process she could make other people understand what she thought, her joy was boundless. Never did a child apply more eagerly and joyfully to any task than she did to this, and in a few months she could make every letter distinctly, and separate words from each other. . . . .

She is so much in company with blind persons that she thinks blindness common; and, when first meeting persons, she asks if they are blind, or she feels of their eyes. She evidently knows that the blind differ from seeing persons, for when she shows blind persons anything, she always puts their fingers on it.

She seems to have a perception of character, and to have no esteem for those who have little intellect. The following anecdote is significant of her perception of character, and shows that from her friends she requires something more than good-natured indulgence. A new scholar entered school, a little girl about Laura's age. She was very helpless, and Laura took great pride and great pains in showing her the way about the house, assisting her to dress and undress, and doing for her many things which she could not do for herself. In a few weeks it began to be apparent, even to Laura, that the child was not only helpless, but naturally very stupid, being almost an idiot. Then Laura gave her up in despair, and avoided her, and has ever since had an aversion to being with her, passing her by as if in contempt. By a natural association of ideas she attributes to this child all those countless deeds which *Mr. Nobody* does in every house; if a chair is broken or anything misplaced, and no one knows who did it, Laura attributes it at once to this child. . . . .

THE RESULT OF TEN YEARS' TEACHING

When she began fairly to comprehend and to use arbitrary language, then she got hold of a thread by which her mind could be guided out into the light; she has held on to it firmly and followed it eagerly, and come out into a world which has been made to her one of joy and gladness by the general welcome with which she has been greeted. Her progress has been a curious and an interesting spectacle. She has come into human society with a sort of triumphal march; her course has been a perpetual ovation. Thousands have been watching her with eager eyes, and applauding each successful step; while she, all unconscious of their gaze, holding on to the slender thread and feeling her way along, has advanced with faith and courage towards those who awaited her with trembling hope. Nothing shows more than her case the importance which, despite their useless waste of human life and human capacity, men really attach to a human soul. They owe to her something for furnishing an opportunity of showing how much of goodness there is in them; for surely the way in which she has been regarded is creditable to humanity. Perhaps there are not three living women whose names are more widely known than hers; and there is not one who has excited so much sympathy and interest. There are thousands of women in the world who are striving to attract its notice and gain its admiration—some by the natural magic of beauty and grace, some by the high nobility of talent, some by the lower nobility of rank and title, some by the vulgar show of wealth; but none of them has done it so effectually as this poor blind, deaf, and dumb girl, by the silent show of her misfortunes, and her successful efforts to surmount them.

Principles of Public Charity[1]

THE FAMILY SYSTEM

In providing for the poor, the dependent, and the vicious, especially for the young, we must take the ordinary family for our model. We must, in a general view of them, bear in mind that they do not as yet form with us a well marked and persistent class, but a conventional, and, perhaps, only a temporary one. They do not differ from other men, except that, taken as a whole, they inherited less favorable moral tendencies, and less original vigor. Care should be taken that we do not by our treatment transform the conventional class into a real one and a persistent one.

In providing for them we are to consider that although there exists in them, as in all men, a strong gregarious instinct, out of which grows society, there are yet stronger domestic instincts out of which grows the family, and upon which depend the affections and the happiness of the individual. We cannot make the gratification of one instinct atone for the disappointment of the others. No amount of instruction and mental culture compensates for stunted affections; no abundance of society compensates for poverty of domestic relations; and the denial of these to the dependent poor, especially to the young, can only be justified by stern necessity. The family has been called the social unit. It is indeed the basis without which there will be no real society, but a multitude of individuals who harden into selfishness as they grow older. By means of the affections growing out of the family, the individual is divided into many; and the interests of others are felt to be his own.

God not only "set the solitary in families," and made "blood thicker

Extract from *Second Annual Report of the Massachusetts Board of State Charities, January, 1866*, pp. xlv–xlvi, xliv–xlv, xli–xliv.

than water," but seems to have ordained that the natural institution of the family, growing out of kindred, and long familiar intercourse, must be at the foundation of all permanent social institutions, and that by no human contrivance should any effectual substitute be found for it. But the family instinct craves a permanent homestead; and the lack of that is one of the greatest evils of poverty.

If we look through history we shall find that none of the attempts to imitate the family, upon a large scale, have been successful, and that most of them have been disastrous failures. They require separation of sexes, and this involves a train of evils. Large numbers of one sex, living together permanently as a family, constitute an unnatural community, which necessarily tends to a morbid condition. Armies, and still more, navies, show this in some degree; but where the congregation is closer and longer continued, as in monasteries, nunneries, knighthood-militant, shakerism, and other establishments on like foundation, the evil effects are multiplied and intensified. The public history of such establishments shows this plainly. . . . .

GENERAL PRINCIPLES OF PUBLIC CHARITY

In considering what measures ought to be taken for the care and treatment of the dependent and vicious classes, we are to bear in mind several principles.

1st. That if, by investing one dollar, we prevent an evil the correction of which would cost ten cents a year, we save four per cent.

2d. That it is better to separate and diffuse the dependent classes than to congregate them.

3d. That we ought to avail ourselves as much as possible of those remedial agencies which exist in society,—the family, social influences, industrial occupations, and the like.

4th. That we should enlist not only the greatest possible amount of popular sympathy, but the greatest number of individuals and of families, in the care and treatment of the dependent.

5th. That we should avail ourselves of responsible societies and organizations which aim to reform, support, or help any class of dependents; thus lessening the direct agency of the State, and enlarging that of the people themselves.

6th. That we should build up public institutions only in the last resort.

7th. That these should be kept as small as is consistent with wise economy, and arranged so as to turn the strength and the faculties of the inmates to the best account.

8th. That we should not retain the inmates any longer than is manifestly for their good, irrespective of their usefulness in the institution. . . . .

PROVISION FOR DISABLED SOLDIERS

There is, indeed, danger at this very moment that the earnest desire of the people to show their gratitude to those who carried the country triumphantly through the war, may lead to the formation of institutions upon unsound principles, which may prove to be nuisances, and cumber the field of charity in the next generation.

We cannot be too grateful for the services rendered; too reverent of the memories of our dead heroes, or too tender and generous to those survivors who need sympathy and aid. But we must remember that the warmer is the public heart, the more need of right direction for its impulses. Many of our soldiers may need *homes*, but such homes as we ourselves need; and a great institution, with its congregation of one sex,—with its necessary discipline, and its monotonous life,—never was and never can be such a home as our deserving veterans ought to have.

Better the poorest hut in a retired hamlet, with its single family gathered round the hearthstone, where,

> The broken soldier, kindly bade to stay,
> Sits by the fire and talks the night away,

than a showy building, set upon a hill, with its corps of officials, its parade of charity, and its clock-work and steam for doing domestic work so thoroughly that it is robbed of all its old and endearing associations. Unless some as yet undiscovered method is found to check the evil tendencies of all institutions which congregate persons of one sex, and substitute artificial for real family influences, soldiers' homes, or asylums, or refuges, will be likely to share the fate of like institutions in older countries. They will degenerate like the Invalides and the Quinze Vingts in France, and the Greenwich Hospital in England; and a succeeding generation will be occupied, as is the present generation abroad, in correcting their evils or cutting at their roots.

There is danger, indeed, that our institutions may not start under as favorable auspices as did some of the foreign ones. They were at first filled with well deserving veterans who had been actually wounded, or blinded, or disabled in war. But the signs already portend that into ours will press hardly any respectable Americans, few deserving foreigners, but a multitude of "bounty-jumpers and shirks," who want to eat but not to work.

Another danger is the very abundance of means of endowing such institutions; for there is not only the exhaustless treasure of the people's gratitude and the people's purse, but there are funds in hands of the government, derived from forfeitures, fines, unclaimed pay, and the like, which can be applied with seeming propriety to such purposes.

Besides, at this moment, there abound unemployed men who think they can do something better than work. Some of these aspire to honor, and some to office, and they will seek to connect themselves as patrons, or as officers, with institutions likely to have temporary popularity.

If the unreasoning impulse to build up special homes for soldiers is not followed with great caution, a large part of these funds will be invested at the outset in lands and buildings; a part of the remainder will be spent in keeping them in order; and a larger part in paying a costly corps of officers and retainers; leaving a small portion only for the immediate benefit of the soldiers. Better far, even as an economical measure, would be some well devised plan by which the money could go directly to the soldier, to be spent, or saved, or even wasted, at his will.

Besides, the natural desire of the deserving soldier, disabled in the war, is with few exceptions, to be at or near his old home and among his old associates; and the people should have him there, and nowhere else; not only for his happiness but their own good; that he may go about among them, wearing his orders of merit—his honorable scars—to keep alive in their hearts the feelings of patriotism and of gratitude.

Better have 500 maimed veterans stumping about the towns and villages of Massachusetts, living partly on their pension and partly by their work, than shut up in the costliest and best structure that art could plan or money build.

Among the establishments of this kind which have already sprung up in various parts of the country, some are under the guidance of men who are not only earnest and honest, but wise and practical; and they will, for a time, keep down the unfavorable tendencies; but their vigilance and care cannot be always enjoyed, while the tendencies are innate, and will crop out sooner or later. In some of the establishments, or homes, they have not begun to do so; but in others they are already painfully visible.

In whatever is done we must not favor the creation of a separate class, but encourage the fusion of the soldier with general society. We must not lessen self-respect, or reluctance to accept direct aid, either in the soldiers themselves or in their widows and children, but merely help them to help themselves.

The board would encourage every popular impulse leading to thought and care for our fellow-men of whatever class; and these remarks are inspired by the wish of making the present sympathy for the soldier productive of the most good and the least evil.

DOROTHEA LYNDE DIX

1802–1887

DOROTHEA L. DIX AND FEDERAL AID

EDITORIAL NOTE

MORE than three-quarters of a century ago, Dorothea Lynde Dix, a pioneer in the field of public welfare administration, presented to the Congress of the United States a moving appeal for federal aid to the states in making provision for the insane.[1] At a time when federal land grants were an approved method of extending federal aid, she asked for a land grant to be used to assist the states in providing humane and curative treatment for what was already a large group in our population.

The beneficial results of improved care had been demonstrated more than half a century earlier by Pinel in Paris and by Tuke in England. In America, as her *Memorial* shows, some of the states had already made an effort to establish hospital care. The need, however, was too great to be met by state funds.

In the *Memorial* we have a flashlight picture of the care of the insane in our American states at the close of the first half of the nineteenth century. To secure the evidence in the *Memorial* showing the inadequacy of the provision for the insane in twenty-seven of the states, she traveled more than 60,000 miles, at a time when traveling involved almost inconceivable hardships. As a result of her effort a measure passed both houses of Congress, providing for a grant to the states of 10,000,000 acres of the public domain to be applied to the care of the insane and 2,500,000 acres for the education of the deaf. This measure was vetoed[2] by President Franklin Pierce on the ground both of power and of policy.

In view of recent discussions of federal aid, the *Memorial* of Miss

[1] The best available account of the work of Dorothea Dix will be found in Francis Tiffany, *Life of Dorothea Lynde Dix* (Boston, 1890).

[2] The veto message appears as one of the documents in the forthcoming volume of the "Social Service Series," *Public Welfare Administration in the United States*, by S. P. Breckinridge. The significance of the controversy between Miss Dix, President Pierce, and the Thirty-Third Congress is also discussed further in this volume.

Dix, the veto of President Pierce after Congress had finally answered her appeal, and the congressional debate following the veto are of timely interest. Space does not permit the publication of the veto message, but the *Memorial* and the extract from the *Debates* will be of interest.

E. A.

Memorial of Dorothea L. Dix[1]

Your memorialist respectfully asks permission to lay before you what seem to be just and urgent claims in behalf of a numerous and increasing class of sufferers in the United States. I refer to the great and inadequately relieved distresses of the insane throughout the country.

Upon the subject to which this *Memorial* refers, many to whose justice and humanity it appeals are well-informed; but the attention of many has not been called to the subject, and a few, but a very few, have looked upon some features of this sad picture as revealed in private dwellings, in poor-houses, and in prisons. . . . .

It is a fact, not less certainly substantiated than it is deplorable, that insanity has increased in an advanced ratio with the fast increasing population in all the United States. For example, according to the best received methods of estimate five years since, it was thought correct to count one insane in every thousand inhabitants throughout the Union. At the present, my own careful investigations are sustained by the judgment and the information of the most intelligent superintendents of hospitals for the insane, in rendering the estimates not less than one insane person in every eight hundred inhabitants at large, throughout the United States.

There are, in proportion to numbers, more insane in cities than in large towns, and more insane in villages than among the same number of inhabitants dwelling in scattered settlements. . . . .

There are twenty State hospitals, besides several incorporated hospitals, for the treatment of the insane, in nineteen States of the Union, Virginia alone having two government institutions of State and incorporated hospitals. . . . .

---

[1] Extract from *Memorial of D. L. Dix Praying a Grant of Land for the Relief and Support of the Indigent Curable and Incurable Insane in the United States, June 23. 1848* (U.S. Thirtieth Congress, 1st sess., "Senate Miscellaneous Document No. 150"). See *Congressional Globe* (Thirty-first Congress, 1st sess., June 25, 1850), p. 1290; (Thirty-second Congress, 1st sess., February, 4, 1852), p. 461; *ibid.*, June, 7, 1852, pp. 1527-29; (Thirty-third Congress, 1st sess., February 9, 1854), p. 389; *ibid.*, April 25, 1854, p. 985.

Well organized hospitals are the only fit places of residence for the insane of all classes; ill-conducted institutions are worse than none at all. The New York City Hospital for the Insane, and the State hospitals of Georgia and Tennessee, cannot take present respectable rank as curative or comfortable hospitals.

Tennessee State Hospital, at Nashville, was opened in 1839. According to an act of the legislature the present year, this hospital is to be replaced by one of capacity to receive 250 patients. In the old hospital are 64 patients. Boston City Hospital for the indigent, which has 150 patients, and Ohio State Hospital at Columbus, were severally opened in 1839. The latter has been considerably enlarged, and has now 329 patients. Maine State Hospital, at Augusta, 1840, patients 130. New Hampshire State Hospital, at Concord, was opened in 1842, and has 100 patients. New York State Hospital, at Utica, was established in 1843, and has since been largely extended, and has 600 patients. Mount Hope Hospital, near Baltimore, 1844–45, has 72 insane patients. Georgia has an institution for the insane at Milledgeville. and at present 128 patients. Rhode Island State Hospital opened, under the able direction of Dr. Ray, early in 1848. New Jersey State Hospital, at Trenton, 1848. Indiana State Hospital, at Indianapolis, will be opened in 1848. State Hospital of Illinois, at Jacksonville, will be occupied before 1849. The Louisiana State Hospital will be occupied perhaps within a year.

I repeat that these institutions, liberally sustained as are most of them, cannot accommodate *one twelfth* of the insane population of the United States which require prompt remedial care.

It may be suggested that though hospital treatment is expedient, perhaps it may not be absolutely necessary, especially for vast numbers whose condition may be considered irrecoverable, and in whom the right exercise of the reasoning faculties may be looked upon as past hope. Rather than enter upon a philosophical and abstract argument to prove the contrary to be the fact, I will ask permission to spread before you a *few* statements gathered, without special selection, from a mass of records made from existing cases, sought out and noted during *eight years* of sad, patient, deliberate investigation. To assure accuracy, establish facts beyond controversy, and procure, so far as possible, temporary or permanent relief, more than sixty thousand miles have been traversed, and no time or labor spared which fidelity to this imperative and grievous vocation demanded. The only States as yet unvisited are North Carolina, Florida, and Texas. From each of these, however, I have had communications, which clearly prove that the conditions of the indigent insane differ in no essential degree from those of other States.

I have myself seen *more than nine thousand idiots, epileptics, and insane, in these United States, destitute of appropriate care and protection;* and of this vast and most miserable company, sought out in *jails,* in *poorhouses,* and in *private dwellings,* there have been hundreds, nay, rather thousands, bound with galling chains, bowed beneath fetters and heavy iron balls, attached to drag-chains, lacerated with ropes, scourged with rods, and terrified beneath storms of profane execrations and cruel blows; now subject to jibes, and scorn, and torturing kicks— now abandoned to the most loathsome necessities, or subject to the vilest and most outrageous violations. These are strong terms, but language fails to convey the astounding truths. I proceed to verify this assertion, commencing with the State of Maine. I will be ready to specify the towns and districts where each example quoted did exist, or exists still.

In B—, a furious maniac confined in the jail; case doubtful from long delay in removing to an hospital; a heap of filthy straw in one corner served for a bed; food was introduced through a small aperture, called a slit, in the wall, through which also was the sole source of ventilation and avenue for light.

Near C—, a man for several years in a narrow filthy pen, chained; condition loathsome in the extreme.

In A—, insane man in a small damp room in the jail; greatly excited; had been confined many years; during his paroxysms, which were aggravated by every manner of neglect, except want of food, he had *torn out his eyes,* lacerated his face, chest, and arms, seriously injured his limbs, and was in a state most shocking to behold. In P—, nine very insane men and women in the poorhouse, all exposed to neglect and every species of injudicious treatment; several chained, some in pens or stalls in the barn, and treated less kindly than the brute beasts in their vicinity. At C—, four furiously crazy; ill treated, through the ignorance of those who held them in charge. 47 cases in the middle district, either scattered in poorhouses, jails, or in private families, and all inappropriately treated in every respect; many chained, some bearing the marks of injuries self-inflicted, and many of injuries received from others. In New Hampshire, on the opening of the hospital for the reception of patients, in 1842, many were removed from cages, small unventilated cells in poorhouses, private houses, and from the dungeons of county jails. Many of these were bound with cords, or confined with chains; some bore the marks of severe usage by blows and stripes. They were neglected and filthy; and some, who yet remain in remote parts of the State, through exposure to cold in inclement seasons, have been badly frozen, so as to be maimed for life. Details in many cases will not bear recital.

In New Hampshire, a committee of the legislature was named in 1832, whose duty it was to collect and report statistics of the insane. Returns were received from only one hundred and forty-one towns: in these were returned the names of *one hundred and eighty-nine* persons bereft of their reason, and incapable of taking care of themselves; ninety men and ninety-nine women. The number confined was *seventy-six*, *twenty-five* of whom were in private houses, seven in cells and cages, six in chains and irons, and four in the jails. Of the number at liberty, many had at various times been confined. Many of the facts represented by this committee are too horrible to repeat, and would lead many to the belief that they could not be correct, were they not so undeniably authenticated. The committee remark that from many towns no returns had been made, and conclude their *Report* with the declaration "that they could not doubt that the numbers of the insane greatly exceeded the estimates rendered."

Where were these insane? "Some were in cells or cages; some in outbuildings, garrets, or cellars; some in county jails, shut up with felons and criminals; some in almshouses, in brick cells, never warmed by fire, nor lighted by the rays of the sun." The facts presented to this committee not only exhibit severe unnecessary suffering, but utter neglect, and in many cases actual barbarity.

Most of the cases reported, I could authenticate from direct investigation. . . . .

The [New Hampshire] committee of 1836 conclude their *Report* as follows:

Neither the time nor the occasion requires us to allude to instances of the aggravated and almost incredible suffering of the insane poor which have come to our knowledge. We are convinced that the legislature require no high wrought pictures of the various gradations of intense misery to which the pauper lunatic is subjected; extending from his incarceration in the cold, narrow, sunless, and fireless cell of the almshouse, to the scarcely more humane mode of *"selling him at auction,"* as it is called, by which he falls into the hands, and is exposed to the tender mercies, of the most worthless of society, who alone could be excited by cupidity to such a revolting charge. Suffice it on this point, your committee are satisfied that the horrors of the *present* condition of the insane poor of New Hampshire are far from having been exaggerated; and of course they find great unwillingness on the part of those having charge of them to render correct accounts, or to have these repeated to the public.

The *Report* of the nine trustees for the hospital, for 1847, states, that from authentic sources they are informed that "in eight of the twenty-four towns in Merrimack county, having an aggregate population of twelve thousand, there are eighteen insane paupers; part supported upon the town-farms, and part *set up and bid off at auction from year to year, to be kept and maintained by the lowest bidder."* According to the data afforded above, there must be in the State several hundred insane supported on the poor-farms, or put up at auction, annually.

In Vermont, the same neglect, ignorance, and sometimes brutal severity, led to like results. Dr. Rockwell, his assistant physicians, and the whole corps of hospital nurses, bear accordant testimony to the sufferings of patients formerly brought to that institution from all parts of the State; and many even now arrive under circumstances the most revolting and shocking, subject to the roughest treatment or the most inexcusable and extreme neglect.

I have seen many of these afflicted persons, men of hardy frames and women of great capacity for endurance, bowed and wasted till almost all trace of humanity was lost in groveling habits, and injuries through severities and privations, which those cannot comprehend who have never witnessed similar cases of misery.

Not many counties, if indeed any towns or parishes, but have their own tales of various woe, illustrated in the miseries of the insane.

In the eighth annual *Report* of the Vermont hospital for 1844 is the following record, which being a repetition in fact, if not almost literal expression of my own notes, I adopt in preference:

One case was brought to the hospital four and a half years ago, of a man who had been insane more than twelve years. During the four years previous to his admission he had not worn any article of clothing, and had been caged in a cellar, without feeling the influence of a fire. A nest of straw was his only bed and covering. He was so violent that his keeper thought it necessary to cause *an iron ring to be riveted about his neck*, so that they could hold him when they changed his bed of straw. In this miserable condition he was taken from the cellar and conveyed to the hospital. . . . .

Examples here, as in *every State of the Union*, might be multiplied of the insane caged and chained, confined in garrets, cellars, corn-

houses, and other outbuildings, until their extremities were seized by
the frost, and their sufferings augmented by extreme torturing pain.

In all the States where the cold of winter is sufficient to cause freez-
ing of the human frame by exposure, I have found many mutilated insane, deprived either of the hands or the feet, and sometimes of both.

In Massachusetts we trace repetition of like circumstances. . . . .

I visited the poor house in W—. In a cage, built under a wood-
shed, fully exposed to all passers upon the public road, was a miserable
insane man, partially enveloped in a torn coverlet. "My husband,"
remarked the mistress of the house, "clears out the cage and puts in
fresh straw once a week; but sometimes it's hard work to master him.
You see him now in his best estate!"

In the adjacent town, at the poorhouse, was a similar case; only,
if possible, more revolting, more excited, and more neglected. There
were also other persons there in different stages of insanity.

In a county jail not distant was a man who had been confined in a
close apartment for many years; a wreath of rags invested his body
and his neck; he was filthy in the extreme; there was neither table, seat,
nor bed; a heap of noxious straw defiled one corner of the room.

One case more must suffice for this section: I would that no others
could be adduced even more revolting than are these so briefly referred
to. In G—, distant from the poorhouse a few rods, was a small wooden
building, constructed of plank, affording a single room; this was un-
furnished, save with a bundle of straw. The occupant of this comfortless abode was a young man, declared to be incurably insane. He was
chained, and could move but a little space to and fro; the chain was
connected to the floor by a heavy staple at one end—the other was attached to an *iron collar which invested his neck*—the device, it seemed,
of a former keeper. In summer the door was thrown open, but during
winter it was closed, and the room was in darkness. Some months after
I saw this poor patient, and after several individuals also had witnessed
his sufferings, the authorities who directed the affairs of the poorhouse
reluctantly consented that he should be placed under the care of Dr.
Bell. The man who was charged to convey the patient the distance of
rather more than forty miles, having bound and chained him (I have
the impression that, by the aid of a blacksmith, he was released at this
time from the torturing iron ring) conveyed him as far as East Cam-
bridge, arriving at dusk. Instead of proceeding with the patient at
once to the hospital, which was distant less than a mile, in Somerville,

he chained him for the night to a post in the stable. After breakfast he was released and carried to the hospital in a state of much exhaustion. While the careful attendants and humane physician were busied in removing the strong bands which chafed his limbs, and lacerated the flesh in many places, he continually endeavored to express his gratitude—embracing them, weeping, and exclaiming, "Good men! kind men! Ah, good, kind men, keep me here."

After some months of careful nursing, he was so much improved that strong hopes were entertained of his complete restoration. These were crushed by an absolute decision of the overseers of the poor, remanding him to his old prison. Remonstrance was ineffectual. The last account stated an entire relapse, not only to the former state, but to a still more hopeless condition. He had become totally idiotic. . . . .

Of the most miserable neglects in the case of large numbers carried for successive years to the Hartford Retreat, Drs. Brigham, Woodward, and Butler can, even now, bear sad testimony; and to the observations of medical men may be added the evidence of that good man and true friend of sufferers, Rev. T. H. Gallaudet.

Rhode Island has nearly or quite four hundred insane, idiots, and epileptics. About 90 recently are receiving the benefit of hospital care, under the enlightened administration of Dr. Ray. In no State, however, have I found more terrible examples of neglect and suffering, from abuse or ignorance, than existed there in the year 1843, and some cases in 1845–47. In the jails were many pining in narrow, damp, unventilated dungeons. In the poorhouses were many examples of misery and protracted distress. In private families these conditions were less frequent; but the suffering, through ill-directed aims at securing the patients from escape, was in many instances equally revolting and shocking. Here, as in the five States first referred to, hundreds of special cases might be cited, did time permit. . . . .

New York, according to the census of 1840, had 2,340 idiots and insane. I am convinced that this estimate was below the certain number by many hundreds. In 1841, the Secretary of State reported 803 supported at public charge. In 1842, the trustees of poorhouses estimated the number of insane poor then confined in the *jails* and *poor houses* at 1,430. In 1843 I traversed every county in the State, visiting every poorhouse and prison, and the insane in many private families. The hospital for the insane at Utica was opened in January, 1843, and during the year received 276 patients, all with the exception of six being residents of the State of New York. On Blackwell's island were above 300; at Bloomingdale more than 100: 26 were at Bellevue. Besides these, I found, chiefly in the poorhouses, more than 1,500 insane and idiots, 500 of whom were west of Cayuga bridge. In the poorhouse at Flatbush were 26 insane, not counting idiots; in that at Whiteplains were 30 insane; at Albany between 30 and 40; at Ghent 18; in Greene county 46. In Washington county poorhouse, besides "simple, silly, and idiotic," 20 insane. Nearly every poorhouse in the State had, and still has, its "crazy house," "crazy cells," "crazy dungeons," or "crazy hall;" and in these, with rare exceptions, the inevitable troubles and miseries of the insane are sorely aggravated.

At A—, in the cell first opened, was a madman. The fierce command of his keeper brought him to the door, a hideous object; matted locks, an unshorn beard, a wild, wan countenance, disfigured by vilest uncleanness; in a state of nudity, save the irritating incrustations derived from that dungeon, reeking with loathsome filth. There, *without light*, without pure air, without warmth, without cleansing, absolutely destitute of everything securing comfort or decency, was a human being—forlorn, abject, and disgusting, it is true, but not the less of a human being—nay more, an immortal being, though the mind was fallen in ruins, and the soul was clothed in darkness. And who was he—this neglected, brutalized wretch? A burglar, a murderer, a miscreant, who for base, foul crimes had been condemned, by the justice of outraged laws and the righteous indignation of his fellow-men, to expiate offences by exclusion from his race, by privations and sufferings extreme, yet not exceeding the measure and enormity of his misdeeds? No; this was no doomed criminal, festering in filth, wearing wearily out the warp of life in dreariest solitude and darkness. No, this was no criminal—"*only a crazy man.*" How, in the touching language of Scripture, could he have said: "My brethren are far from me, and mine acquaintance are verily estranged from me: my kinsfolk have failed, and my familiar friends have forgotten me: my bone cleaveth unto my skin and my flesh. Have pity upon me, have pity upon me, for the hand of God hath touched me!" . . . .

In B—, the cells in the crazy cellar admitted neither light nor pure air.

In T—, the cells for the insane men were in a shocking condition.

In A—, were above twenty insane men and women in the poorhouse, mostly confined *with chains and balls attached to fetters.* "By adopting this plan," said the master of the poorhouse, "I have given them light and air, preventing their escape; otherwise I should have to keep them always in the cells." A considerable number of women, mostly incurables, were "behinds the pickets," in an out-building; there was a passage sufficiently lighted and warmed, and of width for exercise. There was no classification; the noisy and the quiet mutually vexed each other. One woman was restrained by a barbarous apparatus to prevent rendring her clothes: it consisted of *an iron collar investing the throat,* through which, at the point of closing in front, passed a small bolt or bar, from which depended *an iron triangle,* the sides of which might measure sixteen or eighteen inches. To the corners of the horizontal side were attached *iron wristlets:* thus holding the hands confined, and as far apart as the length of the base line of the triangle. When the hands and arms were suddenly elevated, pressure upon the apex of the triangle, near the point of connexion at the throat, produced a sense of suffocation; and why not certain strangulation, it was not easy to show.

Not distant from the poorhouse I found a woman in a private dwelling, supported by two invalid sisters; she was in the highest state of phrensy, and nearly exhausted the patience of love in those who toiled laborously for her and their own scanty maintenance. She had once been transferred to the poorhouse; but patience was never there exercised in behalf of the unruly; and bearing the marks of harsh blows, she was taken again by her sisters, to share "the little they could earn so long as they or she should live."

In E—, the insane, as usual, were unfitly disposed of. To adopt the language of a neighboring farmer, "those damp dreary cells were not fit for a dog to house in, much less for crazy folks."

At R—, and M—, and L—, and B—, were repetitions of the like dismal cells—heavy chains and balls, and hopeless sufferings. After my visit at L—, I found one of the former inmates at the hospital in charge of Dr. Brigham. *He bore upon his ankles the deep scars of fetters and chains, and upon his feet evidence of exposure to frost and cold.*

In B—, several idiots occupied together a portion of a most comfortless establishment. *One gibbering, senseless creature* was the mother of an infant child.

At A—, the most furious were in narrow cells, which were neither cleaned, warmed, nor ventilated. In O— was an insane man, so shockingly neglected and abused that his limbs were crippled, so that he could neither stand nor walk; he was extended on a miserable dirty pallet, untended and little cared for.

At E—, the insane were confined in cells crammed with coarse, dirty straw, in the basement, dark and damp. "They are," said the keeper, "taken out and *washed* (buckets of water thrown over them) *and have clean straw, once every week.*"

In H—, were many furiously crazy. Several of the women were said to be mothers of infants, which were in an adjoining room pining with neglect, and unacknowledged by their frantic mothers.

I pass over hundreds of desperate cases, and quote a few examples from my notes in New Jersey; altogether omitting Canada, East and West, as being without the limits of the United States; though corresponding examples with those in New York were found in almost every direction. In 1841, there were found in New Jersey, upon a rather cursory survey, *two-hundred and fifty-two insane men, one hundred and sixty-three insane women, and one hundred and ninety-six idiots*, of both sexes. I traversed the State in 1844; the numbers in every county were increased, and their miseries were also increased. Sixty patients had been placed in the hospitals in New York and Pennsylvania, but hundreds still occupied the wretched cells and dungeons of almshouses, and of prisons. In the winter of 1845 several froze to death, and several perished through severe exposure and alarm at a fire which consumed a populous poorhouse. At S—, of eight insane patients, several were heavily chained, and two were furiously mad.

In one poorhouse was a man who had been chained by the leg for more than twenty years, and the only warmth introduced into his cell was derived from a small stovepipe carried through one corner. . . . .

In P—, the *cells in the cellar for the insane* were in a most wretched condition. In M—, the insane, and many imbeciles, were miserably housed, fed, and clothed. In the vicinity of the main building was one of brick, containing the poor cells, *from eight to nine feet square.* A straw bed and blanket on the floor constituted the furniture, if I except the *ring-bolts and iron chains for securing the patients.* In P—, I found the insane, as usual, ill provided for. One madman was chained, clothed only with a straight jacket, laced so as to impede the motion of the arms and hands: cold, exposed, and offensive to the last degree, his aspect, wild and furious, was as shocking as his language was coarse and blasphemous. Such care was bestowed as the keepers of the poorhouse best could render; but an hospital alone could afford fit treatment for one so dangerous and so unmanageable. . . . .

In Y— were above thirty insane: those in the basement of the poorhouse occupied cells of sufficient dimensions, being fourteen by ten, and ten feet high; *hobbles* and *chains* in use. The physician estimated the number of insane in the county at more than one hundred, and added that cases of exceeding neglect and suffering often came to his knowledge. Sufficient provision in hospitals might save thousands of honest citizens from becoming a life-long burden to themselves and others, through permanent insanity. In this county above one hundred insane were found; there probably were other cases. In the poorhouse at G— the insane were exposed and suffering; the basement cells measured *eight by eight feet, and eight feet high. Chains, hobbles,* and the miscalled *"tranquilizing chain,"* were in use. There were more than forty insane in the county.

In C—, above twenty insane and idiots in the poorhouse; one was chained near the fireplace of a small room; a box filled with straw was near, in which he slept. Above 60 insane and idiots in this county. In B— I found nearly forty; some chained, others confined in narrow cells. In S—, several insane in the jail; one; *heavily ironed*, had been in close confinement there six years—another for eleven months. In this county the insane and idiots were estimated to be 76 in 1840. I heard of more than 100. One woman has for months wandered in the woods and fields in a state of raving madness.

In G—, several cases in the jail; one chained: above forty in the county.

In N—, in the jail, two madmen in chains; no furniture or decent care. One was rolling in the dust, in the highest excitement: he had been in close confinement for fifteen years. On one occasion he became exasperated at the introduction of a drunken prisoner into his cell, who perhaps provoked him. No one knows; but the keeper, on entering, found the insane man furious, covered with the blood of the other, who was murdered and mutilated in the most shocking manner. Another insane man had been in confinement for seven years, and both are to this day in the same prison. In the poorhouse were above twenty insane and idiots; four chained to the floor. In the adjacent county were above fifty insane and epileptics; several cases of misery through brutal usage, by "kicks and beating," in private families. . . . .

In Maryland, large numbers are at this hour in the lowest state of misery to which the insane can be reduced. At four different periods I have looked into the condition of many cases, counting hundreds there.

Chains, and want, and sorrows, abound for the insane poor in both the western and eastern districts, but especially in the western.

In Delaware, the same history is only to be repeated, with this variation: as the numbers are fewer, so is the aggregate of misery less.

In the District of Columbia, the old and the new jails, and the alms-houses, had, till very recently, their black, horrible histories. I witnessed abuses in some of these in 1838, in 1845, and since, from which every sense recoils. At present, most of these evils are mitigated in this immediate vicinity, but by no means relieved to the extent that justice and humanity demand.

In Virginia, very many cases of extreme suffering now exist. The most observing and humane of the medical profession have repeatedly expressed the desire for additional hospital provision for the insane. Like cases of great distress to those in Maryland and Pennsylvania were found in the years 1844 and '45. In every county through which I passed were the insane to be found—sometimes chained, sometimes wandering free. In the large, populous poorhouse near R— were spectacles the most offensively loathsome. Utter neglect and squalid wretchedness surrounded the insane. The estimate of *two thousand insane* idiots and epileptic patients in this State is thought to be below the actual number. The returns in 1840 were manifestly incorrect.

In the *Report* upon the Western State Hospital of Virginia, at Staunton, for the year 1847, Dr. Stribling feelingly remarks upon the very insufficient means at command for the relief of the insane poor throughout the State. . . . .

North Carolina has more than twelve hundred insane and idiots. . . . .

South Carolina records the same deplorable abuses and necessities as New York. I have found there the insane in pens, and bound with cords and chains, and suffering no less than the same class in States already referred to at the north, except through exposure to the cold in winter, the climate in the southern States sparing that aggravated misery. . . . .

Georgia has, so far as I have been able to ascertain, fewer insane, in proportion to population, than either North or South Carolina, but there is not less injudicious or cruel management of the violent cases throughout the State; chains and ropes are employed to increase security from escapes, in addition to closed doors, and the bolts and bars

which shut the dreary cells and dungeons of jails and other receptacles. . . . .

In Tennessee the insane and idiot population, as in Kentucky, is
numerous and increasing. *The same methods of confinement to cabins,
pens, cells, dungeons, and the same abandonment to filth, to cold, and exposure, as in other States.*

In Kentucky I found one epileptic girl subject to the most brutal
treatment, and many insane in perpetual confinement. Of the *idiots*
alone, supported by the State at a cost of $17,500.62, in indigent pri-
vate families, and of which class there were in 1845 *four hundred and
fifty*, many were exposed to severest treatment and heavy blows from
day to day, and from year to year. In a dreary block-house was confined for many years a man whose insanity took the form of mania.
Often the most furious paroxysms prevented rest for several days and
nights in succession. No alleviation reached this unhappy being; without clothes, without fire, without care or kindness, his existence was
protracted amidst every horror incident to such circumstances. *Chains
in common use.*

In Ohio, the insane population, including idiots, has been greatly
underrated, as I am fully satisfied by repeated but interrupted inquiries in different sections of the State. The sufferings of a great number here are very distressing, corresponding with those referred to in
New York and in Kentucky. *Cells and dungeons, unventilated and
uncleansed apartments, severe restraints, and multiplied neglects, abound.*

Michigan, it was stated, had sixty-three insane in 1840. I think it a
moderate estimate, judging from my investigations, reaching no further north than Jackson and Detroit, that the number in 1847 exceeded
two hundred and fifty. I saw some truly afflicted and lamentable cases.

Indiana, traversed through its whole length and breadth in 1846,
exhibits the usual forms of misery wherever the insane are found; and
of this class there cannot be, including idiots and epileptics, less than
nine hundred. *I found one poor woman in a smoke-house, in which she
had been confined more than twenty years.* In several poorhouses the insane, both men and women, were chained to the floors, sometimes all in
the same apartment. Several were confined in mere pens without clothing or shelter; some furious—others for a time comparatively tranquil.
The hospital now about to be opened, when finished, will not receive
to its care one patient in ten of existing cases.

Illinois, visited also in its whole extent in 1846, has more than four
hundred insane, at the most moderate estimate. . . . .

In Missouri, visited in 1846 and 1847, multiplied cases were found in pens, in stalls, in cages, in dungeons, and in cells; men and women alike exhibited the most deplorable aspects. Some are now dead, others still live only to experience renewed troubles of mind, and tortures of the flesh.

Let these examples suffice; others daily occur. Humanity requires that every insane person should receive the care appropriate to his condition, in which the integrity of the judgment is destroyed, and the reasoning faculties confused or prostrated.

Hardly second to this consideration is the civil and social obligation to consult and secure the public welfare: first in affording a protection against the frequently manifested dangerous propensities of the insane; and second, by assuring seasonable and skilful remedial cares, procuring their restoration to usefulness as citizens of the republic, and as members of communities.

Under ordinary circumstances, and where there is no organic lesion of the brain, no disease is more manageable or more easily cured than insanity; but to this end, special appliances are necessary, which cannot be had in private families, nor in every town and city; hence the necessity for hospitals, and the multiplication, *not enlargement,* of such institutions. The citizens of many States have readily submitted to increased taxation, and individuals have contributed liberal gifts, in order to meet these imperative wants. Hospitals have been constructed, and well organized. The important charge of these has been in most instances confided to highly responsible and skilful physicians—men whose rank in morals and in intellect, while commanding the public confidence, has wrought immeasurable benefits for hundreds and thousands of those in whom, for a time, the light of reason had been hidden.

But while the annual reports emanating from these beneficent institutions record eminent successes in the cure of *recently* developed cases, the provision for the treatment of this malady in the United States is found wholly insufficient for existing necessities, as has been already demonstrated in preceding pages.

To confide the insane to persons whose education and habits do not qualify them for this charge, is to condemn them to a mental death. The keepers of prisons, the masters of poorhouses, and most persons in private families, are wholly unacquainted with bodily and mental diseases, and are therefore incapable of the judicious application of such remedial measures, moral, mental, and medical, as are requisite for the restoration of physical and mental health. Recovery, even of recent cases, not submitted to hospital charge, is known to be very rare; a fact readily demonstrable by examples, and by figures, if necessary. It may be more satisfactory to show the benefits of hospital treatment, rather than dilate upon the certain evils of prison and almshouse neglects or abuses, and domestic mismanagement.

Under well-directed hospital care, *recovery is the rule—incurable* permanent insanity the exception. . . . .

I do not recollect a more satisfactory illustration of the benefits of hospital care upon large numbers of incurable patients, brought under improving influences at one and the same time, than is afforded in the first opening of the hospital for the insane poor at South Boston. Prior to 1839, the insane poor of Suffolk county were confined in a receptacle in rear of the almshouse; or rather all those of this class who were furiously mad, and considered dangerous to be abroad upon the farm grounds. This receptacle revealed scenes of horror and utter abomination such as language is powerless to represent. These wretched creatures, both men and women, exhibited cases of long standing, regarded past recovery, their malady being confirmed by the grossest mismanagement.

The citizens were at length roused to a sense of the enormity and extent of these abuses, matched only, it is believed, (except in individual cases,) by the vile condition of the English private madhouses, as thrown open to the inspection of Parliamentary commissioners, within the last thirty years. The monstrous injustice and cruelty of herding these maniacs in a hall filled with cages, behind the bars of which, all loathsome and offensive, they howled, and gibbered, and shrieked, and moaned, day and night, like infuriated wild beasts, moved the kindling sensibilities of those heretofore ignorant or indifferent. The most sanguine friends of the hospital plan expected no more for these wretched beings than to procure for them greater decency and comfort; recovery of the mental faculties, for such as these, was not anticipated.

The new buildings were completed, opened, and a system of discipline adopted by Dr. Butler, the results of which I witnessed with profound interest and surprise. The insane were removed, disencumbered of their chains, freed from the remnants of foul garments, bathed, clothed, fed decently, and placed by kind nurses in comfortable apartments. Remedial means, medical and moral, were judiciously applied. Behold the result of a few months' care, in their recovered physical health, order, general quiet, and well-directed employments. Now, and since, visit the hospital when you may, at neither set time nor season, you will find this class of *incurable* patients exercising in companies or singly, reading the papers of the day, or books loaned from the library; some busy in the vegetable, some in the flower gardens, while some are found occupied in the washing and ironing rooms, in the kitchen and in the sewing rooms. Less than one-sixth of those who were removed from the almshouse recovered their reason; but, with the exception of three or four individuals, they regained the decent habits of respectable life, and a capacity to be useful, to labor, and to enjoy occupation.

No hospital in the United States but affords abundant evidence of the capacity of the insane to work under direction of suitable attendants, and of recovery from utter helplessness to a considerable degree of activity and capacity for various employments.

I have seen the patient attendants, in many institutions, persevere day by day in endeavors to rouse, and interest, and instruct the demented in healthful occupations; and these efforts after a time have found reward in the gradual improvement of the objects of their care, and their acquisition of power to attend to stated healthful labors. . . . .

I ask of the representatives of a whole nation, benefits for all their constituents. Annual taxation for the support of the insane in hospitals is felt to be onerous, both in the populous maritime States, and in the States and Territories west of the Alleghenies. Much has been done, but much more remains to be accomplished, as I have endeavored to demonstrate in the preceding pages, for the relief of the sufferings and oppressions of that large class of the distressed for whom I plead, and upon whose condition I am solicitous to fix your attention.

I ask for the people that which is already the property of the people; but possessions so holden, that it is through your action alone they can be applied as is now urged.

The whole public good must be sought and advanced through those channels which most certainly contribute to the moral elevation and true dignity of a great people.

Americans boast much of superior intelligence and sagacity; of power and influence; of their vast resources possessed and yet undeveloped; of their free institutions and civil liberty; of their liberally endowed schools of learning, and of their far-reaching commerce: they call themselves a mighty nation; they name themselves a great and wise people. If these claims to distinction above most nations of the earth are established upon undesirable premises, then will the rulers, the political economists, and the moral philosophers of other and remote countries, look scrutinizingly into our civil and social condition for examples to illustrate the greatness of our name. They will seek not to measure the strength and extent of the fortifications which guard our coast; they will not number our vessels of war, or of commerce; they will not note the strength of our armies; they will not trace the course of the thousands eager for self-aggrandizement, nor of the tens of thousands led on by ambition and vain glory; they will search after illustrations in those God-like attributes which sanctify private life, and in that incorruptible integrity and justice which perpetuates national existence. They will note the moral grandeur and dignity which leads the statesman to lay broad and deep the foundations of national greatness, in working out the greatest good for the whole people; in effect, making paramount the interests of mind to material wealth, or mere physical prosperity. *Primarily*, then, in the highest order of means for confirming the prosperity of a people and the duration of government must be the education of the ignorant, and restoring the health and maintaining the sick mind in its natural integrity.

I will not presume to dictate to those in whose humane dispositions I have faith, and whose wisdom I cannot question.

I have approached you with self-diffidence, but with confidence in your impartial and just consideration of the subject submitted to your discussion and righteous effective decision.

I confide to you the cause and the claims of the destitute and of the desolate, without fear or distrust. I ask, for the thirty States of the Union, 5,000,000 acres of land, of the many hundreds of millions of public lands, appropriated in such manner as shall assure the greatest benefits to all who are in circumstances of extreme necessity, and who, through the providence of God, *are wards of the nation*, claimants on the sympathy and care of the public, through the miseries and disqualifications brought upon them by the sorest afflictions with which humanity can be visited.

The Senate Debate on the Veto[1]

Mr. Brown: The President, in the outset of the message, admits that this is a measure of great humanity, and one which commends itself to the warmest sympathies of his heart. I am glad he said so, because I apprehend that the sentiment will find a response in the heart of every American citizen, of every friend of humanity, whether he resides north or south, east or west. The President says that eleemosy-

[1] Extract from *Congressional Globe* (Thirty-third Congress, 1st sess., May 3, 1854), pp. 1063, 1065.

nary objects or purposes are not among those which are provided for in the Constitution. So they are not in express terms; but does Congress never legislate upon any subject in regard to which it has not been expressly authorized to legislate? If not, I want to know where we get our authority to legislate for school purposes? The President makes an argument to show by implication that we have the power to do that. All the grants that have been made from time to time for school purposes are sanctioned by the Constitution, according to his construction of it; and yet, sir, you may read the instrument from one end to the other, and find no specific power to make grants for school purposes. If the President will point to the clause which authorizes grants of land to colleges, I will show him the clause which authorizes the grant proposed in this bill.

But, says the President, if we legislate for the benefit of the insane, where are we to stop? Are we to carry our benevolence so far as to legislate for the protection of all other indigent or unfortunate classes? This, you will see at once, is not an argument which can touch the question of power, but it is simply an argument which reaches the question of the exercise of power. If you have authority to do this, it may follow that you have the power to do something else; but it does not follow that because you do this, you ought therefore to do something else. If you have the power to make an appropriation of land for the protection and benefit of the indigent insane, it may follow that you have the power to make an appropriation of land for the protection and benefit of the indigent who are not insane. But if you exercise the power in the one case, it does not necessarily follow that you must exercise it in the other.

The President seems to think that in this matter the States will be brought to bow to the authority of Congress. I do not think so. When my State and yours, Mr. President, (Mr. Bright occupying the chair) accepted donations of land for school purposes, for common schools, and for schools of a higher grade, did it ever enter into your head or mine that our States were thereby humiliated, and were bowing as paupers, and beggars, and mendicants, to the authority of Congress? No sir; we felt that we were receiving a part of that which belonged to us, that we were not beggars but that Congress was giving its assent to our exercising exclusive jurisdiction over a part of that which belonged to us in common with our fellow-citizens of all the States.

The President seems also to be apprehensive that if we go on legislating in this way, we shall dry up all the sources of benevolence in the

States, and that the people of the States, instead of taking care of their indigent insane, their poor, their blind, and their lame, will habitually look to Congress for the protection of those classes. I think not. With as much justice might you say that, if you receive land from the Government for the education, in part, of your children, this will induce the States to look to Congress for the means of educating all the children. Did it ever enter into your mind, sir, when Congress granted your State the sixteenth section of land in each township for school purposes, that, by the State accepting it, you were in danger of becoming mendicants, begging Congress to make appropriations for the education of all the children in your State? I apprehend there is no more danger of our becoming beggars at the footstool of Congress for the support of our indigent insane, our indigent blind, and our poor of every class, if we accept a grant like this, than there has been that we should become beggars of Congress to educate all our children, because, in days gone by, we accepted aid from Congress to educate a part of them. . . . .

MR. DIXON: I am no latitudinarian in the construction of the Federal Constitution, and perhaps would go as far as any Senator on this floor in maintaining the constitutional rights of the States, and of keeping separate and apart the powers which properly belong to the Federal Government and those justly appertaining to the States. But I cannot understand how it is that, if the Federal Government can exercise the constitutional power of making a grant of lands for one benevolent object, it may not do it for another. It has appropriated lands for roads and canals; it has donated, in effect, a large amount of the public lands to assist a State in paying off her public debt; it has appropriated lands to educational purposes in the States in which the lands lie; it has given them to States within which they do not lie for similar purposes; it has appropriated large sums of money to the building of marine hospitals in different States, to minister to the wants and comforts of the unfortunate and wretched class of citizens described in the different acts making the appropriations. It has given, time and again, large sums of money, and large portions of the public lands, for other purposes—some benevolent and some speculative, and all without any express grant of power under the Federal Constitution; and now, when we are about to vote away thousands and thousands of acres of the public domain to all such as may settle on them, whether they be citizens or foreigners, we are gravely told by the President that a grant, by Congress, of a portion of this same public domain, for an object the most humane and the most benevolent, and which appeals most strong-

ly to the sympathies of every heart capable of feeling for the misfortunes of the most unhappy of mankind, is interdicted by the spirit of
the Constitution, and a violation of the rights and an encroachment on
the sovereignty of the States. . . . .

MR. BELL: I do not mean to cite the occasional appropriations
which have been heretofore made of the public lands with a view to
rely upon them; such, for example, as the township of land to Connecticut to found an institution for the instruction of the deaf and dumb in
1819,—and a similar appropriation to Kentucky at a subsequent period
in 1826. Take out all these occasional appropriations, exclude them
entirely from the argument, throw them aside as being irregular, and
what do we find? I may say here, in passing, that such appropriations
as these constitute a very small, and almost invisible fraction of the
enormous amount of the public land which has been appropriated. I
have not examined the reports or public documents from the Departments in relation to the subject, but I know it is said that a hundred
millions of acres of the public lands have heretofore been appropriated
—not sold, and the money paid into the Treasury; but this large quantity of land has been given to the States in which the lands lie for the
purposes of education, and for the purpose of aiding them in the construction of works of internal improvement. It was only a few years
ago, as you know, sir, that we appropriated seven hundred and fifty
thousand acres of land, with scarcely any debate or controversy in the
Senate, for the construction of a canal around the falls at the Sault St.
Mary—to overcome obstructions in the straits, between Lake Huron
and Lake Superior.

The great mass of these appropriations has been for the support of
internal improvements, and for laying the foundations of a system of
schools and education in the new States. Then again they have received large grants of swamp lands; but take them out of view, regard
them as not constituting one of the items about which the old States
should complain; suppose they should amount to twenty or thirty millions of acres, still there would remain sixty or seventy-five millions of
acres which have been voted away for the general purposes which I
have enumerated—for internal improvements and educational purposes in the new States. . . . .

AN EARLY ADVENTURE IN CHILD-PLACING
CHARLES LORING BRACE

EDITORIAL NOTE

THE experiment of placing New York City children in free homes, largely in rural areas, was begun seventy-five years ago by the Children's Aid Society, which had been organized a year earlier with a young minister, Charles Loring Brace,[1] as its first secretary at a salary of a thousand dollars a year. In 1852 Mr. Brace, then twenty-five years of age, had joined a city missionary who was working in the old "Five Points" district in New York. Later in that same year he helped to organize "Boys' Meetings" among the vagrant, neglected boys who were so numerous in New York City in the middle of the last century. It was early in the next year that he became secretary of the newly formed Children's Aid Society, which he called "a mission to the children." No attempt will be made here to review comprehensively or critically the varied work of Mr. Brace. An extract from his very important book is presented since it gives an interesting picture of an attempt at child-placing in the West by a New York organization before the Civil War.

It is important, however, to keep in mind the fact that the condition of the dependent and neglected children of New York City in the days when there was almost no social work, public or private, in their behalf has no parallel in our American cities today. Children then were not infrequently homeless, and Brace tells of seeing often

---

[1] The most interesting account of the work of Charles Loring Brace will be found in his own book, *The Dangerous Classes of New York and Twenty Years' Work among Them* (New York, 1872). This book was widely read and will be still found in many libraries, although it was published nearly sixty years ago. A biography, *The Life of Charles Loring Brace Chiefly Told in His Own Letters*, edited by his daughter (New York: Charles Scribner's Sons, 1894), is also conveniently available. For a useful brief account of Brace's work, see also *The Children's Aid Society of New York, Its History, Plan and Results* (New York, 1893).

CHARLES LORING BRACE
1826–1890
From a photograph taken at the age of twenty-nine

a dozen small boys piled together to keep warm under the stairs of printing offices. Two little boys slept one winter in the iron tube of the Harlem Bridge.

The *Dangerous Classes of New York* gives a vivid picture of the homeless boys, street-wandering girls, young "city Arabs," and "street rats" who had been bred in the old "fever nests" and "dens of crime." He knew so many children who "slept anywhere and lived by petty pilferings from the iron works and woodyards and by street jobs." He thought their life was a "painfully hard one. To sleep in boxes, or under stairways, or in hay-barges on the coldest winter nights, for a mere child, was hard enough; but often to have no food, to be kicked and cuffed by the older ruffians, and shoved about by the police, standing barefooted and in rags under doorways as the winter storm raged, and to know that in all the great city there was not a single door open with welcome to the little rover— this was harder."

"Most touching of all," he wrote, in describing the early days of the new Children's Aid Society, "was the crowd of wandering little ones who immediately found their way to the office. Ragged young girls who had nowhere to lay their heads; children driven from drunkards' homes; orphans who slept where they could find a box or a stairway; boys cast out by step-mothers or step-fathers; newsboys, whose incessant answer to our question, 'Where do you live?' rang in our ears, 'Don't live nowhere!'; little bootblacks, young peddlers, 'canawl-boys,' who seem to drift into the city every winter, and live a vagabond life; pickpockets and petty thieves trying to get honest work; child beggars and flower-sellers growing up to enter courses of crime—all this motley throng of infantile misery and childish guilt passed through our doors."

Before the days of free and compulsory schools, when the "Fourth Ward Industrial School" was opened by the Society, he tells of going about through the slums in the vicinity of the school to "let it be widely known that a school to teach work, and where food was given daily, and clothes were bestowed to the well-behaved was just forming." The schoolroom was in the basement of a church in Roosevelt Street, where there gathered in December, 1853, the volunteer ladies and "a flock of the most ill-clad and wildest little street-girls that could be collected anywhere in New York." His account of the school gives another vivid contrast between the neglected children of 1850 and those of our own day. The little girls who had been persuaded to come to school were entirely new to the experience. "They flew over the benches, they swore and fought with one another, they bandied vile language, and could hardly be tamed down sufficiently to allow the school to be opened. Few had shoes, all were bonnetless, their dresses were torn, ragged, and dirty; their hair tangled, and faces long unwashed; they had, many of them, a singularly wild and intense expression of eye and feature, as of half-tamed creatures, with passions aroused beyond their years." He tells of one, a little homeless girl, who used to float about the quarter near East Thirty-second Street because her drunken mother "had thrown her out of doors, and she used to sleep under stairways or in deserted cellars, and was a most wretched, half-starved little creature." Mr. Brace said that he talked with her often "but could not induce her to go to school or to seek a home in the country," and at that time there was, of course, no juvenile court with the necessary authority to protect such a child. He wrote that he often walked the narrow lanes of the quarter to watch the ragged, wild children flitting about; or he visited "the damp underground basements which every high tide flooded, crowded with men, women and children; or climbed to the old rookeries, packed to the smallest attic with a wretched population."

It is not surprising that the eager imagination of the young minister saw the great West as a vast and spacious home for the vagrant children of the metropolis. "Our hope in this matter," he wrote, "is in the steady demand for juvenile labor in the country districts and the substantial rewards which await industry there." The plan appealed to practical men. New York had "a large multitude of children" who were young outcasts destined to become the criminals of the future. The western states, of which the good minister and directors of the new Society knew very little, seemed to them full of kindly homes that would provide for the poor children of New York. Mr. Brace thought that the western farms needed labor, and it did not occur to him to question the desirability of transporting the children to meet this need. "The readiness on the part of farmers to receive these children was at once evident. An announcement, by circulars through the city weeklies and rural papers, of the intention of supplying children, brought a speedy response in the form of hundreds of applications from farmers and mechanics."

The first western party started for Michigan from the New York Office of the Children's Aid Society in the fall of 1854. It is typical of the time that the agent was not a professional social worker but a minister, Rev. E. P. Smith. Mr. Brace saw himself "draining the city" of its neglected and ignorant children who were on the threshold of criminal careers.

Statistics published in 1893 showed that the Society had sent more than 50,000 boys and girls out of New York. The following states had received 500 or more children: Colorado, 739; Connecticut, 1,159; Illinois, 7,366; Indiana, 3,782; Iowa, 4,852; Kansas, 3,310; Massachusetts, 876; Michigan, 2,900; Minnesota, 2,448; Missouri, 4,835; Nebraska, 2,343; New Jersey, 4,149; Ohio, 4,418; Pennsylvania, 1,839; Virginia, 1,448; Wisconsin, 2,135.

The work of child-placing agencies has greatly developed in the eighty-five years since Charles Loring Brace sent his first "emigration party" from New York to Michigan. But he was a great pioneer who had courage and faith, enthusiasm and tireless energy. The fact that he was only twenty-eight years old when he sent his first group of children west is one of the astonishing things about his work.[1]

Louisa Lee Schuyler, writing shortly after his death, said:

His genius solved the problem which had baffled the philanthropists of preceding centuries. He saw that home life, and not institution life, was needed for children, and so he set himself to finding homes for homeless children. It seems so simple to us now, now that we know all about it; but it required his penetration, his genius, to reveal to us what is self-evident when once our eyes are opened.

The first circular issued by the New York Children's Aid Society in March, 1853, is of great interest, and we reprint it here.

E. A.

[1] The portrait of Mr. Brace in this volume was painted during the early years when so much of his early experimental work for children was being planned.

First Circular of the Children's Aid Society (1853)[1]

To the Public: This society has taken its origin in the deeply settled feeling of our citizens, that something must be done to meet the increasing crime and poverty among the destitute children of New York. Its objects are to help this class, by opening Sunday meetings and industrial schools, and gradually, as means shall be furnished, by forming lodging-houses and reading-rooms for children, and by employing paid agents, whose sole business shall be to care for them.

As Christian men, we cannot look upon this great multitude of unhappy, deserted, and degraded boys and girls without feeling our responsibility to God for them. We remember that they have the same capacities, the same need of kind and good influences, and the same immortality, as the little ones in our own homes. We bear in mind that One died for them, even as for the children of the rich and the happy. Thus far, almshouses and prisons have done little to affect the evil. But a small part of the vagrant population can be shut up in our asylums; and judges and magistrates are reluctant to convict children, so young and ignorant that they hardly seem able to distinguish good and evil. The class increases. Immigration is pouring in its multitudes of poor foreigners, who leave these young outcasts everywhere abandoned in our midst. For the most part, the boys grow up utterly by themselves. No one cares for them, and they care for no one. Some live by begging, by petty pilferings, by bold robbery. Some earn an honest support by peddling matches, or apples, or newspapers. Others gather bones and rags in the street to sell. They sleep on steps, in cellars, in old barns, and in markets; they hire a bed in filthy and low lodging-houses. They cannot read. They do not go to school or attend a church. Many of them have never seen the Bible. Every cunning faculty is intensely stimulated. They are shrewd and old in vice when other children are in leading-strings. Few influences which are kind and good ever reach the vagrant boy. And yet, among themselves, they show generous and honest traits. Kindness can always touch them.

The *girls*, too often, grow up even more pitiable and deserted. Till of late, no one has ever cared for them. They are the cross-walk sweepers, the little apple-peddlers and candy-sellers of our city; or by more questionable means they earn their scanty bread. They traverse the low, vile

[1] Extract from *The Life of Charles Loring Brace Chiefly Told in His Own Letters*, edited by his daughter (New York: Charles Scribner's Sons, 1894), pp. 489–92.

streets alone, and live without mother or friends, or any share in what we should call *home*. They, also, know little of God or Christ, except by name. They grow up passionate, ungoverned; with no love or kindness ever to soften the heart. We all know their short, wild life, and the sad end. These boys and girls, it should be remembered, will soon form the great lower class of our city. They will influence elections; they may shape the policy of the city; they will, assuredly, if unreclaimed, poison society all around them. They will help to form the great multitude of robbers, thieves, and vagrants who are now such a burden upon the law-respecting community. In one ward alone of the city, the eleventh, there were in 1852, out of 12,000 children between the ages of five and sixteen, only 7,000 who attended school, and only 2,500 who went to Sabbath-school, leaving 5,000 without the common privileges of education and about 9,000 destitute of public religious influence.

In view of these evils, we have formed an association which shall devote itself entirely to this class of vagrant children. We do not propose in any way to conflict with existing asylums and institutions, but to render them a hearty co-operation, and at the same time to fill a gap, which, of necessity, they have all left. A large multitude of children live in the city who cannot be placed in asylums, and yet who are uncared for and ig-norant and vagrant. We propose to give to these work, and to bring them under religious influences. A central office has been taken, and an agent, Charles L. Brace, has been engaged to give his whole time to efforts for relieving the wants of this class. As means shall come in, it is designed to district the city, so that hereafter every ward may have its agent, who shall be a friend to the vagrant child. "Boys' Sunday Meet-ings" have already been formed, which we hope to see extended, until every quarter has its place of preaching to boys. With these, we intend to connect "Industrial Schools," where the great temptations to this class, arising from *want of work*, may be removed, and where they can learn an honest trade. Arrangements have been made with manufacturers, by which, if we have the requisite funds to begin, *five hundred boys* in different localities can be supplied with paying work. We hope, too, especially to be the means of draining the city of these children, by communicating with farmers, manufacturers, or families in the country, who may have need of such for employment. When homeless boys are found by our agents, we mean to get them homes in the families of respectable persons in the city, and to put them in the way of an honest living. We design, in a word, to bring humane and kindly influences to bear on this forsaken class—to preach in various modes the Gospel of Christ to the vagrant children of New York.

Numbers of our citizens have long felt the evils we would remedy, but few have the leisure or the means to devote themselves personally to this work, with the thoroughness which it requires. This society, as we propose, shall be a medium through which all can, in their measure, practically help the poor children of the city. We call upon all who recognize that these are the little ones of Christ; all who believe that crime is best averted by sowing good influences in childhood; all who are the friends of the helpless, to aid us in our enterprise. We confidently hope this wide and practical movement will have its share of Christian liberality. And we earnestly ask the contributions of those able to give, to help us in carrying forward the work.

March, 1853

Trustees

B. J. HOWLAND
JOHN L. MASON
WM. C. GILMAN
WM. L. KING
CHARLES W. ELLIOTT
AUGUSTINE EATON

J. S. PHELPS, M.D.
JAMES A. BURTUS
MOSES G. LEONARD
WM. C. RUSSELL
J. EARL WILLIAMS
A. D. F. RANDOLPH

Secretary, CHARLES L. BRACE

The First Party of Children Sent West by the New York Children's Aid Society[1]

Though without a home the homeless lads and girls were often not legally vagrant—that is, they had some ostensible occupation, some street-trade—and no judge would commit them, unless a very flagrant case of vagrancy was made against them. They were unwilling to be sent to Asylums, and, indeed, were so numerous that all the Asylums of the State could not contain them. Moreover, their care and charge in public institutions would have entailed expenses on the city so heavy, that tax-payers would not have consented to the burden.

The workers, also, in this movement felt from the beginning that "asylum-life" is not the best training for outcast children in preparing them for practical life. In large buildings, where a multitude of children are gathered together, the bad corrupt the good, and the good are not

---

[1] Extract from Charles Loring Brace, *The Dangerous Classes of New York, and Twenty Years' Work among Them* (New York, 1872), pp. 224–66.

educated in the virtues of real life. The machinery, too, which is so necessary in such large institutions, unfits a poor boy or girl for practical handwork.

The founders of the Children's Aid Society early saw that the best of all Asylums for the outcast child, is the *farmer's home*.

The United States have the enormous advantage over all other countries, in the treatment of difficult questions of pauperism and reform, that they possess a practically unlimited area of arable land. The demand for labor on this land is beyond any present supply. Moreover, the cultivators of the soil are in America our most solid and intelligent class. From the nature of their circumstances, their laborers, or "help," must be members of their families, and share in their social tone. It is, accordingly, of the utmost importance to them to train up children who shall aid in their work, and be associates of their own children. A servant who is nothing but a servant, would be, with them, disagreeable and inconvenient. They like to educate their own "help." With their overflowing supply of food also, each new mouth in the household brings no drain on their means. Children are a blessing, and the mere feeding of a young boy or girl is not considered at all.

With this fortunate state of things, it was but a natural inference that the important movement now inaugurating for the benefit of the unfortunate children of New York should at once strike upon a plan of emigration.

Simple and most effective as this ingenious scheme now seems— which has accomplished more in relieving New York of youthful crime and misery than all other charities together—at the outset it seemed difficult and perplexing. . . . .

Among other objections, it was feared that the farmers would not want the children for help; that, if they took them, the latter would be liable to ill-treatment, or, if well-treated, would corrupt the virtuous children around them, and thus New York would be scattering seeds of vice and corruption all over the land. Accidents might occur to the unhappy little ones thus sent, bringing odium on the benevolent persons who were dispatching them to the country. How were places to be found? How were the demand and supply for children's labor to be selected? And, when the children were placed, how were their interests to be watched over, and acts of oppression or hard dealing prevented or punished? Were they to be indentured, or not? If this was the right scheme, why had it not been tried long ago in our cities or in England?

These and innumerable similar difficulties and objections were offered to this projected plan of relieving the city of its youthful pauperism and suffering. They all fell to the ground before the confident efforts to carry out a well-laid scheme; and practical experience has justified none of them.

To awaken the demand for these children, circulars were sent out through the city weeklies and the rural papers to the country districts. Hundreds of applications poured in at once from the farmers and mechanics all through the Union. At first, we made the effort to meet individual applications by sending the kind of children wanted; but this soon became impracticable.

Each applicant or employer always called for "a perfect child," without any of the taints of earthly depravity. The girls must be pretty, good-tempered, not given to purloining sweetmeats, and fond of making fires at daylight, and with a constitutional love for Sunday Schools and Bible-lessons. The boys must be well made, of good stock, never disposed to steal apples or pelt cattle, using language of perfect propriety, and delighting in family-worship and prayer-meetings more than in fishing or skating parties. These demands, of course, were not always successfully complied with. Moreover, to those who desired the children of "blue eyes, fair hair, and blond complexion," we were sure to send the dark-eyed and brunette; and the particular virtues wished for were very often precisely those that the child was deficient in. It was evidently altogether too much of a lottery for bereaved parents or benevolent employers to receive children in that way. . . . . .

Having found the defects of our first plan of emigration, we soon inaugurated another, which has since been followed out successfully during nearly twenty years of constant action.

We formed little companies of emigrants, and, after thoroughly cleaning and clothing them, put them under a competent agent, and first selecting a village where there was a call or opening for such a party, we dispatched them to the place.

The farming community having been duly notified, there was usually a dense crowd of people at the station, awaiting the arrival of the youthful travelers. The sight of the little company of the children of misfortune always touched the hearts of a population naturally generous. They were soon billetted around among the citizens, and the following day a public meeting was called in the church or town hall, and a committee appointed of leading citizens. The agent then addressed the assembly, stating the benevolent objects of the Society, and something of the history of the children. The sight of their worn faces was a most pathetic enforcement of his arguments. People who were childless came forward to adopt children; others, who had not intended to take any into their families, were induced to apply for them; and many who really wanted the children's labor pressed forward to obtain it.

In every American community, especially a Western one, there are many spare places at the table of life. There is no harassing "struggle for existence." They have enough for themselves and the stranger too. Not, perhaps, thinking of it before, yet, the orphan being placed in their presence without friends or home, they gladly welcome and train him. The committee decide on the applications. Sometimes there is almost a case for Solomon before them. Two eager mothers without children claim some little waif thus cast on the strand before them. Sometimes the family which has taken in a fine lad for the night feels that it cannot do without him, and yet the committee prefer a better home for him. And so hours of discussion and selection pass. Those who are able, pay the fares of the children, or otherwise make some gift to the Society, until at length the business of charity is finished, and a little band of young wayfarers and homeless rovers in the world find themselves in comfortable and kind homes, with all the boundless advantages and opportunities of the Western farmer's life about them. . . . . .

OUR FIRST EMIGRANT PARTY[1] (1854) (FROM OUR JOURNAL)

BY A VISITOR

On Wednesday evening, with emigrant[2] tickets to Detroit, we started on the "Isaac Newton" for Albany. Nine of our company, who missed the boat, were sent up by the morning cars, and joined us in Albany, making forty-six boys and girls from New York, bound westward, and, to them, homeward. They were between the ages of seven and fifteen—most of them from ten to twelve. The majority of them orphans, dressed in uniform—as bright, sharp, bold, racy a crowd of little fellows as can be grown nowhere out of the streets of New York. The other ten were from New York at large—no number or street in particular. Two of these had slept in nearly all the station-houses in the city. One, a keen-eyed American boy, was born in Chicago—an orphan now, and abandoned in New York by an intemperate brother. Another, a little German Jew, who had been entirely friendless for four years, and had finally found his way into the Newsboys' Lodging-house. Dick and Jack were brothers of Sarah O——, whom

[1] [This section is transposed from the place where it appears in the book in order to make the entire account more nearly consecutive.]

[2] [A footnote in the original explains that after this first experience, the children were always sent by regular trains, in decent style.]

we sent to Connecticut. Their father is intemperate; mother died at Bellevue Hospital three weeks since; and an older brother has just been sentenced to Sing Sing Prison. Their father, a very sensible man when sober, begged me to take the boys along, "for I am sure, sir, if left in New York, they will come to the same bad end as their brother." We took them to a shoe-shop. Little Jack made awkward work in trying on a pair. "He don't know them, sir; there's not been a cover to his feet for three winters."

Another of the ten, whom the boys call "Liverpool," defies description. Mr. Gerry found him in the Fourth Ward, a few hours before we left. Really only twelve years old, but in dress, a seedy loafer of forty. His boots and coat and pants would have held two such boys easily—filthy and ragged to the last thread. Under Mr. Tracy's hands, at the Lodging-house, "Liverpool" was soon remodeled into a boy again; and when he came on board the boat with his new suit, I did not know him. His story interested us all, and was told with a quiet, sad reserve, that made us believe him truthful. A friendless orphan in the streets of Liverpool, he heard of America, and determined to come, and after long search found a captain who shipped him as cabin-boy. Landed in New York, "Liverpool" found his street condition somewhat bettered. Here he got occasional odd jobs about the docks, found a pretty tight box to sleep in, and now and then the sailors gave him a cast-off garment, which he wrapped and tied about him, till he looked like a walking rag bundle when Mr. G. found him.

As we steamed off from the wharf, the boys gave three cheers for New York, and three more for "Michigan." All seemed as careless at leaving home forever, as if they were on a target excursion to Hoboken.

We had a steerage passage, and after the cracker-box and ginger bread had passed around, the boys sat down in the gang-way and began to sing. Their full chorus attacted the attention of the passengers, who gathered about, and soon the captain sent for us to come to the upper saloon. There the boys sang and talked, each one telling his own story separately, as he was taken aside, till ten o'clock, when Captain S. gave them all berths in the cabin; meanwhile, a lady from Rochester had selected a little boy for her sister, and Mr. B., a merchant from Illinois, had made arrangements to take "Liverpool" for his store. I afterwards met Mr. B. in Buffalo, and he said he would not part with the boy for any consideration; and I thought then that to take such a boy from such a condition, and put him into such hands, was worth the whole trip.

At Albany we found the emigrant train did not go out till noon, and it became a question what to do with the children for the intervening six hours. There was danger that Albany street-boys might entice them off, or that some might be tired of the journey, and hide away, in order to return. When they were gathered on the wharf, we told them that *we* were going to Michigan, and if any of them would like to go along, they must be on hand for the cars. This was enough. They hardly ventured out of sight. The Albany boys tried hard to coax some of them away; but ours turned the tables upon them, told them of Michigan, and when we were about ready to start, several of them came up bringing a stranger with them. There was no mistaking the long, thick, matted hair, unwashed face, the badger coat, and double pants flowing in the wind—a regular "snoozer."

"Here's a boy what wants to go to Michigan, sir; can't you take him with us?"

"But, do you know him? Can you recommend him as a suitable boy to belong to our company!" No; they didn't know his name even. "Only he's as hard up as any of us. He's no father or mother, and nobody to live with, and he sleeps out o' nights." The boy pleads for himself. He would like to go and be a farmer—and to live in the country—will go anywhere I send him—and do well if he can have the chance.

Our number is full—purse scant—it may be difficult to find him a home. But there is no resisting the appeal of the boys, and the importunate face of the young vagrant. Perhaps he will do well; at any rate, we must try him. If left to float here a few months longer, his end is certain. "Do you think I can go, sir?" "Yes, John, if you will have your face washed and hair combed within half an hour." Under a brisk scrubbing, his face lights up several shades; but the twisted, tangled hair, matted for years, will not yield to any amount of washing and pulling—barbers' shears are the only remedy.

So a new volunteer is added to our regiment. Here is his enrollment:

"John———, American—Protestant—13 years—Orphan—Parents died in R——, Maine—A 'snoozer' for four years—Most of the time in New York, with an occasional visit to Albany and Troy, 'when times go hard'—Intelligent —Black, sharp eye—Hopeful."

As we marched, two deep, round the State House to the depot, John received many a recognition from the "outsiders," among whom he seems to be a general favorite, and they call out after him, "Goodby, Smack," with a half-sad, half-sly nod, as if in doubt whether he was playing some new game, or were really going to leave them and try an honest life.

At the depot we worked our way through the Babel of at least one thousand Germans, Irish, Italians, and Norwegians, with whom nothing goes right; every one insists that he is in the wrong car—that his baggage has received the wrong mark—that Chicago is in this direction, and the cars are on the wrong track; in short, they are agreed upon nothing except in the opinion that this is a "bad counthry, and it's good luck to the soul who sees the end on't." The conductor, a red-faced, middle-aged man, promises to give us a separate car; but, while he whispers and negotiates with two Dutch girls, who are traveling without a protector, the motley mass rush into the cars, and we are finally pushed into one already full—some standing, a part sitting in laps, and some on the floor under the benches—crowded to suffocation, in a freight-car without windows—rough benches for seats, and no back—no ventilation except through the sliding-doors, where the little chaps are in constant danger of falling through. There were scenes that afternoon and night which it would not do to reveal.

Irishmen passed around bad whisky and sang bawdy songs; Dutch men and women smoked and sang, and grunted and cursed. . . . .

Night came on, and we were told that "passengers furnish their own lights!" For this we were unprepared, and so we tried to endure darkness which never before seemed half so thick as in that stifled car, though it was relieved here and there for a few minutes by a lighted pipe. One Dutchman in the corner kept up a constant fire; and when we told him we were choking with smoke, he only answered with a complacent grunt and a fresh supply of the weed. The fellow seemed to puff when he was fairly asleep, and the curls were lifting beautifully above the bowl, when smash against the car went the pipe in a dozen pieces! No one knew the cause, except perhaps, the boy behind me, who had begged an apple a few minutes before.

At Utica we dropped our fellow-passenger from Germany, and, thus partially relieved, spent the rest of the night in tolerable comfort.

In the morning we were in the vicinity of Rochester, and you can hardly imagine the delight of the children as they looked, many of them for the first time, upon country scenery. Each one must see everything we passed, find its name, and make his own comments. "What's that, mister?" "A cornfield." "Oh, yes; them's what makes buckwheaters." "Look at them cows [oxen plowing]; my mother used to milk cows." As we whirled through orchards loaded with large, red apples, their enthusiasm rose to the highest pitch. It was difficult to keep them within doors. Arms stretched out, hats swinging, eyes swimming, mouths watering, and all screaming—"Oh! oh! just look at 'em! Mister, be they any sich in Michi*gan?* Then I'm in for *that* place—three cheers for Michi*gan!*" We had been riding in comparative quiet for nearly an hour, when all at once the greatest excitement broke out. We were passing a cornfield spread over with ripe yellow pumpkins. "Oh! yonder! look! Just *look* at 'em!"—and in an instant the same exclamation was echoed from forty-seven mouths. "Jist *look* at 'em! What a heap of *mushmillons!*" "Mister, do they make mushmillons in Michi*gan?*" "Ah, fellers, *ain't* that the country though!— won't we have nice things to eat?" "Yes, and won't we *sell* some, too?" "Hip! hip! boys; three cheers for Michi*gan!*"

At Buffalo we received great kindness from the freight-agent, and this was by no means his first service to the Children's Aid Society. Several boys and girls whom we have sent West have received the kindest attention at his hands. . . . . Also, the agent for the Michigan Central Rail Road gave me a letter of introduction, which was of great service on the way.

We were in Buffalo nine hours, and the boys had the liberty of the town, but were all on board the boat in season. We went down to our place, the steerage cabin, and no one but an emigrant on a lake-boat can understand the night we spent. The berths were covered with a coarse mattress, used by a thousand different passengers, and never changed till they are filled with stench and vermin. The emigrants spend the night in washing, smoking, drinking, singing, sleep, and licentiousness. It was the last night in the freight-car repeated, with the addition of a touch of sea-sickness, and of the stamping, neighing, and cleating of a hundred horses and sheep over our heads, and the effluvia of their filth pouring through the open gangway. But we survived the night; *how* had better not be detailed. In the morning we got outside upon the boxes, and enjoyed the beautiful day. The boys were in good spirits, sang songs, told New York yarns, and made friends generally among the passengers. Occasionally, some one more knowing than wise would attempt to poke fun at them, whereupon the boys would "pitch in," and open such a sluice of Bowery slang as made Mr. Would-be-funny beat a retreat in double-quick time. No one attempted that game twice. During the day the clerk discovered that three baskets of peaches were missing, all except the baskets. None of the boys had been detected with the fruit, but I afterwards found they had eaten it.

Landed in Detroit at ten o'clock, Saturday night, and took a first-class passenger car on Michigan Central Rail Road and reached D——c, a "smart little town," in southwest Michigan, three o'clock Sunday morning. The depot-master, who seldom receives more than three passengers from a train, was utterly confounded at the crowd of little ones poured out upon the platform, and at first refused to let us stay till morning; but, after a deal of explanation, he consented, with apparent misgiving, and the boys spread themselves on the floor to sleep. At day-break they began to inquire, "Where be we?" and, finding that they were really in Michigan, scattered in all directions, each one for himself, and in less than five minutes there was not a boy in sight of the depot. When I had negotiated for our stay at the American House and had breakfast nearly ready, they began to straggle back from every quarter, each boy loaded down—caps, shoes, coat-sleeves, and shirts full of every green thing they could lay hands upon—apples, ears of corn, peaches, pieces of pumpkins, etc. "Look at the Michi*gan* filberts!" cried a little fellow, running up, holding with both hands upon his shirt bosom, which were bursting out with *acorns*. Little Mag (and she is one of the prettiest, sweetest little things you ever set eyes upon), brought in a "nosegay," which she insisted upon sticking in my coat—a mullen-stock and corn-leaf, twisted with grass!

Several of the boys had had a swim in the creek, though it was a pretty cold morning. At the breakfast table the question was discussed, how we should spend the Sabbath. The boys evidently wanted to continue their explorations; but when asked if it would not be best to go to church, there were no hands down, and some proposed to go to Sunday School, and "boys" meeting, too.

The children had clean and happy faces, but no change of clothes, and those they wore were badly soiled and torn by the emigrant passage. You can imagine the appearance of our "ragged regiment," as we filed into the Presbyterian church (which, by the way, was a school-house), and appropriated our full share of the seats. The "natives" could not be satisfied with staring, as they came to the door and filled up the vacant part of the house. The pastor was late, and we "occupied the time" in singing. Those sweet Sabbath School songs never sounded so sweetly before. Their favorite hymn was, "Come, ye sinners, poor and needy," and they rolled it out with a relish. It was a touching sight, and pocket handkerchiefs were used quite freely among the audience.

At the close of the sermon the people were informed of the object of the Children's Aid Society. It met with the cordial approbation of all present, and several promised to take children. I was announced to preach in the afternoon; but, on returning to the tavern, I found that my smallest boy had been missing since day-break, and that he was last seen upon the high bridge over the creek, a little out of the village. So we spent the afternoon in hunting, instead of going to church. (Not an uncommon practice here, by the way.)

We dove in the creek and searched the woods, but little George (six years old) was not to be found; and when the boys came home to supper there was a shade of sadness on their faces, and they spoke in softer tones of the lost play-mate. But the saddest was George's brother, one year older. They were two orphans—all alone in the world. Peter stood up at the table, but when he saw his brother's place at his side vacant, he burst out in uncontrollable sobbing. After supper he seemed to forget his loss, till he lay down on the floor at night, and there was the vacant spot again, and his little heart flowed over with grief. Just so again when he awoke in the morning, and at breakfast and dinner.

Monday morning the boys held themselves in readiness to receive applications from the farmers. They would watch at all directions, scanning closely every wagon that came in sight, and deciding from the appearance of the driver and the horses more often from the latter, whether they "would go in for *that* farmer."

There seems to be a general dearth of boys, and still greater of girls, in all this section, and before night I had applications for fifteen of my children, the applicants bringing recommendations from their pastor and the justice of peace.

There was a rivalry among the boys to see which first could get a home in the country, and before Saturday they were all gone. Rev. Mr. O. took several home with him; and nine of the smallest I accompanied to Chicago, and sent to Mr. Townsend, Iowa City. Nearly all the others found homes in Cass County, and I had a dozen applications for more. A few of the boys are bound to trades, but the most insisted upon being farmers, and learning to drive horses. They are to receive a good common-school education, and one hundred dollars when twenty-one. I have great hopes for the majority of them. "Mag" is adopted by a wealthy Christian farmer. "Smack," the privateer from Albany, has a good home in a Quaker settlement. The two brothers, Dick and Jack, were taken by an excellent man and his son, living on adjacent farms. The German boy from the "Lodging-house" lives with a physician in D——.

Several boys came in to see me, and tell their experience in learning to farm. One of them was sure he knew how to milk, and being furnished with a pail, was told to take his choice of the cows in the yard. He sprang for a two-year-old steer, caught him by the horns, and called for a "line to make him fast." None seemed discontented but one, who ran away from a tinner, because he wanted to be a farmer.

But I must tell you of the lost boy. No tidings were heard of him up to Monday noon, when the citizens rallied and scoured the woods for miles around; but the search was fruitless, and Peter lay down that night sobbing, and with his arms stretched out, just as used to throw them around his brother.

About ten o'clock a man knocked at the door, and cried out. "Here is the lost boy!" Peter heard him, and the two brothers met on the stairs, and before we could ask where he had been, Peter had George in his place by his side on the floor. They have gone to live together in Iowa.

On the whole, the first experiment of sending children West is a very happy one, and I am sure there are places enough with good families in Michigan, Illinois, Iowa, and Wisconsin, to give every poor boy and girl in New York a permanent home. The only difficulty is to bring the children *to* the homes.

A LATER PARTY TO THE WEST

January, 1868

DEAR SIR: It will, perhaps, be interesting for you to know some facts connected with the disposal of my party at the West. We numbered thirty-two in all: two babies—one a fine little fellow one year old, and the other twenty-one years old, but nevertheless, the greatest babe in the company. Just before I reached Chicago, I was surprised to find that my party numbered only about twenty, instead of thirty-two. I went into the forward car. You may imagine my surprise to find my large babe, W—— D——, playing upon a concertina, and M—— H——, alias M—— B——, footing it down as only a clog dancer, and one well acquainted with his business at that, could do, while eight or ten boys, and perhaps as many brakesmen and baggagemen, stood looking on, evidently greatly amused. It was plain to see that I was an unwelcome visitor. Order was at once restored, and the boys went back and took their seats. As we neared A——, a gentleman by the name of L—— came to me, and, after making some inquiries, said: "I wish you would let me take that boy," pointing to G—— A——, a little fellow about eight years old. I told him we never allowed a child to go to a home from the train, as we had a committee appointed in A——, to whom application must be made. I promised, however, that I would keep the boy for him until Monday and if he came, bringing satisfactory recommendations, he should have him. He said if money was any inducement, he would give me twenty-five dollars if I would let him have the boy. I said five thousand dollars would not be an inducement without the recommendations. The little fellow was really the most remarkable child I ever saw, so amiable and intelligent, and yet so good looking. When I reached A——, I had not been out of the cars five minutes when a gentleman went to G——, and placing his hand on his shoulder, said, "This is the little man I want." I told him he had been engaged already. We passed through the crowd at the depot, and finally reached the hotel. We had been there but a short time when I had another application for G——. The first applicant came up also, and asserted his claim; said that, if L—— did not come and get the boy, he had the first right to him. L—— did not come, and I had some difficulty to settle the matter between the two applicants. Didn't know but I should have to resort to Solomon's plan, and divide the boy, but determined to let him go to the best home.

Matters went off very pleasantly the first day. I found *good* homes for some ten or twelve boys; but, in the evening, I missed the boys from the hotel, and, in looking for them, was attracted to a saloon by the dulcet tones of my babe's concertina, and entered. D—— was playing, and two of the boys were delighting the audience with a comic Irish song. All the rowdies and rum-drinkers in the town seemed to have turned out to meet them. I stepped inside of the door, and, with arms folded, stood looking very intently at them, without uttering a word. First the music ceased, then the singing, and one by one the boys slunk out of the room, until I was left alone with the rabble. It was rather amusing to hear their exclamations of surprise. "Halloo! what's up?" "What's broke loose now?" I went to the hotel, found the boys there, and a more humble set I never saw. I gave them a lecture about a yard long, and professed to feel very much hurt at the idea of finding a boy who came out with me, in a rum-shop. I gave them to understand what I should expect of them in future, and ended by having the door opened and extending an invitation to leave to those boys who thought they could do better for themselves than I should do for them. As no disposition to leave manifested itself, I then put the question to vote whether they would remain with me and do just as I wished, or go and look out for themselves. Every hand went up, and some of the boys expressed themselves very sorry for what they had done. W—— D—— left a day or two after, taking the concertina with him, which I afterward learned belonged to another boy. The most of my trouble seemed to take wing and fly away with him. He was the scapegoat of the party.

Illinois is a beautiful farming country. All the farmers seem to be wealthy. The large boys, with two exceptions, were placed upon farms. Quite a number of boys came back to the hotel to say goodby, and thank me for bringing them out. I will note a few of the most interesting cases: John Mahoney, age 16, with Mr. J—— T—— (farmer); came in town Sunday to show me a fine mule his employer had given him. J—— C——, age 14, went with Mrs. D——, who has a farm; came in to tell me how well pleased he is with his place; says he will work the farm as soon as he is able, and get half the profits. D—— M——, age 17, went with A—— H. B—— (farmer); came back to tell me his employer had given him a pig, and a small plot of ground to work for himself. J—— S——, age 17, went with J—— B——; saw him after the boy had been with him three or four days; he likes him very much, and has given him a Canadian pony, with saddle and bridle. I might mention other cases, but I know the above to be facts.

The boys met with a good deal of sympathy. One old gentleman came in just for the purpose of seeing a little boy who had lost an eye, and was a brother to a boy his son had taken. When I told the little fellow that the gentleman lived near the man who had taken his brother, he climbed up on his knee, and putting his arms around his neck, said: "I want to go home with you, and be your boy; I want to see my brother." The old gentleman wept, and wiping the tears from his eyes, said: "This is more than I can stand; I will take this boy home with me." He is a wealthy farmer and a good man, and I am sure will love the little fellow very much, for he is a very interesting child.

PROVIDING COUNTRY HOMES
THE OPPOSITION TO THIS REMEDY—ITS EFFECTS

This most sound and practical of charities always met with an intense opposition here from a certain class, for bigoted reasons. The poor were early taught, even from the altar, that the whole scheme of emigration was one of "proselytizing," and that every child thus taken forth was made a "Protestant." Stories were spread, too, that these unfortunate children were re-named in the West, and that thus even brothers and sisters might meet and perhaps marry! Others scattered the pleasant information that the little ones "were sold as slaves," and that the agents enriched themselves from the transaction.

These were the obstacles and objections among the poor themselves. So powerful were these, that it would often happen that a poor woman, seeing her child becoming ruined on the streets, and soon plainly to come forth as a criminal, would prefer this to a good home in the West; and we would have the discouragement of beholding the lad a thief behind prison-bars, when a journey to the country would have saved him. Most distressing of all was, when a drunken mother or father followed a half-starved boy, already scarred and sore with their brutality, and snatched him from one of our parties of little emigrants, all joyful with their new prospects, only to beat him and leave him on the streets.

With a small number of the better classes there was also a determined opposition to this humane remedy. What may be called the "Asylum-interest" set itself in stiff repugnance to our emigration scheme. They claimed—and I presume the most obstinate among them still claim—that we were scattering poison over the country, and that we benefited neither the farmers nor the children. They urged that a restraint of a few years in an Asylum or House of Detention rendered these children of poverty much more fit for practical life, and purified them to be good members of society.

We, on the other hand, took the ground that, as our children were not criminals, but simply destitute and homeless boys and girls, usually with some ostensible occupation, they could not easily, on any legal grounds, be inclosed within Asylums; that, if they were, the expense of their maintenance would be enormous, while the cost of a temporary care of them in our Schools and Lodging-houses, and their transference to the West, was only trifling—in the proportion of fifteen dollars to one hundred and fifty dollars, reckoning the latter as a year's cost for a child's support in an Asylum. Furthermore, we held and stoutly maintained that an Asylum-life is a bad preparation for practical life. The child, most of all, needs individual care and sympathy. In an Asylum, he is "Letter B, of Class 3," or "No. 2, of Cell 426," and that is all that is known of him. As a poor boy, who must live in a small house, he ought to learn to draw his own water, to split his wood, kindle his fires, and light his candle; as an "institutional child," he is lighted, warmed, and watered by machinery. He has a child's imitation, a desire to please his superiors, and readiness to be influenced by his companions. In a great caravansary he soons learns the external virtues which secure him a good bed and meal—decorum and apparent piety and discipline—while he practices the vices and unnamable habits which masses of boys of any class nearly always teach one another. His virtue seems to have an alms-house flavor; even his vices do not present the frank character of a thorough street-boy; he is found to lie easily, and to be very weak under temptation; somewhat given to hypocrisy, and something of a sneak. And, what is very natural, *the longer he is in the Asylum, the less likely he is to do well in outside life.* I hope I do no injustice to the unfortunate graduates of our Asylums; but that was and continues to be my strong impression of the institutional effect on an ordinary street boy or girl. Of course there are numerous exceptional cases among children—of criminal and inherited habits, and perverse and low organization, and premature cunning, lust, and temper, where a half-prison life may be the very best thing for them; but the majority of criminals among children, I do not believe, are much worse than the children of the same class outside, and therefore need scarcely any different training.

One test, which I used often to administer to our different systems, was to ask—and I request any Asylum advocate to do the same—"If your son were suddenly, by the death of his parents and relatives, to be thrown out on the streets, poor and homeless—as these children are—where would you prefer him to be placed—in an Asylum, or in a good farmer's home in the West?"

"The plainest farmer's home rather than the best Asylum—a thousand times!" was always my sincere answer.

Our discussion waxed warm, and was useful to both sides. Our weak point was that, if a single boy or girl in a village, from a large company we had sent, turned out bad, there was a cry raised that "every New York poor child," thus sent out, became "a thief or a vagabond," and for a time people believed it.

Our antagonists seized hold of this, and we immediately dispatched careful agents to collect statistics in the Central West, and, if possible, disprove the charges. . . . .

The effort of tabulating, or making statistics, in regard to the children dispatched by our society, soon appeared exceedingly difficult, mainly because these youthful wanderers shared the national characteristic of love-of-change, and, like our own servants here, they often left one place for another, merely for fancy or variety. This was especially true of the lads or girls over sixteen or seventeen. The offer of better wages, or the attraction of a new employer, or the desire of "moving," continually stirred up these latter to migrate to another village, county, or state.

In 1859 we made a comprehensive effort to collect some of these statistics in regard to our children who had begun their new life in the West. The following is an extract from our report at this time:

During the last spring, the secretary made an extended journey through the Western States, to see for himself the nature and results of this work, carried on for the last five years through those States, under Mr. Tracy's careful supervision. During that time we have scattered there several thousands of poor boys and girls. In this journey he visited personally, and heard directly of, many hundreds of these little creatures, and appreciated, for the first time, to the full extent, the spirit with which the West has opened its arms to them. The effort to reform and improve these young outcasts has become a mission-work there. Their labor, it is true, is needed. But many a time a bountiful and Christian home is opened to the miserable little stranger, his habits are patiently corrected, faults without number are borne with, time and money are expended on him, solely and entirely from the highest religious motive of a noble self-sacrifice for an unfortunate fellow-creature. The peculiar warm heartedness of the Western people, and the equality of all classes, give them an especial adaptation to this work, and account for their success.

"Wherever we went" (we quote from his account) "we found the children sitting at the same table with the families, going to the school with the children, and every way treated as well as any other children. . . . .

"The estimate we formed from a considerable field of observation was, that, out of those sent to the West under fifteen years, not more than two per cent turned out bad; and, even of those from fifteen to eighteen, not more than four per cent. . . . ."

Of course, some of the older boys disappear entirely; some few return to the city; but it may generally be assumed that we hear of the worst cases—that is, of those who commit criminal offenses, or who come under the law—and it is these whom we reckon as the failures. One or two of such cases, out of hundreds in a given district who are doing well, sometimes make a great noise, and give a momentary impression that the work is not coming out well there; and there are are always a few weak-minded people who accept such rumors without examination. Were the proportion of failures far greater than it is, the work would still be of advantage to the West, and a rich blessing to the city.

It is also remarkable, as years pass away, how few cases ever come to the knowledge of the Society, of ill-treatment of these children. The task of distributing them is carried on so publicly by Mr. Tracy, and in connection with such responsible persons, that any case of positive abuse would at once be known and corrected by the community itself.

"On this journey," says the secretary, "we heard of but one instance even of neglect. We visited the lad, and discovered that he had not been schooled as he should, and had sometimes been left alone at night in the lonely log house. Yet this had roused the feelings of the whole country-side; we removed the boy, amid the tears and protestations of the 'father' and 'mother,' and put him in another place. As soon as we had left the village, he ran right back to his old place! . . . ."

In some cases, those who have become disobedient and troublesome are said to have been so principally through the fault of their employers; few instances, comparatively, from this four or five thousand, are known to have committed criminal offenses—in some States not more than four per cent. This is true of Michigan; and in Ohio, we do not think, from all the returns we can gather, that the proportion is even so large as that. The agent of the American and Foreign Christian Union for Indiana, a gentleman of the highest respectability, constantly traveling through the State—a State where we have placed five hundred and fifty-seven children—testifies that "very few have gone back to New York," and that "he has heard of no one who has committed criminal offenses."

The superintendent of the Chicago Reform School, one of the most successful and experienced men in this country in juvenile reform, states that his institution had never had but three of our children committed by the Illinois State Courts, though we have sent to the State two hundred and sixty-five, and such an institution is, of course, the place where criminal children of this class would at once be committed. . . . .

The immense, practically unlimited demand by Western communities for the services of these children shows that the first-comers have at least done moderately well, especially as every case of crime is bruited over a wide country-side, and stamps the whole company sent with disgrace. These cases we always hear of. The lives of poor children in these homes seem like the annals of great States in this, that, when they make no report and pass in silence, then we may be sure happiness and virtue are the rule. When they make a noise, crime and misery prevail. Twenty years' virtuous life in a street-boy makes no impression on the public. A single offense is heard for hundreds of miles. A theft of one lad is imputed to scores of others about him.

The children are not indentured, but are free to leave, if ill-treated or dissatisfied; and the farmers can dismiss them, if they find them useless or otherwise unsuitable.

This apparently loose arrangement has worked well, and put both sides on their good behavior. We have seldom had any cases brought to our attention of ill-treatment. . . . .

On the whole, if the warm discussion between the "Asylum-interest" and the "Emigration party" were ever renewed, probably both would agree (if they were candid) that their opponents' plan had virtues which they did not then see. There are some children so perverse, and inheriting such bad tendencies, and so stamped with the traits of a vagabond life, that a Reformatory is the best place for them. On the other hand, the majority of orphan, deserted, and neglected boys and girls are far better in a country home. The Asylum has its great dangers, and is very expensive. The Emigration-plan must be conducted with careful judgment, and applied, so far as is practicable to children under, say, the age of fourteen years. . . . .

The experience we have thus had for twenty years in transferring such masses of poor children to rural districts is very instructive on the general subject of "Emigration as a Cure for Pauperism." . . . .

With reference to the cost of this method of charity, we have usually estimated the net expenses for the agent, his salary, the railroad fares, food and clothing for the child, as averaging fifteen dollars per head for each child sent. Whenever practicable, the agent collects from the employers the railroad expenses, and otherwise obtains gifts from benevolent persons; so that, frequently, our collections and "returned fares" in this way have amounted to $6,000 or $8,000 per annum. These gifts, however, are becoming less and less, and will probably eventually cease altogether; the farmer feeling that he has done his fair share in receiving and training the child.

We are continually forced, also, toward the newer and more distant States, where labor is more in demand, and the temper of the population is more generous, so that the average expense of the aid thus given will in the future be greater for each boy or girl relieved. . . . .

Were our movement allowed its full scope, we could take the place of every Orphan Asylum and Alms-House for pauper children in and around New York, and thus save the public hundreds of thousands of dollars, and immensely benefit the children. We could easily "locate" 5,000 children per annum, from the ages of two years to fifteen, in good homes in the West, at an average net cost of fifteen dollars per head.

If Professor Fawcett's objection[1] be urged, that we are thus doing for the children of the Alms-house poor, what the industrious and self-supporting poor cannot get done for their own children, we answer that we are perfectly ready to do the same for the outside hard-working poor; but their attachment to the city, their ignorance or bigotry, and their affection for their children, will always prevent them from making use of such a benefaction to any large degree. The poor, living in their own homes, seldom wish to send out their children in this way. We do "place out" a certain number of such children; but the great majority of our little emigrants are the "waifs and strays" of the streets in a large city.

[1] See Fawcett on "Pauperism."

APPENDIX I

THREE AMERICAN POOR RELIEF DOCUMENTS
1870–1885

EDITORIAL NOTE

ON THE twelfth of last April, Governor Roosevelt of New York signed the new Public Welfare Act, which takes the place of the century-old state poor law. In view of the widespread interest aroused by the introduction and passage of this measure there is today new hope that our old pauper laws may be modernized in other states.

The relief of the poor in our American states was a local problem from the earliest times. In the last number we published an article dealing with poor relief in the Colonial period,[1] and we present in this number another article dealing with this subject. We also present below three documents showing the opinions of the early state charitable authorities on outdoor and almshouse relief. Fifty years ago, Mrs. Josephine Shaw Lowell was an influential member of the New York State Board of Charities, Frederic H. Wines was the vigorous secretary of the newly created Illinois Board, and Edward L. Pierce was the secretary of the older Massachusetts Board. Their theories of the problems and causes of pauperism as well as their attitudes toward the poor, which will be found in the documents here, show that there were early differences of opinion as to poor-relief policy; but whether or not there was agreement as to the wisdom of granting outdoor relief, there was a widespread belief that if given, it must be given under conditions of deterrence. A study of poor-law history in America is a subject of great importance at the present time.   E. A.

[1] See the Social Service Monographs (Poor Law Series), including Margaret Creech, *Three Centuries of Poor Law Administration;* Aileen Kennedy and S. P. Breckinridge, *The Ohio Poor Law;* Alice Shaffer, Mary Wysor Keefer, and S. P. Breckinridge, *The Indiana Poor Law;* Isabel Bruce, Edith Eichoff, and S. P. Breckinridge, *The Michigan Poor Law;* Grace Browning, *Poor Relief Legislation in Kansas;* and Marcus Wilson Jernegan, *Laboring and Dependent Classes in Colonial America*, Part IV. See also, Robert W. Kelso, *Public Poor Relief in Massachusetts;* E. W. Capen, *Poor Law of Connecticut;* William C. Heffner, *Poor Relief in Pennsylvania;* and Roy M. Brown, *Public Poor Relief in South Carolina.*

Public Outdoor Relief—Theory and Practice in 1883[1]

The only justification for the spending of public money is that the result is a public benefit, that is, that it is better for the whole mass of the people that the money should be spent.

It is not right to tax one part of the community for the benefit of another part; it is not right to take money by law from one man and give it to another, unless for the benefit of both. The public funds are always somebody's money; they are composed of the taxes which are very often hard to pay, or it would be safe to say, which are usually hard to pay; for the men to whom the payment of taxes is an unimportant item are the exceptions in every community, and pay but a very small proportion of the amount raised by taxation. The bulk comes from the many, who are struggling to keep or to obtain their own homes, and to whom a slight increase or decrease is a great matter.

Therefore, the policy of public poor relief, or the feeding and maintenance of one part of the people by money taken by law from the rest, can be justified only on the ground that it is better both for those who are so fed and maintained, and for those who supply the food and maintenance, that this should be done.

There are persons who argue that compulsory or public relief in all its forms tends in the end to do harm by diminishing prudence and industry, in consequence of removing not only the most pressing incentive to those virtues (the fear of suffering and starvation) but also by diminishing the rewards of industry and forethought, which is necessarily done, when a part of what they gain is seized upon to feed indolence and improvidence. Those who argue thus are undoubtedly right in the abstract, but they forget, apparently, that there are in every community persons who cannot maintain themselves, and who have no friends upon whom they have a claim, and that it would not be well, even for others, that these should be driven to desperation by the absolute pressure of want; in this view, public relief is a benefit to the whole people, acting as a preventive of violence. Those who object to public relief in all its forms also seem to forget that human pity is imperative and that were there no final resort for those who cannot maintain themselves, nor assurance against their dying by starvation, it would be absolutely impossible to refuse food and money to all who asked for it. They would ask on the ground that they were starving, and the possibility that such might be the case would open every hand, and in this way a far greater temptation to idleness, improvidence, and fraud would be afforded than any public relief system could present, and a larger share of the earnings of hard-worked men and women would be absorbed by idleness and vice.

It will scarcely be denied by any one that, if possible, all the members of any civilized community must live. To live, they must be maintained by the produce of those members who work, and so create the means of living. The question is as to the way in which this produce shall be taken from those who create it, and given to those who cannot create it. Shall it be done systematically, so that it will supply only those who actually cannot create it, and thus reduce the amount to be taken to a minimum, or shall it be distributed by the producers themselves, who will be a prey to all who pretend that they cannot create it? In other words, shall there or shall there not be public relief? . . . .

In every community the amount given to unknown and often unworthy beggars is undoubtedly a decided tax on industry, which would be increased almost indefinitely were there no public and systematized means of relieving the poor. Public relief, then, appears to be not only a benefit to the whole community, but a necessity. The next point is as to the best form it can assume, and to decide upon this it is necessary to define clearly the objects of public relief. They seem to be all included under the following heads:

1. To provide that no one shall starve, or shall suffer for the absolute physical necessaries of life.

2. To make this provision in such a way as shall do as little moral harm as possible, both to the recipient of relief and to the community at large.

3. To use every means to render the necessity for relief of short duration.

4. To take as small a sum from the tax-paying (that is the working) part of the community as is consistent with the accomplishment of the first three objects.

5. To convince the community that all these objects are attained, and that consequently they need not take upon themselves the provision of the necessaries of life for those who have no direct or personal claim upon them.

Such being the objects, how are they to be attained? What are the methods by which public relief may be wisely given—that is, by which a certain part of the people may be fed and maintained by the rest?

There are only two methods with which we need now to concern ourselves—these are outdoor relief and relief in a workhouse or almshouse, or in other words, relief given to poor persons at their own homes (outside the doors of the workhouse or almshouse) and relief administered inside of an institution, built and maintained at the public expense and controlled by public officials.

It would seem that, a priori, every argument was in favor of the first method—of outdoor relief. Given a community of which some of the members are to be fed and clothed at the cost of the rest, it would be said at once that the right and simple way was to furnish to them, in their own homes, such relief as they required, and that in this way all the objects aimed at would be attained.

1. They would be saved from starvation or suffering.

2. Neither they, nor any other person, would suffer moral injury, because they, living in their own homes, would not be brought in close contact with anyone else, either to corrupt or be corrupted—none of the natural relations, either of the family or the community, would be interrupted.

3. The relief would be of short duration, because the need having passed the relief would stop as a matter of course.

4. It would be much the cheapest method of giving relief, because all the expense incurred would be for absolute necessaries, food, fuel, and clothing, and even this would be reduced to a minimum, because often all that would be required would be a small sum to supplement the means of living, which would be cut off were relief inside an institution to be substituted; while in the latter case the cost of the building and of supervision would also have to be added.

5. The public would certainly be satisfied when assured that the wants of every poor person were supplied at their own homes, while on the other hand the public would certainly not be reconciled to the fact that, simply because a man was poor, therefore his home was to be broken up and he and his family were to be sent into a workhouse to become paupers.

These are the arguments on the side of outdoor relief, arguments which, as arguments, are unanswerable. Considered a priori, the decision would seem to be inevitably in favor of outdoor relief. Fortunately, however, or unfortunately, considering the results of experiment, the effect on a community of outdoor relief is not a field for a priori argument; not only in our own country have partial experiments in this direction been made but in other countries, more especially in England, has the whole question been put to a practical test and proved the very extreme of danger, the results being the exact opposite of what it seemed reasonable to expect. . . . .

Happily for the United States, the practice of distributing public outdoor relief has not as yet obtained a very firm hold among us, but it has been the custom in many of our cities to a limited extent, and . . . . its evil effects are the same here as elsewhere. . . . .

George E. McGonegal, the wisest and most experienced superintendent of poor of New York State, says:[1]

We have a system in our State of furnishing what is called temporary or out-door relief, the object of which is to relieve families, who from sickness or other disability, become temporarily incapacitated from wholly maintaining themselves. This is a worthy object, and deserving of all praise; but the great bulk of what is called temporary relief, is not temporary, but permanent relief. Families are furnished a stated amount weekly or monthly, and this is continued week after week and year after year; and I know of nothing which does so much to encourage pauperism and educate paupers for the next generation, as this system, which I think is in operation in most of the counties, cities and towns in this State. There is nothing except intemperance in the use of alcoholic liquors which is more demoralizing to the head of a family, or more ruinous to children, than to become imbued with the idea that the public is bound to provide for them. And if people could only realize, when they recommend, bring or send a family, composed, in part of bright, intelligent children, who have never yet received public aid, to the superintendent or overseer of the poor, and insist upon aid being furnished, that such an act was almost sure to ruin those bright children, and educate them for paupers or criminals when they become men and women, it seems to me that such people should exhaust every other resource to provide a way for such family to overcome its immediate difficulty, before incurring the fearful responsibility of being instrumental in making them paupers.

People, very soon after commencing to receive public aid, lose their energy and self-respect, find it easier to rely upon the industry of others to furnish them their daily bread than to exert themselves to earn a livelihood; their children learn to think that getting provisions and fuel from the overseer of the poor is perfectly right and proper, and they are almost certain to follow in the footsteps of their parents, especially as it requires a great deal less exertion than to earn their living by honest labor.

There are cases where temporary relief is undoubtedly necessary, and if judiciously disbursed and discontinued at the earliest possible moment, before it becomes permanent relief and before the recipients become chronic paupers, then I have no doubt it is a real benefit to those who receive it. But after an experience of nearly twelve years in the care of the poor, and carefully studying, during that time, the effects of this so-called temporary relief, I am thoroughly convinced that the harm done by means of it greatly over-balances the good,

[1] From the *Proceedings of the Convention of the Superintendents of the Poor of the State of New York*, held at Rochester, N.Y., June 6, 7, 8, 1882. From paper read by Mr. McGonegal of Monroe County.

and I think it is a question well worth considering, whether it would not be better to abolish it entirely. I believe that three-fourths of what is called temporary or out-door relief, furnished in the State of New York, is not only a direct injury to those who receive it, but is a great damage to society by encouraging indolence, and is an enormous unnecessary burden upon the industrious, provident class which is compelled to pay the expense.

A few words from the last annual report of the State Board of Charities and Reform of the state of Wisconsin are also suggestive:

All experience shows that the demand for poor relief grows with the supply, and that a large amount for poor relief does not indicate a large amount of suffering which needs to be relieved, but a large amount of laxity or corruption on the part of officers and a large amount of willingness by able-bodied idlers to be fed at the public expense.

The argument which always has the most weight in favor of continuing public outdoor relief is that many deserving poor persons may suffer should it be cut off. It has already been proved by experience, however, that not only many suffer, but all suffer, by the continuance of a system which undermines the character of those it pretends to relieve, and at the same time drags down to their level many who never, but for its false allurements, would have been sufferers at all, while, on the contrary, the suffering which is looked for in consequence of the stopping of outdoor relief does not occur. These seem to be anomalies, but they may be easily explained. The first fact, that poverty and suffering are increased and even caused by the relief intended to cure them, has already been shown to be due to the moral effects of such relief. . . . . Private charity can and will provide for every person who should be kept from resorting to public sources of relief.

The statement that it can and will do this is not based on the theory that it ought to but on experience in the cities and towns in this country where public outdoor relief has been abolished, not only without causing the suffering among special and worthy cases which it is always feared will follow such a radical change but with the most beneficial effects on the character and, as a natural consequence, on the condition of the people who formerly depended on it.

In Kings County, in our own state, containing a city of almost half a million inhabitants, we have one example; in Philadelphia, with her 890,000 inhabitants, another; and in smaller communities the same effects follow the same causes.

We have comparatively full statistics from Kings County of the amount expended each year for her dependent classes, both from public and private funds in and out of institutions, for the ten years ending September 30, 1882. Until 1879, public outdoor relief was given by the county to the amount of $100,000 or more yearly; it was then cut off in the middle of winter, without warning, without any substitute being provided, and the result was—nothing.

In fact, except for the saving of the money and the stopping of petty political corruption which had been carried on by means of the relief, and the cessation of the spectacle of hundreds of people passing through the streets with baskets of provisions furnished by the public, it would have been impossible to discover that the relief had been stopped. And there was, besides, in 1879 and 1880, a smaller number of persons supported in the almshouse than in any other of the ten years from 1873 to 1882. . . . . .

With an increase of population of about 100,000, the amount of relief given in 1880, in Kings County, was not so large as in 1873, and the largest amounts spent were in 1875, 1877, and 1882.

There could scarcely be a stronger proof that the stopping of outdoor relief does not cause the suffering that is anticipated, or, in other words, that the need supplied by public outdoor relief is in fact created by it.

The following letter from the Secretary of the Philadelphia Society for Organizing Charity gives the results of the abolition of public outdoor relief in that city:

PHILADELPHIA, 23d October, 1883

Mrs. J. S. Lowell, Commissioner, etc.,
New York

DEAR MADAM—In reply to your favor of the 19th inst., I can say that the out-door poor-law relief in this city amounted to from fifty to eighty thousand dollars annually for many years preceding 1880, when it was discontinued. It was dispensed by twelve officials, termed "visitors," appointed, in most instances, for *political* reasons. At the time it was abolished, we, for a few weeks, felt an increased pressure for relief upon the private charities; but that was only temporary, and although the population of the city increased during the past three years, the numbers of the in-door poor have decreased.

Very respectfully yours,

JAS. W. WALK, M.D. (*General Secretary*)

Here we have the experiences of two of the largest cities in the United States, and it may be well to add to this record that of New York City, in which the public outdoor relief for some years has not exceeded $65,000 yearly, and has been confined to the distribution of coal, of medical relief, and of a small annual cash donation to certain blind persons, all of which, in the opinion of many well-informed persons, it would be well to discontinue, trusting to private charity to supply whatever might be required in its place.

We have shown in the foregoing that public outdoor relief may, with advantage, be discontinued in large cities—and we have also the records of two smaller and rural or mixed communities, which point to the same conclusion.

The town of Castleton, in Richmond County, New York, has a population of 12,679, and, since 1879, not one cent of public outdoor relief has been given in the town. In former years, the public relief varied from $1,500 to $3,000 per annum, with from 100 to 300 persons on the pauper list.

The poor have not suffered by the entire cessation of public relief; but there is less idleness, and the proportion of the poor from Castleton who are in the poorhouse is smaller than that from the other towns of the county, where public outdoor relief is still distributed.

In Herkimer County, New York, there was in 1870 a population of 39,929, and public outdoor relief amounted to $21,290; in 1875, the population was 41,589, and the relief $1,084; in 1882, the population was 42,-667, and the relief $2,000.

The following letter from the superintendent of the poor requires no explanation:

Office of the Superintendent of the Poor
HERKIMER, N.Y., October 25, 1883

Mrs. C. R. Lowell, Commissioner, etc., New York City:

Your favor of the 23d inst. at hand, and in reply would say that I have compared the figures quoted by you with the itemized accounts published in the proceedings of the Board of Supervisors, and find them substantially correct.

"As to the cause of the change," or the difference in the amount expended in 1870 and 1882, it may be a little difficult to make an explanation that would be entirely just and satisfactory to all concerned. In the year 1870, very loose and extravagant notions of expenditures in all departments of government prevailed, and our county was no exception; double the numbers of people were kept in the county poor-house, and the cost of supplies being no greater than now, it cost nearly double the amount *per capita* to keep them that it does now. In the year 1878, when all kinds of supplies reached the lowest point, it cost $2 per week in our poorhouse; in 1882, it cost $1.27½ per week, and they were kept in a building warmed by steam and lighted by gas. The following facts may explain the situation to some extent, viz.:

1. The building of a new county poorhouse.

2. Sending all disabled transients to the poorhouse instead of keeping them in hotels or boarding-houses.

3. Cutting off all those able to work and making them earn their living or go to the poorhouse.

4. No men supported because they vote this or that ticket.

5. When a family applies for relief, their circumstances are fully investigated and a record kept, so that we know the exact condition of all such families.

6. We grant outside relief only to those having a family of young children; in such cases we consider it more economical and humane to keep the family together if the circumstances will warrant it.

The above facts may have something to do with producing the results which you note.

As to the effects of cutting off such large expenditures, I can safely say that there are not as many paupers in our poorhouse, that there are not as many destitute in our villages, and that there are no complaints from any class of people.

There is but one drawback to our present condition, and that is that the number of our insane is increasing; while pauperism is slightly decreasing, insanity is increasing with us.

Very respectfully yours,

JOHN CROWLEY, Superintendent

Outdoor relief, then, it appears from the foregoing facts and arguments, fails to attain any one of the objects which should be aimed at by relief from the public funds.

1. It fails to provide that no one shall starve or suffer for the common necessaries of life, because, however lavish may be the relief, unless self-restraint and providence be conferred upon those who receive it, all that is bestowed will often be wasted by them in riotous living, and the innocent and helpless beings dependent upon them will be left to suffer far more than had the relief been denied.

2. It fails to save the recipient of relief and the community from moral harm, because human nature is so constituted that no man can receive as a gift what he should earn by his own labor without a moral deterioration, and the presence in the community of certain persons living on public relief has the tendency to tempt others to sink to their degraded level.

3. Outdoor relief cannot be of short duration, because when it has once been accepted, the barrier is broken down and rarely, or never, thereafter, is the effort made to do without it, and thus all such relief has the tendency to become regular and permanent.

4. The taxpayers are the losers by outdoor relief, because, although the amount given to each individual is, undoubtedly, smaller than would be required for that individual in an institution, yet outdoor relief is so infectious and, once obtained, is so easy a way of getting a living, that

far larger numbers demand and receive it than could be induced to enter an institution, and thus the total cost of public relief is always increased by giving it outside of the workhouse or almshouse.

5. The chief object, to convince the public that the poor are adequately cared for by public officials, has never been attained by either system, and may be left for time, experience, and education.

Outdoor relief, in fact, cannot be defended; it has none of the redeeming features of private charity, because there is nothing personal or softening in it, nor has it the advantages which might, perhaps, be derived from an acknowledged and openly advocated communism, for the principle underlying it is not that the proceeds of all men's labor is to be fairly divided among all, but that the idle, improvident, and even vicious man has the right to live in idleness and vice upon the proceeds of the labor of his industrious and virtuous fellow-citizen.

We have already accepted in this paper the postulate that the community should save every one of its members from starvation, no matter how low or depraved such member may be, but we contend that the necessary relief should be surrounded by circumstances that shall not only repel everyone, not in extremity, from accepting it, but which shall also insure a distinct moral and physical improvement on the part of all those who are forced to have recourse to it—that is, discipline and education should be inseparably associated with any system of public relief.

And there is still another point to be insisted on; while the acknowledgment is made that every person born into a civilized community has a right to live, yet the community has the right to say that incompetent and dangerous persons shall not, so far as can be helped, be born to acquire this right to live upon others. To prevent a constant and alarming increase of these two classes of persons, the only way is for the community to refuse to support any except those whom it can control—that is, except those who will submit themselves to discipline and education. It is certainly an anomaly for a man and woman who have proved themselves incapable of supplying their own daily needs to bring into the world other helpless beings, to be also maintained by a tax upon the community.

If, then, outdoor relief is proved to be not only useless as a means of relieving actual, existing suffering, but an active means of increasing present and future want and vice, the only other means of giving public relief is within an institution, and this will be found to render possible the attainment of all the objects that should be aimed at by public relief.

It is easy to provide that all the inmates shall have the necessaries of life, and besides being fed and clothed, they can be subjected to the best sanitary regulations, they can be kept clean and be required to live regularly, to work, to exercise, to sleep, as much or as little as is good for them, and this brings us to the second object, for in an institution the inmates, besides being prevented from receiving moral harm, can be brought under such physical, moral, mental, and industrial training as will render them far better members of society than they ever were before, and will eventually make them self-supporting, and so attain the third object.

The fourth object (saving money to the workers of the community) will, of course, follow from the measures enumerated in the foregoing. To cure paupers and make them self-supporting, however costly the process, must always be economical as compared with a smaller but constantly increasing and continual outlay for their maintenance.

To accomplish the objects set forth as desirable, it is not sufficient simply to shelter, feed, and clothe the public dependents inside of institutions supported by taxation. Such institutions may, and unhappily do, often, become the means of still further degrading the miserable beings who crowd into them.

To make them useful at all, it is necessary that they should be governed by those who recognize that the prevention and permanent cure of pauperism, vice, and disease are the objects to be sought, and the whole system of public relief must be based upon that principle.

Experience of the Overseers of the Poor, Collated and Reviewed[1]

With the view of obtaining the results of the system of outdoor relief from the experience of overseers of the poor, the secretary [of the Massachusetts Board of State Charities], in June last, prepared and issued a circular, which was mailed to those officers in each town and city of the commonwealth. . . . . So much of the circular as concerns outdoor relief is as follows.

1. What is the effect, and what are the advantages and disadvantages of the practice of "out-door relief"; that is, of relief given by your city or town to poor persons at their homes, and outside of almshouses? and, particularly,

2. Does it or not increase pauperism, by encouraging persons to apply for public aid who would have supported themselves, having the ability to do so, if they were to receive support only in almshouses?

3. To what extent in your city or town have persons received such aid who could have supported themselves, or been supported by their near kindred?

[1] Extract from "Report of the Secretary," Edward L. Pierce, in *Eighth Annual Report of the Massachusetts Board of State Charities, January, 1872,* pp. 41–53.

4. Would the entire abolition of the practice, so as to confine the support of poor persons to support in almshouses, result in inhumanity to any considerable part of those now relieved at their homes, or tend to make them permanent instead of *temporary* paupers, or otherwise be attended with injurious results?

5. Do the persons receiving "out-door relief" in your city or town generally continue to receive it from year to year, or do they after receiving it a year or two cease to receive it by being again able to support themselves,—in other words, does the "out-door relief" prove to be *permanent* or only *temporary* with the larger class who receive it?

6. What proportion of the "out-door relief" is given to State paupers?

7. What limitations or principles of administration in cases of "out-door relief" are, in your judgment, expedient?

Answers were received from 160 towns, enough to give a complete view of the system. Some were given in a perfunctory way, but many were thoughtfully prepared. In determining the preponderance of testimony it will be necessary here, as always, to weigh rather than count the witnesses. As a whole, they present fully the general views of the overseers as to the workings of the system, and many valuable illustrations of its advantages and disadvantages. Never before in this state, probably not in any state of the Union, has there been brought together such an accumulation of experience and opinion from those having immediately to do with the care of the poor; and such experience and opinion are always essential in correcting a priori reasoning and adjusting a system to the requirements of public opinion. They are worthy of careful attention, and the secretary returns his sincere acknowledgments to the overseers who have kindly obliged him with their answers. Under assurances given in order to secure greater freedom and confidence in replies, the names of towns must be withheld in references and extracts.

It is the purpose to give here the general results of the answers without being confined to the particular questions calling for the information. After such a statement, extracts representing the different features of the system and varying experiences in its administration will be given, as far as is consistent with the just limits of this report.

NECESSITY OF SUCH RELIEF

Outdoor relief for the poor, or support of some kind and to some extent outside of almshouses and at their own homes or with relatives or friends, is *a necessary part of a wise and humane pauper system.* This is the general, though not quite the unanimous opinion. While its evil tendencies are confessed, it is maintained that they can, with proper precautions, be kept within bounds and substantially defeated. A certain proportion, perhaps one-tenth, repudiate it in all cases, as not required by good policy or humanity; but the main current is the other way.

The *occasions* calling for outdoor relief in preference to almshouse relief may be briefly indicated.

To prevent the breaking up of families and the increase of pauperism.— The *death* of the father of a family may leave it destitute. This is particularly true in manufacturing and seafaring communities. Removal to an almshouse breaks up the home and all its associations, deadens natural affections, disrupts the family relation, places the children in the almshouse to be contaminated by pauper associations, or distributes them by indentures. The breaking up of a home dispirits and demoralizes the whole family, taking away self-respect, ambition, and the best incentives to effort, and affecting not merely the family itself with the pauper name and character, but transmitting the taint to other generations. Timely outdoor relief, instead of removal to an almshouse, preserves these ties and inspirations, and keeps the family together until the older children are able to earn money for the common support.

The *sickness* of the head of a family, want of work in a hard winter, or some other calamity may create the same necessity and justify the same relief. The hardship of refusing public aid to an industrious family stricken down by some sudden misfortune, other than in a part of a room of an almshouse, is felt by all. It is true, one may say, that there should have been greater forecast, and something should have been laid by for just such an emergency, and that the refusal of outdoor relief would be likely to stimulate the laboring classes to greater prudence. But it will not do to press this view, though it may have much truth in it, too far. With the best appliances, it is likely to be a remote point in social progress when poverty will disappear; and this consideration cannot fail to temper and limit the rigid theories of the economist.

The preservation of the home and family by means of outdoor relief is made more important by the consideration of the welfare of the *children.* . . . . This Board, through the Visiting Agency, has made every effort to segregate the children from the mass of paupers at the earliest possible moment, and to distribute them in industrious and worthy families. Outdoor relief, in case of the death or sickness of the head of the family, instead of removal to an almshouse, saves children from such corrupting association.

The *hereditary* tendency of pauperism is supposed to be prevented, in many cases, by outdoor relief in preference to almshouse relief. This is a point kindred to that concerning children. While both kinds of relief imply pauperism more or less continued, in the one case it is far more pronounced than in the other. Support in an almshouse draws the line distinctly between a dependent and a self-supporting condition, and throws the inmates into the pauper class, both in repute as well as in fact. The character ends not with the residence in it or with them; but if they pass out they do so only to return, either themselves or their children and grandchildren. A pauper grandfather, a pauper father, and a pauper grandchild is not an uncommon genealogy. It is therefore important, as far as may be, to adjust relief so as not to aggravate or develop the corrupting tendency.

Outdoor relief is commended in the cases already referred to, as keeping pauperism temporary, rather than making it permanent. The family or person relieved, retaining its self-respect, may be expected to support itself when the pressure has been lifted or children become older; whereas when it takes up its abode in an almshouse, all hope of better things must be abandoned. The danger, too, of transmitting pauper blood is diminished by the temporary outside provision.

On the other hand, outdoor relief, while nominally occasional and temporary, becomes, in a large proportion of cases, continuous and permanent. One application is often followed by another as certainly as new moons are to come. To some, though not to an equal extent, it has the same demoralizing effect upon recipients as life in an almshouse.

What proportion of outdoor relief is *permanent*, that is, continuing from year to year, either as full or partial support, and what proportion is *temporary*, that is limited to one year or less than five years, cannot be determined. The estimate may be ventured that the former in *amount* is larger than the latter, but in *number* the recipients of the latter class exceed those of the former.

The evils accompanying the separation of families, the destruction of self-respect and ambition in those likely to recover the capacity of self-support, the corruption of children by pauper reputation and associations, the tendency of pauperism, when demonstrated by residence in an almshouse, to become permanent and hereditary rather than temporary and individual, present the strongest cases for the intervention of outdoor relief.

When required by humane sentiments.—Humanity, as distinct from merely prudential or moral considerations, like those involved in the separation of families that include children, and in relief given to persons

temporarily in want is, in a certain class of cases, the chief reason for
outdoor relief. Aged persons of temperate and correct lives, who have
seen better days, cling to familiar associations, and shrink from a pauper
home, are the leading instance under this head. Younger persons permanently disabled and idiots present a similar case. If these classes have
kindred who can do something for them, and whom they can serve by
some little offices about the house, as caring for children, doing chores,
and the like, they are more likely to receive outside relief. Their growing
infirmities call for peculiar aid and wearisome attention, rarely to be expected except from kindred and friends. It is thought harsh to sever them
from their accustomed resorts and fellowships. Public charity cannot indeed go much beyond physical wants, but on the other hand cannot count
out entirely the natural feelings.

Outdoor relief for the aged and others afflicted with chronic disability
is generally permanent and not temporary. It is not demanded by the
same reasons as in temporary distress, or when the preservation of a family of children is concerned. Usually the amount allowed is limited to
the cost of support in an almshouse, or reduced to something less. Relatives or friends are expected to make up the rest.

Some overseers, however, exclude aged and permanently disabled
persons from outdoor relief, as being better off and more cheaply supported, on the whole, in almshouses, and confine it to cases calling for only
temporary relief. And in towns where outdoor relief is both more liberally
dispensed and restricted to a few cases, it is the custom to place in almshouses aged persons destitute of relatives or friends especially interested
in them.

Outdoor relief is given to paupers *too sick to bear removal to the almshouse.* The humanity and necessity of this practice are evident.

Relief given in one town to paupers having settlements in *other* towns,
with the right of reimbursement, is stated to be liable to much abuse,
being furnished when not needed.

Some of the overseers recommend that the towns be authorized to give
temporary relief to state paupers, with the right to reimbursement from
the state treasury, that is, an extension of the present practice in the case
of state paupers "too sick to be removed" to all other state paupers needing relief. But it is evident that it is liable to the same abuse as is now
practiced between towns, and even greater, and the danger is that it
could not be kept within bounds, at least without extensive and constant
supervision.

AMOUNT OF THE RELIEF

The amount and kind of outdoor relief vary. Except in cases of sickness or peculiar disability, it is rare that $1.00 a week, or its equivalent, for each person, is exceeded. Sometimes only half that amount is allowed. Some overseers allow money, but generally it is refused for fear that it will be misapplied or wasted. Fuel or provisions, or both, are given, and sometimes rent, without further aid, is paid. One limitation is frequently stated to be that the amount is not allowed to exceed the cost of support, or half the cost of support in the almshouse. This is a plausible rather than a safe measure, as is indicated in the next paragraph.

COST OF THE RELIEF

The *comparative* economy of the two systems invites attention. The most frequent reason given for outdoor relief is that it is the cheaper; as for instance, that it involves only partial support, as the expenditure of a dollar a week, or less, or the price of half a ton of coal with a small quantity of provisions in the winter, or the payment of rent—the relatives or the beneficiary himself supplying the rest; while almshouse relief, which is partial support, involves the expenditure, on an average, of $2.50 a week, or about $125.00 a year.

The question, however, cannot be settled simply by comparing the cost per week of outside support for one or more persons (even when full support) with inside support, as the comparative cost of the systems, and not of any two cases, is the issue. The former may be cheaper in a given case, but dearer by increasing the number of dependents. Besides, it being necessary to have an almshouse for some classes of paupers and as a deterrent to the indolent poor, additional inmates, while there is room, do not proportionately increase the expense.

If outdoor relief were refused in all cases, there is a proportion of persons now receiving it, but not really needing it, who would cease to apply for it. Also some poor persons of reputable lives rather than go to the almshouse would get along in some way, either suffering or relying on private charity, or being burdensome to relatives of limited means. So sensitive are some of this class that they would rather starve and freeze than become the inmates of an almshouse. The treasury might be a gainer by ignoring their feelings, but it would be difficult for the state, upon grounds of economy, to maintain so harsh and rigid a system. The mean to be sought is a system which shall deter, as far as may be, from unnecessary resort to public charity without doing violence to humane and honorable instincts.

It may be remarked that the foreign-born are said to show more aversion than natives to the almshouse, but less reluctance than natives to apply for and receive outdoor relief.

The tendency of outdoor relief to make those once receiving it apply again when proper effort might have saved them from such a resort, and also to invite applications from others who can get along without it, is admitted by all, even by those who approve the system. With those who have once received it the second lapse is easier than the first, and with those not yet recipients, the spectacle of others receiving it, who are in the same or not substantially different circumstances, is a tempting one.

The difficulty, and in some cases the impossibility, of discriminating between meritorious and undeserving applicants is likewise admitted. This difficulty is greater in large towns and cities, and much less in rural districts. In the latter, where the habits and character of the applicants are well known, it hardly exists.

In comparing the expense of the two systems, while the tendency of outdoor relief to increase the number of applicants is admitted, on the other hand in a large view the tendency of the almshouse system to make some *permanent* paupers, who with temporary relief would not become such, must be taken into account. The two systems cannot therefore be compared in a single year, but only in a series of years.

LIMITATIONS PROPOSED

The answers are suggestive of but few limitations or principles of administration for securing the system of outdoor relief from abuse. The following are some of them:

The giving or refusing of relief should be left, it is generally stated, to the *discretion* of the overseers.

The overseers should be men governed by humanity, but not by any weak sentiment, and doing their duty without fear or favor. On their care, shrewdness, and firmness, not merely in one year, but from year to year, nearly all depends.

They should be chosen, not as now for a single year, but for a longer period, so as to insure for them larger experience and a less dependent tenure. This change has already been made with school committees, and should be made with overseers, each to be chosen for three years, with terms ending with different years. A more continuous body, thus composed, would keep the overseers in possession of necessary information as to paupers, and insure uniform and better records.

The names of parties receiving outdoor relief are usually published in the annual town reports.

The recipients of relief should ordinarily, particularly in cities, be visited from time to time, in order to see if their need still continues, and that relief is properly applied. Each order should be for a limited period, not as a continuing allowance, and should be renewed only on a fresh examination.

As an illustration of the need of close scrutiny, an instance has come to the knowledge of the secretary in which $2 a week was paid, for some years, as outside relief, to an aged person who left an estate worth nearly $1,000 dollars. The imposition was afterwards justified on the ground that the person "might as well have it as not."

Some overseers recommend that the aid should not in any one case exceed $50 a year, or be extended beyond two years.

The outdoor relief should be limited to *worthy* persons, who have led virtuous and industrious lives. Those whose poverty arises from indolence, intemperance, and wasteful habits, or who are otherwise vicious and troublesome, should be sent to the almshouse. The practice of notifying these classes in summer that, on applying for aid in the winter following they would receive it only in the almshouse, is stated to have a good effect. Some of the overseers call attention to the fact that the father of a family which they are obliged to relieve is often an idle person, or one who spends his wages in drink, leaving his family destitute. Further legislation is requested to meet the evil, and to compel him to support his own. But the law already gives a remedy, to wit, a prosecution for vagrancy (General Statutes, chap. clxv, sec. 28), which is declared to cover "persons who neglect their calling and employment, misspend what they earn, and do not provide for themselves, or for the support of their families." Another provision (chap. xxii, sec. 1) designates as proper inmates of a workhouse

persons who, being able of body to work, and not having estate or means otherwise to maintain themselves, refuse or neglect to work; persons who live a dissolute, vagrant life, and exercise no ordinary calling or lawful business; persons who spend their time and property in public houses to the neglect of their proper business, or who, by otherwise misspending what they earn to the impoverishment of themselves and their families, are likely to become chargeable to the city or town.

The penalties of vagrancy have already been stated in the chapter upon that subject. The overseers, therefore, have at hand an ample remedy.

Near kindred, though able to support the persons seeking relief, often fail to do so. It would appear that the provisions of the General Statutes, chapter lxx, requiring this of parents, children, grandparents, and grandchildren are not always enforced. This obligation is not imposed by our statutes upon brothers and sisters and other collaterals.

Some of the answers suggest that legislation is required to enable towns to recover for aid given to persons *subsequently acquiring* property. The General Statutes, chapter lxx, section 21, already provide such a remedy against the estate of a *deceased* pauper, chargeable to a town at the time of his decease. But a person relieved or supported by the town has not been liable to compensate therefor, except from 1817 to 1836. It has been held by the Supreme Court that one, who being in need of immediate relief and support has received the same from the town of his lawful settlement, is not, in the absence of fraud, liable to any action by the town therefor, although he was possessed of property at the time. The relief is considered to be furnished as a charity, and not under a contract; and it is added,

In this case the rule of law operates hardly. But there is no danger that the rule will often work injustice. In almost all cases where relief is furnished by a town to persons who have property not at their immediate command, we cannot help believing that they would be disposed to indemnify the town. And if hidden or unknown property of a person who has received support should be discovered after his death, it is to be hoped that those to whom such property legally belongs would not often insist on holding it (*Stow* vs. *Sawyer*, 3 Allen's Reports, 515; *Groveland* vs. *Medford*, 1 *ibid.*, 23).

An almshouse is an important, indeed a necessary part of a proper pauper system. It must always be held in reserve for certain classes. It deters some, who can support themselves, from pressing for relief, as well as enables overseers to be more resolute in refusing relief to those apparently not in need of it. They can refer such applicants to the almshouse without the possible chance of the denial of all relief turning out to be unjust. Towns having neither almshouses nor any arrangements for sending to the almshouse of some other town are without a valuable check.

Some towns are too small to sustain an almshouse of their own, and many almshouses are not more than half filled. The General Statutes make full provision for the purchase and support of a common almshouse by two or more towns jointly (chap. xxii, secs. 3–10).

The almshouse is also the proper receptacle for others who, on account of vicious propensities or disabled and friendless condition, cannot be provided for elsewhere without great expense.

Paupers may do much toward their own support in a well-conducted almshouse, which, it is asserted by some, can be made in many cases well-nigh self-supporting.

It may be remarked that however great the disadvantages of outdoor relief, it would be impracticable oftentimes, particularly in cities, to exclude it entirely. The almshouse, unless built of mammoth proportions, would not hold all the paupers. . . . .

TENDENCIES OF THE SYSTEM

While outdoor relief seems to be a necessary department of a pauper system, particularly under existing conditions of public sentiment, it is always important to keep in view its dangerous tendencies and its great liability to abuse. We may be as yet exempt from its evils as developed in an aggravated form in older countries, but without perpetual care we shall not be able to escape them when our population has become dense and the resources of new territory and new enterprises have become restricted. Even now in some of the towns, according to the letters of the overseers, a large proportion of the outdoor relief, sometimes one-half, is distributed to those who stand in no need of it, and is therefore worse than wasted. This has come to pass, probably, from loose methods of administration from which it is difficult to escape, as the poor have acquired exaggerated notions of their claims to support, and public sentiment has become demoralized. It becomes us, for the welfare of this generation, and still more of posterity, to resist such vicious tendencies at the beginning, *obstare principiis*, to put in motion all counteracting agencies that are available, and to regulate public charity with a tender but a firm hand. Above all, it should be inculcated on the poor by the pulpit, the press and the authorities, that it is alike the social and religious duty of every human being to make every effort to take care of himself. The notion that one, on the first pressure or deprivation of usual comforts, can fly to the public treasury for support, that one has some right to poor rates or outside relief derived from a fancied mutual insurance arising from the social compact, or from the assumption that the world owes him a living, has no foundation in philosophy, and ought not to be tolerated in administration. Upon this point the moralists are in harmony with the economists.

The County Almshouses of Illinois, 1872[1]

To avoid making the report unnecessarily long, we have decided . . . . to confine ourselves, in treating of pauperism, to a few general remarks. . . . .

[1] Extract from *Second Biennial Report of the Board of State Commissioners of Public Charities of the State of Illinois Presented to the Governor, December, 1872* (Frederic H. Wines, Secretary), pp. 186–90.

The almshouses of Illinois are of several distinct types.

The most common ideal is that of a county farmhouse, corresponding in its general style to the average farmhouses of the district in which it is situated, with, perhaps, a tendency to be a little below the average, in respect of convenience and comfort. In the larger counties, there is ordinarily to be found upon the county farm a group of houses, and this is often the case in the smaller counties as well—one house, better than the rest, for the family of the keeper, and the others for the use of male and female paupers and the insane, to each of whom separate buildings, when the number is sufficient to justify classification, are allotted. The life, in an almshouse of this description, is that of a family in the country, rather poorly clothed and fed, and bearing the marks of a listless poverty.

Another type of almshouse is the hospital, of which St. Clair County probably affords the best illustration. The St. Clair County almshouse, only a mile distant from the courthouse at Belleville, and almost on the outskirts of the town, differs from all ordinary almshouses in this respect. The whole air of the establishment, the internal arrangements, the management and discipline resemble those of a well-organized, well-kept hospital proper, in which are collected not only the temporarily sick or disabled but the permanently helpless and infirm, and no others. A flower garden blooms in front of the premises; a pesthouse has been erected at some distance in the rear; and a thoroughly well-planned, well-built, and every way comfortable receptacle for the insane has been provided. The county judges visit the place daily, and it exhibits, in its entire aspect, the marks of thorough oversight and intelligent care. It is a credit to the county and to the state.

A third type is modeled after the idea of the state or public institution, with a large brick building or buildings, divided into center and wings, and approximating more or less nearly (generally less) in its plan of organization to the commonly received notion of what an institution should be. A very favorable instance of this style of almshouse is to be seen in Knox County, at Knoxville. It was built after plans of which Dr. McFarland, of Jacksonville, furnished the preliminary sketches, and although not yet completed, one wing only having been erected, it is ably and satisfactorily presided over by a lady superintendent, Mrs. Cleveland, who has been in charge for a number of years. In this institution also, proper provision has been made for the care of the hopelessly insane, in an "L" at the extremity of the wing. The house is heated by steam, by Gold's apparatus, matting is laid down all over the house, facilities furnished for bathing, and in all respects what has been done deserves the highest praise.

In a number of counties, however, there is no almshouse, and the paupers are boarded out, sometimes in mass, sometimes in detachments, and they go, in this case, usually, to the lowest bidder—a system that deserves the severest reprobation.

The first fault in the management of the majority of county farms that strikes a visitor is the excessive quantity of land commonly contained in them. The objections to large farms are the loss of interest on the original investment, the impossibility of working them profitably with pauper labor, and the diversion of the attention of the keeper from the care and oversight of the paupers to the care of the farm. There are few instances in which forty acres are not amply sufficient for all practical purposes, and oftentimes ten or twenty would be enough. Yet it is not uncommon for a county to own a poor farm (and poor farms the most of them are, in fact) of three or four hundred acres. In several of the counties visited by us, we have been informed that the original purchase was a speculation, on the part of some prominent and influential citizen, who wished to dispose of comparatively worthless land for a price far in excess of its actual value.

A second fault is often observable in the nature of the selection of a keeper, and in the nature of the contract made with him. Many of the counties appear indifferent as to the character and capacity of the keeper employed, and only anxious to secure the cheapest man who will do, whether really competent or not. Some of the almshouse keepers in this state are only a degree above the paupers under their charge, in point of efficiency or intelligence. When the care of the paupers is let to the lowest bidder, this must ordinarily be so. The contracts made with the men employed are often loosely drawn, so as not to guard the interests either of the county or of the unfortunate inmates. The worst of all contracts is that in which an individual agrees to take all the paupers that are sent to him, and furnish everything, medicines and medical attendance included, at his own cost, for a stipulated sum per annum. This is simply an attempt on the part of county officials to throw off all responsibility for the care of the poor, by hiring a proxy to do their duty for them. Under such a system, it is the interest of the keeper to mistreat his victims, for the sake of personal profit. If complaint is made to him, he alleges that he cannot afford to keep them better at the price allowed him by the county. If complaint is made to the county authorities, they wash their hands of all responsibility in the matter; they have made their contract; they feel no personal interest in paupers; and they presume the contractor keeps them well enough. Very little better are the contracts in which the same agreement is made for a stipulated sum per capita. The true method of caring for paupers in almshouses is for the county to employ the best man and wife that can be had for the price, especial pains being taken to secure a kind but efficient woman, as head of the domestic department, and to pay them a fixed salary; to require an account to be kept of the production and consumption of supplies on the farm, and insist upon the farm being made to yield as much for the support of the paupers as possible; and all purchases should be made by authority of the county at county expense, the bills to be carefully audited before being paid. This is the usual practice, and it is altogether the best and most satisfactory. The farm should be worked in the interest of the county and not of the keeper—the object not being to make money, but to secure proper attention to the paupers.

A very important point in the management of almshouses is the selection of a physician, who should be possessed of fair ability and attainments, and should be required to visit the establishment not simply when sent for but at stated intervals. Stated visits of inspection by a physician have the effect of improving the general management, and often prevent the rise and spread of epidemics, or arrest individual cases of sickness by securing medical attention at the right moment. Of course the physician should be required to make visits as frequently as necessary, in sickness. It is immaterial whether he receive an annual salary or a fee for each visit paid.

Great care ought to be taken in the admission of inmates, not to exclude any who are actually in need of assistance, not on the other hand to allow lazy and vicious persons to become pensioners upon public bounty. Thoroughness in the discipline and employment at hard labor, in proportion to their strength, will present serious imposition because able-bodied beggars will not submit to it. Those who do, and whose misfortunes are irremediable, are entitled to sympathy, and should not be permitted to suffer, because they are poor and unfortunate. They should be made thoroughly comfortable, and the small expense necessary to accomplish this ought not to be grudgingly bestowed.

Special attention should be paid, for their benefit, to the garden and orchard. There is no reason why they should not have fruit and vegetables in abundance. In Morgan County, the keeper, a German, is an extraordinarily skilful gardener, and every summer fruit and vegetables are canned, under his direction, in sufficient quantity to supply the table profusely during the winter and spring. None but pauper labor is employed, and the inmates are simply eating what they themselves have produced, while the diet furnished costs the county nothing, and so diminishes the cash expense.

Another point that needs attention is the care of the hopelessly insane, of whom a greater or less number are to be found in all our almshouses. They are the victims of disease, they suffer greatly, and no pains should be spared to make them as comfortable as circumstances will admit. Where receptacles are built for them they should be well lighted, well warmed, well ventilated, provided with suitable bedding and other conveniences, protected against peril from fire, so arranged as to protect the insane from each other, in case of violent excitement, and under no circumstances should they be allowed to degenerate into the living tombs that they too often are. The horrors that we have seen in some of the county almshouses are too shocking to repeat—nakedness, filth, starvation, vice, and utter wretchedness, which a very slight exercise of common sense and of humanity might have entirely prevented.

The improvement of our almshouse system must be a work of time. It would be greatly facilitated were these abodes of misery more often visited by the better class of citizens in each county. A voluntary association for relief of pauperism and crime, by regular and methodical inspection of the county almshouses and jails at least as often as once in every month, might be organized in Illinois, with a branch or auxiliary society in each county, and might accomplish a world of good.

The almshouses can be made self-sustaining only to a very limited extent. Pauper labor is worth little, and what labor is expended will be more effective if directed to the production of supplies for home consumption than for the market.

The presence of children in such places is their saddest feature. What can be more dreary than the future prospects of a pauper child? All such should be provided with homes, if possible, and, at the almshouse, should be given every facility for obtaining the rudiments of an education, in the hope of lifting them out of their forlorn condition.

Closely connected with the question we have been discussing is that of outdoor relief, or assistance granted outside the almshouses. We find, in different counties directly opposite principles and practices, in this particular, prevailing. In some of the counties, the authorities grant outdoor relief to an extent that is appalling—multitudes of persons receiving aid, to whom aid is a positive injury, inasmuch as it fosters a spirit of dependence which undermines all energy and personal effort to obtain a livelihood. One case was reported to us of an able-bodied man who received aid from the county in which he lived to support his wife, living at home with him in his own house. Other counties, to avoid this drain upon the treasury, go to the opposite extreme, and refuse relief to anyone who will not first give his consent to become an inmate of the county house. This policy is as cruel and short-sighted as the other is unwise, since it has a tendency to convert temporary misfortune into permanent poverty, for it is difficult for one who has once been forced to seek admission to an almshouse ever to fully regain his self-respect. On the other hand judicious temporary assistance often enables a man struggling with adversity to regain his feet. Wisdom seems to dictate a medium course, namely, the reduction of outdoor relief to a minimum, in order to prevent the growth of paupersim by undue indulgence, but the granting of temporary aid, at home, whenever the suffering is so great that it ought to be relieved, and it is probable that only temporary relief will be necessary. The great problem of all charity, public or private, is how to diminish suffering without increasing, by the very act, the number of paupers; how to grant aid, in case of need, without obliterating the principle of self-reliance and self-help. To accomplish this, a mixture of the two systems appears to be essential.

The registration of paupers ordered by the last General Assembly has gone into general effect throughout the state, and promises to be of great service, not simply as an aid to the collection of uniform and trustworthy statistical information, but in securing a more thorough oversight and control of the almshouses by county authorities. We regret to say that the provision of the law requiring county clerks to make semiannual returns to his office has not been complied with by all, and it may be necessary to enforce the penalty for non-compliance, which is a fine of $100. The system of registration adopted in this state has been copied by the state of Wisconsin.

It is difficult, in some of the counties, to ascertain from the records the precise cost of pauperism. We suggest the propriety and expediency of separating, upon the record, the pauper and criminal expenses of the several counties from other payments made on other accounts, and the distinguishing also between almshouse expenses and the cost of outdoor relief.

APPENDIX II

THE FIRST PUBLIC WELFARE ASSOCIATION

EDITORIAL NOTE

IN CONNECTION with the publication of the proceedings of the first annual meeting of the newly formed Association of Public Welfare Officials,[1] it seemed appropriate to publish at the same time an extract from the proceedings of the first "Conference of Boards of Public Charities," which met in New York in 1874. This organization afterward became the National Conference of Charities and Correction and, still later, the National Conference of Social Work.

An early portrait of Frank Sanborn, of Massachusetts, is published here because he was largely responsible for the organization of what may be called the first public welfare conference. In 1863 Mr. Sanborn became the first secretary of the first state board of charities—that of Massachusetts—and the portrait is from a photograph of a crayon drawing[2] made about the time when he began his pioneer work for the pioneer state board in this country. In 1874 Mr. Sanborn was general secretary of the American Social Science Association, under whose wing the Conference of the State Boards was assembled. A Department of Social Economy had been organized in the American Social Science Association, and it was under the auspices of this department that the Conference of State Boards was assembled. There were in 1874 nine state boards, but only four of them were represented at the meeting of 1874. It was, of course, difficult for the western members to attend a meeting held in New York City, and some of the western boards preferred regional conferences to eastern meetings.

The new emphasis in recent years on the importance of the vari-

[1] This organization, formed in 1930, later became the American Public Welfare Association, now included as one of the constituent organizations in the Public Administration Clearing with headquarters near the University of Chicago Quadrangles and closely associated with the University of Chicago program.

[2] This portrait of Mr. Sanborn, who was also the eighth president of the National Conference of Charities and Correction, is taken from his *Recollections of Seventy Years* (Boston: Richard G. Badger, 1909), I, 188.

F. B. SANBORN, 1860, ÆT 28
From a crayon by Miss H. Cheney

ous forms of public social service has led to a new interest in public welfare organization. The continuous development of the state welfare services over a period of nearly seventy years is evidence of the permanent character of these great state departments for social welfare.

The extract from the report of the proceedings of the first "Conference of the Boards of Public Charities in the United States," was first published in the *Journal of Social Science* in 1874.

E. A.

The First Conference of Boards of Public Charities[1]
Held at New York, May 20 and 22, 1874

In accordance with an invitation extended to the Boards f Public Charities in the States of New York, Pennsylvania, Illinois, Massachusetts, Michigan, Wisconsin, Connecticut, Rhode Island, and Kansas, a Conference of these Boards was held on May .20th. At first, only delegates of these Boards and members of the Executive Committee of the Association were present; but after the organization, on motion of Dr. Bishop, the reporters were admitted, and members of the Association or others having experience in the matters discussed were invited to take part in the Conference. Hon. J. V. L. Pruyn, President of the New York Board, was appointed Chairman, and F. B. Sanborn, delegate from the Massachusetts Board, was chosen Secretary. There were also present from the New York Board, Dr. Nathan Bishop, of New York; William P. Letchworth, Esq., of Buffalo; Hon. Samuel F. Miller, of Delaware County, and Dr. Charles S. Hoyt, of Albany, the Secretary. The State Board of Wisconsin was represented by Hon Henry H. Giles, the President, and Mrs. W. P. Lynde, a member of the Wisconsin Board of Charities; and Connecticut by Mrs. Mariette E. Pettee, Secretary of the State Board of Connecticut. A dispatch was received from George L. Harrison, Esq., of Philadelphia, President of the Pennsylvania Board, announcing that his attendance was prevented.

Letters were read from the Boards of Rhode Island, Pennsylvania, Michigan, and Kansas. The city Board of New York, which had been invited, was occupied with a public investigation during the sessions of the Conference, and was not represented therein; but gentlemen representing the State Charities Aid Association and the Bureau of Charities in New York City were present.

[1] From *Journal of Social Science Containing the Transactions of the American Association*, No. VI (July, 1874), pp. 60–96; No. VII (September, 1874), 374–407.

The first subject considered was, "The Duty of the States toward the Insane Poor," upon which Dr. J. B. Chapin, of the Willard Asylum for the Insane, at Willard, New York, made some brief remarks [which concluded as follows]:

A word is necessary on the subject of the maintenance of the insane, and here, again, we are confronted with the financial aspect of the question. In those States where the expense of maintenance of the insane poor is a direct charge upon the counties or towns, there is a manifest reluctance, except in extreme cases, to transfer them to the state asylums, where the views as to their requirements differ, and the expense is greater than in the county poor-houses. We do not believe the differences which prevail on this point can be reconciled except by positive legislation. In conclusion, we deem it of the highest importance that entire harmony should exist and be cultivated between the boards of public charities of the several States, and the medical profession, as to the best policy to be pursued.

In these remarks Dr. Chapin was understood to express the views not only of himself, but of the trustees of his asylum, which is a large State establishment, with more than 800 patients, chiefly of the chronic insane. One of these trustees, Mr. Darius A. Ogden, of Penn Yan, N.Y., was present, and took part in the debate which followed the remarks of Dr. Chapin.

The Secretary, Mr. Sanborn, submitted a copy of an act lately passed in Pennsylvania, giving the Board of Charities in that State power to transfer the insane poor, who are found neglected or abused in almshouses and prisons, to the State hospitals and asylums, where they will be under medical supervision. This statute, and the others given on another page, grew out of the controversial discussion of the treatment of the insane poor in Pennsylvania, which was carried on last winter between the State Board of Charities and the superintendents of State establishments for the insane. Taken together, Mr. Sanborn said they give Mr. Harrison and his colleagues substantially the same powers and duties as were imposed on the Massachusetts Board by a law of 1864. In the discussion which followed it was evident that the experience of other States in regard to the chronic insane poor has been, or is becoming, very similar to that of Massachusetts.

Mention was made in this connection of the asylum for chronic insane attached to the great State Almshouse at Tewksbury, Mass., and of the excessive mortality among its inmates in the year 1873. The whole number under treatment being 43 5, during the year ended October 1, 1873, not less than 60 had died, or nearly 14 per cent of the whole number.

Various causes had been assigned for this mortality, but it had been found that there was a lack of proper medical supervision and of sanitary provision for the patients; and, this evil having been exposed and in part remedied by the Board of Charities, the mortality had much declined during the past seven months. Mrs. Pettee spoke of the generally good condition of the Connecticut Hospital for the Insane Poor at Middletown, and Mrs. Lynde related some instances of neglect which had come under her notice in the county almshouses of Wisconsin. Dr. Bishop spoke in condemnation of the present costly architecture of establishments for the poor, both the sane and the insane; and, upon his motion, a committee of five was appointed to consider and report upon the subject of Buildings for the Indoor Poor. This committee consists of Dr. Nathan Bishop of New York, Chairman; Mrs. Lynde of Wisconsin, Dr. Diller Luther, Secretary of the Pennsylvania Board of Charities; Rev. F. H. Wines, Secretary of the Illinois Board, and Mr. D. A. Ogden, of the Willard Asylum, New York.

In opening the debate on the second topic considered by the Conference, *The Laws of Pauper Settlement, and the Best Mode of Administering Poor-law Relief*, Mr. Sanborn, the Secretary, submitted two Reports from Departments of the Association. The first, from the Department of Jurisprudence, related to the Settlement Laws of Massachusetts. . . . .

The second Report submitted was read the afternoon of Friday, May 22d, when it was ably discussed in the General Meeting of the Association. This report on "Pauperism in the City of New York" was prepared by the Committee of the New Department of Social Economy [of the American Social Science Association] and was read by Dr. Robert T. Davis, of Fall River, Massachusetts, a member of the Committee.[1] It is signed by all the members of the Committee; but it is proper to state that the original draft was prepared by Charles L. Brace, Esq., of New York; and that the modifications made by the Committee affected chiefly the general statements of the Report, and not those relating to last winter's experience in New York, in regard to which Mr. Brace is a very competent witness. Appended to this paper will be found an imperfect record of the debate concerning it, in the General Meeting.

Mr. J. W. Skinner, of the Children's Aid Society, New York, next spoke, dwelling chiefly upon out-door relief. Pauperism was like an ulcer which gradually undermined the health of the body politic. Wherever out-door relief had

[1] The report is signed by W. B. Rogers, Chairman; Dr. S. G. Howe, Charles L. Brace, Mrs. S. Parkman, Mrs. Henry Whitman, John Ayres, Lucy Ellis, George S. Hale, Charles F. Coffin, Robert T. Davis, F. B. Sanborn, Secretary.

been put in practice, pauperism, so far from being checked, had invariably continued to increase faster than before. The only systematic and well-working charity was that which was accompanied by work. But it was the prevention not the cure of the disease that was the primary consideration, and the speaker believed that the only possible way of checking pauperism was by educating the lower classes.

Dr. Nathan Bishop did not think compulsory education would be successful. He spoke of what he called the street schools,—academies where children learned to repeat a fearful catalogue of home suffering. There were thousands of children in this city who went from door to door repeating the sorrows of their home, the suffering, the poverty of their parents. They went to the kitchen-doors, and the servants believed their stories. These children were taught daily lessons of this kind of story-telling by men and women who profited by their gains; and the result was, that at least 6,000 children were every day going about in this way, becoming chronic liars, and getting schooled in crime and vice of all kinds. When they grew up, what were they going to do? They dropped into the worst forms of degradation. They made up the worst of our dangerous classes in the end. Then there were the children who beg in the street. He illustrated the evil of this street-begging by telling how, one winter's day, he had met two little girls, bare-legged and ragged, begging. He noticed several gentlemen give them money, and he asked them several questions, and finally told a policeman that he thought they were impostors, and that they had shoes and stockings hidden in the neighborhood. This, on investigation, was found to be true, and their shoes and stockings and shawls were discovered under a near-by woodpile. This kind of deception, he said, was very prevalent in the city. It was a kind that did more than anything else to swell the current of vice and crime and pauperism in the city. His advice was not to give anything to the street-beggars, or to those who called at the doors of dwellings. Let those in want go to the regular places of charity. Then, again, never listen to those who meet you in rags at night time, or call at your doors, complaining and whimpering and asking for aid. In 999 cases out of 1000 they were frauds who followed this way to make a living, and who, in the day-time, went about well dressed.

Dr. Hall was asked to give the result of the attempt made last winter to establish in New York a bureau of charities, and did so briefly, saying that the principal obstacles to the success of the bureau were the unwillingness of one large society to assist it, owing to a misunderstanding of its objects, and the opposition of a large religious denomination. It was to ferret out impostors and to make charity reach only those who were in real need, that the Bureau of Charities was established,—a sort of clearing house of charities. The great majority of the charitable institutions responded to the plans of the bureau; but there were a few which refused to cooperate. No one could have walked the streets during the past winter without being struck with what is very humiliating,—the observation that this city is rapidly travelling in the track of the worst capitals of Europe, in the direction of abundant street paupers. Many of them are of the fancy kind, made up for effect, purely spectacular, intended to operate upon the generous sympathies of the people at the moment. Others are quasi beggars,—among them the street musicians. When I think of the many poor boys and girls who are being trained in that way in this city, educated in the worst direction, I must anticipate a crop of the most adroit thieves and the most abandoned women within the next few years. I find that one society, admirable in its principles and organization, whose operations extend over the whole of the city, states in its printed report that there were 20,000 persons, impostors, in this city living by the misdirected charity of the city. We have the Commissioners of Charities and Correction to look after paupers and criminals, —a most unfortunate grouping,—who expend $1,250,000 per year. We have the Commissioners of Emigration to attend, with certain restrictions, to those who come to our shores, who expend over $600,000 per year. There is more than $1,750,000 per year. But take the 20,000 who are living by fraud and imposture. These people live very comfortably. It is very low to put their living at a dollar per day. That makes over $7,000,000 a year going into the hands of the most degraded and corrupting class in the community. What is our reward? These clever, cunning, degraded people, despise and laugh at us, and think that our very Christianity is something that only gets hold of people who are a little soft in the brain. Men have very much to unlearn, and then much to learn, before they will get courage to persevere; and then, though they may not accomplish all they desire, they bequeath a trust to their fellow-creatures for them to carry out.

Mrs. Caroline H. Dall, of Boston, moved that the paper be printed as a pamphlet in an edition so large and a form so cheap as to permit of its being widely circulated gratuitously. In speaking for Boston, she fully indorsed all that had been set forth as resulting from the ill-organized method of distributing alms, and cited instances as coming within her own experience immediately after the Boston fire, and during the late distress among the poor.

Dr. Davis said that inasmuch as so much commendation was bestowed upon this paper, he felt it his duty to state that he had not prepared the paper himself, and that it had been simply revised by the committee of which he was a member.

Mr. Robert H. McCurdy spoke of the progress of pauperism in this city since he was a young man. In 1833, he lived on Fifth Avenue, near Tenth Street, and in the neighborhood was an immense number of shanties. Great poverty existed among the inmates, and it was traced to the same cause which is now really the cause of pauperism—the rum shops. Everybody in those days drank freely, and in all the social customs of the day liquor was never wanting. Rum was really at the bottom of all our poverty, and when we swept away the rum shops we would have undermined the pauperism and made a clear and bright way for a better future for that class of people who are now suffering from want and misery.

Mr. James M. Barnard, of Boston, also spoke, relating some of his European observations on pauperism in Italy and Germany at different periods.

REPORTS OF COMMITTEES

During the first session of the Conference a committee was appointed, consisted of F. B. Sanborn, of Massachusetts, W. P. Letchworth, of New York, and Henry H. Giles, of Wisconsin, to report a plan for the Uniformity of Statistics, and a better cooperation among the Board of Charities throughout the United States. At the second session, on Friday, May 22, this committee made a preliminary report, to the effect that it was desirable to have the statistics of pauperism, crime, insanity, and the other topics discussed in the board's reports, made as completely as possible upon a uniform plan, and include a general statement of all the facts for the whole State in which the report is published, and asked further time to prepare a form for use by the different boards. It was also reported that a plan for better cooperation between boards could not be prepared without some correspondence with all the boards; and further time was asked for, which was granted. It was stated that a conference in the spring of 1875, at Buffalo or Detroit, had been proposed, and would probably be called. Dr. Bishop, for the Committee on Public Buildings for the Poor, the Insane, etc., made a preliminary report setting forth the present evils of extravagant architecture, and asking time for the preparation of a more complete report, which was voted. It was also voted that the Chair appoint a committee of five to consider the condition of destitude and delinquent children, and the prevention of pauperism.

In the debate on Dr. Bishop's report, the latter spoke of the unsatisfactory condition and unsuitableness of the buildings now used for the detention and cure of insane persons, and of the amount of money expended on them.

Mr. Sanborn spoke of the plan in Massachusetts to build a new state prison at a cost of $2,000,000 when it was quite useless to expend so much money upon that object. Dr. Bishop spoke of the bad influence of giving the rascals and rogues who were preying upon society better accommodations than honest men. Dr. Stephen Smith said one essential point was, that each building,—hospital, prison, or reformatory,—should be built with a regard to the peculiar wants of the class for which it was designed. Many of those in New York had failed, particularly the inebriate asylum, for the reason that they were too much like prisons. Mr. Letchworth, of Buffalo, defended the expenditure of the public money on public institutions. . . . . .

THE STATISTICS OF CRIME AND PAUPERISM

The committee appointed at the Conference of Boards of Charities to consider a plan for uniformity of Statistical Reports have met since the

Conference and considered a form of Questions and some suggestions relating thereto, prepared by Dr. Harris, of New York, and submitted to the Committee by Mr. Letchworth, of the New York Board of Charities. Although it is doubtful how far these questions can be generally used in all the States, the Committee have printed them, for the public information, along with the concise and clear summary of the subject by Dr. Harris. . . . .

EXPLANATIONS OF THE QUESTIONS

(Extracts from the Correspondence of ELISHA HARRIS, M.D., Cor. Sec'y of the Prison Association, with the Board of Charities of the State of New York.)

NEW YORK, May 30, 1874.

As the Executive Committee of the Prison Association, on Thursday evening last approved and ordered the circular and a schedule of inquiries for use of all Prison Committees, I have so framed the whole as to make the points we seek, in this field to correspond, and to be pressed forward with inquiries to be made by the State Boards of Charities, as I hope their schedules of points will provide. It will be apparent that no statistics which have been gathered in your Reports of 1872, or 1873, will be of any use to guide the needed inquiry into causes and increase of pauperism, etc. The question is, what is the pathway by which each person arrived at the state of misfortune and dependence?

As in our inquiries (for the Prison Association) into sources of crime, we must go back to the home and the two preceding generations of parentage, so in the record of misfortune and dependence, the physical, mental, moral and social defects are linked with nearly all personal histories found closing up the series of woes at the doors of the Almshouse and the Asylum. The educational and early disciplining and industrial record of every inmate whose history is accessible in the Almshouses and the Asylums and Refuges, will need to be obtained, and upon that basis of twenty thousand individual records, in sixty counties in which an expert physician or educator has given attention to every record, conclusions can be reached which will command the attention and study of the world. It will be too great a task for any one mind to frame and inspire those inquiries; but what is worth doing at all in this field is worth doing well.

June 5th, 1874

It has given me some pleasure to arrange the outlines of a system, for an inquiry into the causes that produce increase of pauperism, insanity, idiocy and crime. The final draft of a *method*, and the requisite questions and forms, have been completed in a shape that would enable all thoughtful citizens to see that certain investigations are practicable, though no State in America has ever attempted such inquiry in a thorough manner. Our new Schedule of Inquiry into Causes of Crime, is in harmony with the outlines I have sketched for inquiry into the Causes of Dependence, for the consideration of your Board. . . . .

In transmitting the above papers to the Secretary of this Association, Mr. Letchworth, of the New York Board of Charities, wrote as follows, on the 24th of June:

Dr. Elisha Harris, Secretary of the Prison Association of New York, has been engaged in preparing a set of inquiries into the causes of crime. His questions have been approved, I believe, by the Executive Committee of the Prison Association, and will before long be issued to their committees. The State Board of Charities of New York have decided to make an examination into the causes of pauperism in this State, basing their work upon the fifteen thousand inmates in the various poorhouses and almshouses in the State. The inquiry will go back to parents and grandparents of each subject. This will be a laborious work, involving the directing of not less than six hundred thousand separate questions. The Legislature have made an appropriation to aid in carrying this work out. As it was considered desirable that whatever tables should be made, should be comparative with the work carried on by the Prison Association, Dr. Harris was asked to outline a plan for our work and it is now being printed in such a form as to admit of revision and for the purpose of submitting it to others interested; a copy or copies of it will be sent you in a few days. My object now is to call your attention to what I deem the great importance of your taking immediate action as the Chairman of the Committee appointed by the various State Boards at the last convention of the American Social Science Association, to bring about harmony in the work of gathering statistics by the various State Boards. The work done in this State will probably not be gone over again for many years, and it seems to me of the greatest importance, that it should be comparative with whatever may be done hearafter in other States; and while steps are being taken to harmonize action in the work upon pauperism and crime, with due energy, it seems to me *all* the work to be done this year might be harmonized and made comparative. It has seemed to me that the only way to bring this desirable result about would be for you to correspond with and call together the Secretaries of the various State Boards, and after you have agreed upon a plan among yourselves, to submit it to the various Boards for approval, and have what is done this year done in a way it should be, instead of waiting for another year, when there will not be the incentive to unity that there now is in view of the great work to be undertaken this year in the State of New York. Some of my colleagues incline to the opinion that uniformity of action can be brought about only with reference to the work relating to the *causes* of pauperism, insanity and crime; but I am strongly of the belief, that by prompt and decisive action all the work of the various Boards for this year may be brought into harmony. If it should be found that the plan for uniform action is not perfect, improve it next year. This will be better, I think, than to expect to make a perfect plan now. It is probable that after the Boards get working all together, modifications will need to be made in their plans every year. I sincerely hope you will deem this subject worthy of your earnest and prompt consideration.

In transmitting this letter to the Secretaries of the State Boards, the General Secretary wrote thus to each:—

I have copied this letter in order that your Board may understand the general nature of the New York investigations, before the forms and questions themselves come to hand. Meantime, permit me to ask you a few questions.

1. To what extent can the statistics of *your State* in regard to pauperism, insanity, and crime be made *complete*, so as to show what is the actual amount of those evils in your State?

2. To what extent can they be made uniform with those of Massachusetts, as given in the Reports of the Board of Charities in that State, or with a fuller and better method, if such is known to you?

3. To what extent can this be done in your next report?

The replies to this communication, and the general subject of Dr. Harris's forms, and the feasibility of adopting them, came before a meeting of the Committee held at Buffalo, on the 18th of July, and a report embodying the conclusions of the Committee will probably appear in the next number of the *Journal*, along with a preliminary report from the Committee of which Dr. Bishop is chairman. . . . .

In concluding this preliminary report on a question of infinite detail and of great and growing importance, your Committee would call attention to the fact that the average number of convicts in the United States is now nearly double what it was ten years ago, as appears by the carefully prepared statistics of Dr. Wines, the Secretary of the National Prison Association, and that a considerable part of this increase in punished crime is due, more or less directly, to the late civil war. It was an old saying in France in the days of the Fronde, that "War makes thieves and Peace brings them to the gallows," and now that we have substituted imprisonment for the gallows, the end of the civil war naturally fills up our prisons. They are crowded, and with a class of convicts among whom are many that might be reformed. In the convict prisons of Ireland, under a system of punishment, labor, and instruction, judiciously blended and ably administered, the number of convicts has decreased from 4,000 in 1854, to less than 1,200 in 1874. We cannot hope for so great a diminution of crime in our rapidly growing country, but we ought at least to prevent it from gaining upon the natural increase of our population, as has been the case for at least ten years past.

F. B. SANBORN
JOHN AYRES

COMMITTEES OF THE NEW YORK MEETING

Some report has been made of the action taken by the Committees appointed at the New York meeting in May. That of which Dr. Bishop is Chairman, is engaged in its work, but will make no report until 1875.

The Committee on Destitute and Delinquent Children, as appointed by Dr. Smith, Chairman of the Conference of May 22, consists of Samuel D. Hastings, Madison, Wis., *Chairman*, Charles L. Brace, of New York, Mrs. W. P. Lynde, of Milwaukee, George L. Harrison, of Philadelphia, and Rev. Horatio Wood, of Lowell, Mass. They have power to fill vacancies and to add to their own number, and are to report in 1875.

The Committee on Uniformity of Statistics, appointed at the Conference of Boards of Public Charities, May 20, has been considering the subject ever since that time, and on the 9th of September, reported in part at a special Conference of Secretaries of the State Boards of Charities, convened at the rooms of the Prison Association in New York, (58 Bible House, Astor Place). Their report was accepted, the forms of questions therein proposed were adopted by the Boards represented, and the Committee undertook to consider another statistical subject, in regard to the Insane In Hospitals, upon a suggestion made by Dr. Luther, Secretary of the Pennsylvania Board of Charities.

The following is the

REPORT OF THE COMMITTEE.

The undersigned, a Committee appointed at the New York Conference of Boards of Charities in May last, to consider and report a plan for uniformity of statistics of pauperism and crime, and for better cooperation among the Boards of Public Charities, have attended to that duty, and would report in part as follows:—

I. THE EXISTING BOARDS OF PUBLIC CHARITY

It appears that there are at present in the United States nine State boards or commissions charged with the general oversight of charitable work in the States where they exist. These boards, named in the order of seniority, are:—

1. The Massachusetts Board of State Charities, established in 1863.

2. The New York State Board of Charities, established in 1867.

3. The Rhode Island Board of State Charities and Corrections, established in 1869.

4. The Pennsylvania Board of Commissioners of Public Charities, established in 1869.

5. The Illinois Board of State Commissioners of Public Charities, established in 1869.

6. The Wisconsin State Board of Charities and Reform, established in 1871.

7. The Michigan Board of State Commissioners for the supervision of the Penal, Pauper, and Reformatory Institutions, established in 1871.

8. The Connecticut State Board of Charities, established in 1873.

9. The Kansas Board of Commissioners of Public Institutions, established in 1873.

The present officers and members of these boards are as follows:—

1. Massachusetts

Dr. Samuel G. Howe, Boston, *Chairman;* F. B. Sanborn, Concord; S. C. Wrightington, Fall River, *General Agent;* Sidney Andrews, Boston, *Secretary.*

2. New York

John V. L. Pruyn, Albany, *President;* William P. Letchworth, Buffalo, *Vice-President;* Dr. Charles S. Hoyt, Albany, *Secretary.*

3. Rhode Island

George I. Chace, Providence, *Chairman;* William W. Chapin, Providence, *Secretary; Superintendent of State Charities and Corrections,* George W. Wightman, Providence.

4. Pennsylvania

George L. Harrison, Philadelphia, *Chairman;* Diller Luther, M.D., Reading, *Secretary.*

5. Illinois

S. M. Church, Rockford, Illinois, *President;* Rev. F. H. Wines, Springfield, Illinois, *Secretary.*

6. Wisconsin

Hiram H. Giles, Madison, *President;* A. C. Parkinson, Madison, *Secretary.*

7. Michigan

Charles I. Walker, Detroit, *Chairman;* Charles M. Croswell, Adrian, *Secretary.*

8. Connecticut

Benjamin Stark, New London, *Chairman;* Mrs. Mariette R. Pettee, West Meriden, *Secretary.*

9. Kansas

C. S. Brodbent, Wellington, *Chairman.*

II. THE FORMS FOR STATISTICAL INQUIRY

It is proposed that all these Boards shall unite in answering [certain] questions in their next published reports.

[A list of inquiries to be answered in the Annual Reports of the Boards of Public Charities, beginning with the Reports for the year 1874, then in preparation, are included under six heads as follows:]

I. The Powers and Duties of the Boards Themselves.

II. The Number of Public Dependents.

III. The Cost of Public Charity and Correction.

IV. The Public Provision for Blind, Deaf Mute and Idiotic Persons.

V. Hospital Provision for the Sick.

VI. Private Charities [under which head the secretaries were instructed to "estimate the sums expended in private charity in your State *by organized societies*, and the annual number of their beneficiaries, classifying the same as clearly as possible, and excluding *educational* charities, except for the benefit of the classes named above."]

III. REMARKS ON THE QUESTIONS

It will be noticed that the above questions apply to each State in which a Board of Charities exists, and are intended to elicit such statements in the next Reports of these Boards as will present all the material facts of a general nature in regard to Pauperism, Insanity and Crime, and their cost to the State for which the Report is made. It is not expected that all the questions can be exactly answered, but it is hoped that where definite statistics cannot be given *for the whole State*, a careful estimate will be made, under each head, and, if possible, in reply to each question. Even in cases where, as in the State of New York, the Board of Charities divides with the Commissioners of Emigration, the Lunacy Commissioner, and the Prison Association, the supervision of charitable and penal establishments, it is hoped that the statistics of Pauperism, Insanity, and Crime for the whole State may be brought together in the Report of the Board of Charities, after obtaining the needful information from the other State authorities. In Pennsylvania and Massachusetts, and perhaps in other States, the attempt is now made, in the Annual Reports, to bring all these statistics together, so as to present an aggregate by means of which the condition of one State can be closely compared with that of another.

It will be further observed that no attempt has been made, in the above questions, to get at the statistics of the *causes* of Pauperism and Crime, as it was suggested in the first session of our Committee might possibly be done. This work—a very delicate and difficult one—has been undertaken in the great State of New York, by the diligent and experienced Secretary of the State Board of Charities, Dr. Hoyt, and is going on at this moment. When it shall have been so far completed that the first general abstract of results can be published, other States will have guide, of much value, to aid them in a similar task. Until then we would recommend the Boards in other States to make use of Dr. Hoyt's Questions, printed herewith, so far as may be found practicable where the legal and administrative machinery has not been so fully provided as seems to be the case in New York. It is understood that the form of Questions suggested by Dr. Harris, and printed in the Sixth number of the *Journal of Social Science*, had not received his final revision, and was, indeed, rather a brief for use in consultations concerning the investigation to be set on foot, than a completed plan. . . . .

IV. GENERAL COOPERATION IN CHARITABLE WORK

It is hoped that the Boards of Public Charity enumerated above, and such others as may be from time to time established in the other States, will find it convenient, as it certainly would seem to be useful, to maintain a constant correspondence with each other, and to meet together for conference at least once a year. There can hardly be a too zealous cooperation between such Boards, having common interests, and an intelligent desire to improve the methods of charitable and penal administration throughout the country,—since a bad system anywhere in use, affects, more or less directly all those States which may have a better system. A good example of such cooperation among the officials of a single State (larger, to be sure, than all New England), is to be found in the Annual Convention of the County Superintendents of the Poor in New York, which, for the present year was held at Rochester on the 9th of June. Thirty-four of the counties were represented on that occasion, by more than fifty delegates; and there were also present three members of the State Board of Charities, and the Secretary of the New York Prison Association. The new legislation and the recent administrative experience of the whole State, in regard to pauperism, were there ably discussed, and the published proceedings, are of value to students of Social Science, all over the land. If what is here done in a single State could be done in all the States, great advantage would result. Even if this is not possible, for years to come, it will be possible to bring together the fifty or sixty persons who serve on the State Boards of Charities, for a yearly conference and comparison of methods and results. The undersigned, having been empowered to do so, have invited a conference of the Secretaries of these Boards in the City of New York to-day, and propose to call a general meeting of all the members of Boards at some convenient time and place next year.

Respectfully submitted.

F. B. SANBORN, of Massachusetts
WILLIAM P. LETCHWORTH, of New York
H. H. GILES, of Wisconsin

NEW YORK, September 9, 1874